CW00726631

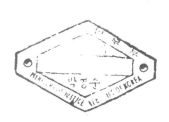

DEPARTMENT OF IMMIGRATION
PERMITTED TO ENTER
AUSTRALIA.

24 APR 1986

on

For stay of 12 Month

SYDNEY AIRPORT 54

IMMIGRATION DIVISION BANGKOK THAILAND
A
72
DEPARTED
- 6 FEB 1988
SIGNED

IMMIGRATION & ETHNIC AFFAIRS
..........Person
30 OCT 1989
DEPARTED
AUSTRALIA
SYDNEY 32

T R A V E L E R ' S
INDONESIA
C O M P A N I O N

上陸許可
ADMITTED
15. FEB. 1986
Status: 4-1-   4
Duration: 90 days
NARITA(N)
Immigration Inspector
日本国

ADMITTED
20 OCT. 1988
Status: 4-1-16
Duration   180 day
Port: HANEDA
Signature

№ 011278

THE UNITED STATES
OF AMERICA
NONIMMIGRANT VISA
ISSUED AT

U.S. IMMIGRATION
170 HHW 1710
JUL 2 0 1998

...SED
Air Port

HONG KONG
(1038)
- 7 JUN 1987
IMMIGRATION
OFFICER

The 1998–1999 Traveler's Companions

ARGENTINA • AUSTRALIA • BALI • CALIFORNIA • CANADA • CHINA • COSTA RICA • CUBA • EASTERN CANADA • ECUADOR • FLORIDA • HAWAII • HONG KONG • INDIA • INDONESIA • JAPAN • KENYA • MALAYSIA & SINGAPORE • MEDITERRANEAN FRANCE • MEXICO • NEPAL • NEW ENGLAND • NEW ZEALAND • PERU • PHILIPPINES • PORTUGAL • RUSSIA • SPAIN • THAILAND • TURKEY • VENEZUELA • VIETNAM, LAOS AND CAMBODIA • WESTERN CANADA

Traveler's INDONESIA Companion
First Published 1998
World Leisure Marketing Limited
9 Downing Road, West Meadows Industrial Estate
Derby, DE21 6HA, England
Web Site: http://www.map-world.co.uk

ISBN: 1-84006-060-3

By arrangement with Kümmerly+Frey AG, Switzerland
© 1998 Kümmerly+Frey AG, Switzerland

Created, edited and produced by Allan Amsel Publishing
53, rue Beaudouin, 27700 Les Andelys, France
E-mail: Allan.Amsel@wanadoo.fr
Editor in Chief: Allan Amsel
Editor: Fiona Nichols
Original design concept: Hon Bing-wah
Picture editors and designers: David Henry and Laura Purdom

Printed by Samhwa Printing Company Limited, Seoul, Korea

TRAVELER'S
INDONESIA
COMPANION

by David DeVoss and Chris Taylor
Photographed by Nik Wheeler

Kümmerly+Frey

Contents

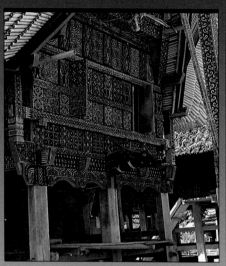

TOP SPOTS

A Symphony in Stone

THREE HISTORICAL SITES IN ASIA MERIT MENTION ABOVE ALL OTHERS, one of which — Borobudur — is in Indonesia. Bagan in Myanmar (Burma) and Angkor Wat in Cambodia both rival Borobudur, it's true, and Angkor Wat gets most of the glory — it's bigger, more awe-inspiring and less accessible. But Java's **Borobudur** is the most ancient of the three. It was probably the model for an inspired temple-building frenzy three centuries later that culminated in the building of Angkor Wat by the Khmer.

Like so many activities in this early-rising nation, a trip to Borobudur is a dawn expedition. This can be done from Yogyakarta or, better, from the **Manohara Hotel** which lies within the grounds of Borobudur itself, and provides spotless mid-range comforts in rooms that look out onto the monument. The temple opens at 5:15 AM, and this is the time to go if you want to mount the stairs at the main eastern entrance in solitude like a latter-day Buddhist pilgrim.

Borobudur is a stupa, a Buddhist reliquary of the kind scattered all over Asia. But a stupa of such vast proportions! Imagine the toiling armies of peasant laborers who brought this massive structure into being, amassing what was finally to amount to more than a million cubic feet of stone, and piling them into the monolithic pyramid that now completely obscures what was once a hill on the Kedu Plain amongst the palms and villages of central Java.

As you mount the steps and emerge on the top terrace in the first glimmerings of dawn, the light gathers, and the shapes around you begin to take on discernible forms, resolving into seemingly innumerable bell-shaped miniature stupas. There are 72 of them in all, and through the stone latticework inside each can be seen a meditating Buddha — reach in and touch the Buddha's hands and feet for good luck. Look for the Buddha who has been unhoused and who sits in quiet meditational repose oblivious of the daily traffic of tourists and pilgrims. Cameras shutters begin snapping from amongst the stupas as light permeates the plain and illuminates

OPPOSITE: Borobudur, Indonesia's superlative cultural attraction, shrouded in early morning mist. ABOVE: A reclining detail from Borobudur's busy wall reliefs.

the cone of nearby Mt. Merapi. The scholarly will be reminded, perhaps, that Borobudur is a mountain too; like Angkor Wat, Borobudur is a symbolic representation of Mt. Mehru, the navel of the universe.

After you've found a quiet spot on the summit and watched the sun rise, retrace your steps to the bottom terrace of Borobudur to begin a second journey of discovery. Like the Bayon at Angkor, Borobudur's stone terraces are lined with bas reliefs that provide detailed depictions of life in Java a millennium ago. Pilgrims follow the reliefs from the east entrance in a clockwise direction, a walk of around five kilometers (three miles), through narrow corridors past a rich pageant of elephants, ships, dancing girls, princes, musicians and monks — a Buddhist *Canterbury Tales* in stone, some 2,700 narrative and decorative panels. Look, too, for the Buddhas who sit peacefully overhead in the relief galleries. There are 432 of them in all. As you file past under their abstracted gaze, pause for a moment and think: They have been watching pilgrims do the rounds for over 1,000 years (see also YOGYAKARTA in JAVA, page 114).

Climb a "Fire Mountain"

GUNUNG API — "FIRE MOUNTAIN" — IS WHAT THE INDONESIANS CALL VOLCANOES,

AND THERE ARE NO SHORTAGE OF THEM IN THIS MOUNTAINOUS ARCHIPELAGO. The fallout from their eruptions brings great fecundity to the soil… and causes great destruction. When Krakatoa, which lies between Java and Sumatra, self-destructed in 1883 it was the biggest bang in recorded history. Lake Toba, one of the world's deepest lakes, was created in a volcanic explosion that is thought to have been the biggest in the history of the planet.

Not that you should let this put you off. Eruptions are rare, explosions even rarer, and the opportunity to scramble up onto the lip of a smoking volcano and come face to face with one of nature's most extraordinary phenomenon is not to be missed. All you need is a reasonable bill of health, some warm clothes (no matter how hot it is at sea-level it will be cold at the summit) and a willingness to be up early: A sunrise view is obligatory.

Indonesia's most famous volcano excursion is **Mt. Bromo**, 2,392 m (7,848 ft), in eastern Java. There are several approaches to the mountain, but

the most popular is via the town of Probolinggo. Probolinggo itself is a squalid bottleneck; travel on to **Cemoro Lawang** on the lip of Bromo's crater where the Hotel Bromo Permai has excellent rooms that look out over Bromo's bizarre lunar landscape.

You will be woken at 3 AM. In the chill darkness outside, travelers and their guides are gathering, stamping their feet. Ponies are a popular mode of conveyance, and there is something particularly romantic about jolting along at an easy pace, the stars overhead, the sleep barely banished from your eyes. If you're walking, it takes around two hours to the summit; if you're riding, around one and a half. Either way, the short journey takes you across Bromo's surreal crater plain and then, via a steep climb, up Bromo's volcanic cone to the summit, where you shiver and wait in the gathering light for the rising of the sun.

Mt. Bromo is not the only volcano in Indonesia that attracts climbers. In Bali **Mt. Agung**, 2,750 m (9,500 ft), is a stiff proposition, taking two days up and

down, much of it slipping and slithering in loose scree. **Mt. Batur**, Bali's other active volcano is an easy climb. Though the top is 1,700 m (5,600 ft) above sea-level, the ascent is a short one. This is because Batur rises from within the crater (or, to use its technical name, the caldera) of a much older and bigger volcano, so you start climbing at a point that's already some 1,000 m (3,000 ft) above sea-level. Three hours will usually see you up and down Mt. Batur.

For a challenge, serious climbers might like to take on Lombok's **Mt. Rinjani**, 3,700 m (12,200 ft), the fourth highest mountain in Indonesia. You'll need a guide, camping equipment and sturdy hiking gear for this climb, which can take three days one-way.

One caveat: Always ask about how a volcano has been behaving recently before climbing it. They are "fire mountains" after all, and at times are best left to their own fiery moods.

OPPOSITE: Into the heart of Kalimantan's jungle. ABOVE: Sunrise over Indonesia's most climbed volcano, Mt. Bromo.

Explore the Art Deco Capital of the East

ART DECO, A WHIMSICAL EUROPEAN ART STYLE THAT HAD ITS HEYDAY FROM 1920 TO 1940, is architecturally best represented in the most far-flung and unconnected places: Miami Beach in Florida, Napier in New Zealand... and Bandung in Java.

When art critics talk about art deco they reach, as art critics will, for words such as "plastic" and "organic." Abstractions such as this give away little; but anyone who has seen America's archetypal art deco skyscraper, the Chrysler Building, a soaring structure that improbably suggests the fins and curves of the American dream machine, will know what the critics are talking about. And look at those sunbeam motifs on the Chrysler Building's domed roof: Art deco is one of those rare fun moments in modern architecture, a product of the Jazz Age, its adherents drawing on a host of eclectic influences from Gothic stained glass to Aztec and Egyptian stone to Brave New World chrome and platinum (or at least look-a-like substitutes for the latter).

For the best in Bandung's art deco heritage take a look at — or better still stay at — the **Savoy Homann Hotel**, which has been lovingly restored both inside and out. The streamlined look of the building is a typical art deco feature. The **Grand Hotel Preanger** was given an art deco gloss in a 1928 renovation by the acclaimed Dutch architect Wolff Shoemacher, who designed over 100 buildings in Bandung. On the **Gedung Merdeka**, also known as the Asia Afrika Building, Shoemacher teamed up with another Dutch architect whose work can be seen in Bandung, A.F. Aalbers. For an interesting example of the latter's work look for the three houses Jalan Ir. H. Juanda N°113–117, that are collectively known as the **Three Locomotives**. Like the Savoy Homann, which evokes an ocean liner both inside and out, the "locomotives" are in the so-

called "streamline" style, an effect evocative of transportation and movement, forces that were turning the world of the early twentieth century on its head.

Take a stroll too along **Jalan Braga**, once Bandung's proudest avenue. Today, decay has set in and the façades only hint at their former glory. One of the best here is the **Bank of Indonesia**, designed by Ed Cuypers, another Dutchman, and flanked by a couple of Schoemacher-designed churches.

Bandung is teeming with fascinating art deco creations. Many of them are private homes tucked away in residential districts, making them difficult to find. Go to the helpful Bandung Visitor Center on the City Square for more information on where to find Bandung's architectural heritage, or better yet, join one of the Visitor Center's art deco tours.

See the Running of the Bulls

RAW EGGS AND HONEY, BEER AND HERBAL POTIONS SUPPLEMENT THEIR DIET; proud owners massage their flanks and sing them to sleep; when they go out into the streets they are draped with tinsel garlands, ribbons and flowers: On **Madura**, an island off the northeast coast of Java, the local bulls are probably the best looked after bulls in the world.

What's all the fuss about? The Madura bull races, or *kerapan sapi.* It all started centuries ago, when farmers plowing their fields raced each other with their teams of bulls to be the first to finish. In time, these impromptu races developed into today's post-harvest season that culminates in the all-Madura **Kerapan Besar**, the Grand Finale held in the Madurese capital Parmekasan every year in October.

The October Kerapan Besar is one of the most boisterous and exciting festivals in all Southeast Asia. If your trip to

An art deco classic, the Savoy (top and bottom) announces its pedigree in its graceful curves before you even reach the lobby.

Indonesia coincides with it, do your best to be there. A boom-crash gamelan orchestra bursts into sound, heightening the tension in the air. The bulls are stripped of their finery and teamed up in pairs. The jockeys give them a generous slug of *arak*, before taking one themselves and mounting the wooden sleds drawn by the teams. The jockey's job is to hit and prick the bulls into being the first whose front legs (not noses) cross the winning line 120 m (400 ft) down the track. Despite their lumbering size, the animals cover the course in around 10 seconds: Faster than record-breaking human sprinters can do the same distance.

The season starts in August and runs through to the Kerapan Besar in October. During this period races are to be seen all over the island, and travel agents in Surabaya can whisk you over and have you back the same day. Races are usually held on weekends.

Be warned that the heat, the crowds, the clashing music and the thunder of the racing bulls is not for the faint hearted. Most of all a front row seat is not advisable. It's not unheard of, particularly at the height of the finals, for teams of bulls to go crashing into the spectators. It's all part of the fun — unless, of course, you happen to be sitting in the front row yourself (see MADURA in CENTRAL JAVA, page 137).

Visit the Son of Krakatoa

LIKE ITS PARENT, WHICH IS NOW USUALLY SPELLED KRAKATAU, THIS IS NO ORDINARY CHILD. Boisterous and capricious, the progeny of great forces, Anak Krakatau — the Son of Krakatau — fascinates, but is best appreciated at a distance.

Krakatau was thought to be dormant until in mid-1883 passing ships noted that it had bestirred itself. On August 27 at 10 AM it exploded with the biggest bang in recorded history: It was heard 4,000 km (2,500 miles) away in Brisbane, Australia. A towering plume of ash

hurtled 80 km (50 miles) into the upper atmosphere, casting much of Indonesia into darkness. The settling ash and dust produced fantastic tropical sunsets as far away as Los Angeles and London for three years afterwards.

It was catastrophic of course. The sea surged into the sudden cavity caused by the collapse of the volcano (it was erupting faster than magma was accumulating beneath it, leaving a vast empty cavity into which the volcano and the sea fell) and met superheated molten rock. Huge tsunamis resulted, one of them more than 40 m (133 ft) high. The tsunamis barreled relentlessly into the coast of west Java and south Sumatra, destroying over 160 villages and

accounting for approximately 36,000 deaths.

In moments Krakatau turned itself into a 300-m (980-ft)-deep hole in the ocean floor. But by 1927 a new steaming and rumbling volcanic cone was nudging its way out of the sea. Today it stands more than 150 m (490 ft) above sea level.

Krakatau is not far offshore from the beach resorts of **Anyer**, **Carita** and **Labuan**, all of which are easy day trips from Jakarta. The journey out to Krakatau, however, requires a full day, which means you will have to stay overnight at one of the resorts. Don't stint on costs. Take one of the more expensive hotel tours, such as the one offered by the

Mambruk Quality Resort at Anyer. A journey out to the Son of Krakatau is not to be taken lightly.

And what a trip it is! For the adventurous souls who make the effort, it will be the experience of a lifetime. As your boat chugs out to sea you will see Anak Krakatau, its blunt and gently sloping cone issuing a dark plume of ash, and if it is particularly active, perhaps spitting boulders from its molten maw. As you get closer, you will hear it booming and roaring, a huge elemental sound that brings your heart into your mouth.

A day at the races in Madura.

It is best to survey the boy volcano from the nearby island of **Krakatau Kecil** — Little Krakatau — rather than Anak Krakatau itself. Like its explosive parent the son is a creature of unpredictable and sometimes destructive moods (see WEST JAVA in JAVA, page102; LAMPUNG in SUMATRA, page 178).

Dolphins at Dawn

IMAGINE BOBBING AROUND ON A SLIGHT SWELL IN THE LIMPID FIRST LIGHT OF DAY, the sky brushed with fading strokes of pink and vermilion, only to be startled from your bleary-eyed reverie by a whoosh and a flash of streamlined gray.

Splash!

"A dolphin!" comes the shout. "Another one!" shouts someone else.

Dolphins, it must be said, are show-offs. Give them a huddle of camera-toting humans and they'll take to the air in a display *of joie de vivre* as if to remind their audience that humans are clumsy landlubbers, inelegant in both air and water, neither fish nor fowl. Not every day, mind you. This is not a circus. The dolphins perform when they feel like it.

One thing is certain, though: Be at **Lovina Beach** in North Bali and take a fisherman's *prahu* out to sea, and you'll see dolphins. Not just the lithe, slippery Flipper variety; some of these dolphins are big, weighing more than a ton.

Organize your dawn dolphin excursion the afternoon before you wish to go, at any of the Lovina Beach guesthouses or restaurants. You will be woken the next morning at around 6 AM, around 15 minutes before the boats set off. The *prahu*, with their outriggers connected to the main vessel by bamboo arms, must be among the most stable boats in the world (choose one of the bigger ones with wooden outriggers so that you're not bobbing about so much that you get seasick). They're certainly among the most colorful. A dozen or so chug out in search of dolphins most mornings, and at the first sighting the race is on to be the first party there.

The excursions last around two hours, if you're just out at sea watching the dolphins. By 7:30 AM the dolphins have headed out to deeper waters to feed. Breakfast — *pisang goreng* (fried bananas with rice) and sweet tea — is served on board, often as dozens of dolphins frolic on either side. You can lengthen the trip by combining it with snorkeling on the reef — an experience akin to being plunged into a vast tropical aquarium — on the way back.

Dolphin watching at Lovina is inexpensive: approximately US$6. At remoter locations around Bali, you will have to pay more. In south Bali, **Bali Diving Perdana (** (361) 286493, for instance, will pick you up from your hotel at the crack of dawn and ship you from Sanur to the Ulu Watu area, with its dramatic cliffs, for dolphin-sighting. Great scenery, same dolphins.

Seven Nights of Dance and Drama

NOT EVERYONE IS UP TO IT BUT, IF STAMINA ALLOWS, A WEEK IN THE BALINESE VILLAGE OF UBUD will thrust you into a heady nightly pageant of dance and drama. Get a program from the local tourist office and then plan your evenings around the performances that most interest you. There are several performances at different locations every night, which means that if you find yourself particularly entranced by a dance you can usually see it performed again (often by another troupe) on another night of the same week. For the Balinese dance and life co-mingle in a way that is difficult for non-Balinese to understand. The dancers you see performing rarely devote their lives to dance. It is simply something they do, that everyone does, though the dances themselves are of course the product of hundreds of hours of diligent practice.

An entranced dancer reaches the climactic moment in the Balinese *kris* dance.

great battle between the forces of good and evil. Similarly, in the **Barong** dance, the *barong*, a lion-like personification of the force of good does fierce battle with a witch-like personification of evil, known as Rangda. Rangda puts the *barong*'s *kris*-bearing armies into a trance, and the sight of the young Balinese men wrestling with their *kris* in an entranced state, seemingly hell-bent on doing away with themselves as the *barong* frantically careens in their midst attempting with his own magic to dispel the trance is one not quickly forgotten.

Everybody soon discovers they have a favorite. For some it will be the *wayang kulit* shadow puppets. There is something magical about the *wayang kulit*, with its fantastic leather puppet characters acting out the age-old drama of the *Ramayana* or the *Mahabharata*, against a white backlit sheet. It is like chancing upon some ancient forerunner of the cinema, and if you have the good fortune to find yourself amongst an Indonesian audience, who understand the proceedings, you will see that the effect is hypnotic.

For others, Bali's trance dances are irresistible. The **Kecak**, for example, earns its name from the "kecak-kecak" chant of a shoulder-to-shoulder chorus of male singers whose rhythmic chanting induces a trance state as the performers act out a

But probably the most beloved of Balinese dances is the **Legong** a breathtakingly graceful dance that traditionally is performed by girls from the age of eight into their early teens, though nowadays you will see adult dancers too. The movements are still-frame staccato and performed in attitudes of beatific concentration. Don't think for a moment, though, that these diminutive performers, cling-wrapped in lustrous lamé, are in a trance: Every movement has been choreographed, the child performer's limbs stretched and molded until they achieve the suppleness to act in the startling but always formalized vernacular of Balinese dance. Their perfect poise and otherworldly posturing will be just one of the moments that linger in your memory, a chaotic jumble of gamelan chimes, entranced warrior armies, shadows acting out epic tales, after a week in the village of Ubud.

Here There Be Dragons

ONE THING YOU DON'T WANT HAPPENING ON YOUR TRIP TO INDONESIA IS A LONE ENCOUNTER WITH A HUNGRY DRAGON ON THE ISLAND OF KOMODO. Indonesians like to claim they were the inspiration for the Chinese dragons of myth. Others claim they are the cousin of an even bigger Australian species that is now extinct. Whatever the case, the Komodo dragon is big: a meat-eating giant that grows up to over three meters (10 ft) long and weighs as much as 136 kg (300 lbs).

You might scoff, but the world's largest lizard can indeed kill an adult human: They are fast runners, they can climb, their tails can deliver crushing blows, and if that weren't enough, a Komodo bite will leave a nasty hole infected with bacteria so virulent that the victim normally only hangs on for a few days. But don't let this put you off. The dragons of Komodo are well fed and far more interested in freebies from the tourists than hunting them down. The last known foreign victim of a dragon was in 1973, an unusual situation in which an elderly traveler was deserted by his guide after an accident.

Known as *ora* in Indonesian, the Komodo dragon is a monitor lizard, and despite its fearful appearance and the potential for lethal encounters, a dragon will generally only attack if threatened. Dragons are more interested in wild boar and deer, which they spring upon in ambush by lurking inconspicuously on their victims' habitual trails.

Komodo, a barren (for most of the year) islet, seems the perfect home for this unique animal. The small village, comprising a couple of hundred bamboo houses on stilts, is populated by the descendants of convicts banished here, the island of monsters, for crimes we can only imagine now. What a hard place it must have seemed in centuries past! From April, blistering winds blow off the Australian continent, scorching the island's scant vegetation and making it impossible for the convicts to grow rice. And up on the highlands water buffalo, deer and wild hogs are stalked by the dragons. They can be seen hiding from the heat in burrows too small for their massive bulk, their tongues flicking idly in and out. When they bring down their prey, they converge on the victim, a writhing confluence of as many as 20 beasts.

Visitors observe the dragons from a viewing platform which overlooks a feeding area. This is the most convenient place to see them, but if you have time you should hire a guide to take you out to remoter location, where dragon encounters (safe ones) have more of a safari flavor. The **Poreng Valley**, around five kilometers (three miles) from the

OPPOSITE: A Komodo dragon's tongue TOP can "sniff" out its surroundings, while those claws BOTTOM can bring down a goat. ABOVE: A dragon basks indolently in the sun, belying its swift agility.

camp at Loh Liang (where all visitors are obliged to stay if they are not on a cruise ship), is an excellent hike and one that brings a good chance of seeing dragons and other wildlife. Don't forget to bring a telephoto lens (see also KOMODO in NUSA TENGGARA, page 222).

Gaze on the Colored Lakes of Flores

A WORD OF WARNING: IF ANOTHER BLEARY-EYED SUNRISE ON A MOUNTAIN IS SIMPLY OUT OF THE QUESTION, READ NO FURTHER. If on the other hand, the splendor of mounts Agung and Batur in Bali, Bromo in Java and Rinjani in Lombok has merely whetted your appetite, then continue farther off the beaten track to Flores Island in Nusa Tenggara, where the three lakes of **Mt. Keli Mutu** are not to be missed.

Visitors find themselves reaching for words such as "surreal" and "otherworldly" when they describe the lakes, each a different color, that lie at the top of Mt. Keli Mutu, an extinct volcano. Locals concur, ascribing supernatural qualities to each of them. At least part of the fascination is the way the colors regularly change. The lakes are featured on the 5,000 rupiah note, but the colors you see today are altogether different: The maroon lake for example, has turned almost black, while the other two are shades of green.

From the village of Moni you can hike up to the summit of Mt. Keli Mutu in a few hours, but most people choose to hop on a truck and drive up at 4:30 AM to be there in time for the sunrise. The lakes look their best on a clear morning. Most people head back on the truck at 7 AM for breakfast after a cursory look at the lakes and a few photographs. Don't follow their example. Prepare a light breakfast the night before and bring it up with you. Once the crowds (usually small) have gone you can strike off alone into a landscape that looks as if it has been lifted from the cover of a science fiction novel.

For those who wonder about such things, despite the claims of most travel writers, the shifting colors of Mt. Keli Mutu's lakes are not a scientific mystery. To be sure the reasons are complex, having to do with minerals in the water, rainfall and hydrothermal activity, but the main determinant is the amount of oxygen in the water: the more oxygen, as with your blood, the redder (or even blacker) the color.

Then again, perhaps the travel writers know best. Forget the rationalist world of science as you stand looking over these curiously colored lakes on a crisp early morning on the faraway island of Flores.

Who knows perhaps the locals are right? That dark lake there is the home

of the souls of evil doers; that light green lake the home of the souls of departed old people. And that bright green lake there, that must be the home of the young, departed before their time (see MT. KELI MUTU in NUSA TENGGARA, page 225).

Float off to Market

ALL OVER ASIA YOU FIND CITIES VYING FOR THE COVETED TITLE OF "VENICE OF THE EAST." Bangkok held the title for the first half of the twentieth century, but these days the famous *khlongs* — canals — are incidental to the reality of traffic-clogged Bangkok. Besides, even 30 years ago travelers were

complaining that the floating markets of Bangkok were a tourist trap. If the East has a Venice today, it is little known **Banjarmasin** in Indonesian Borneo, otherwise known as Kalimantan.

This obscure city of around half a million grew up at the confluence of the Barito and Martapura rivers, which flow out of the mountainous jungles of Borneo into the Java Sea. It's a watery place. Only the city center is on dry land. Most of the inhabitants live in pile houses on a maze of canals.

A boat journey through the canals is *de rigueur*. Early morning and late afternoon are the times to set out. The

The ever-shifting hues of Keli Mutu's colored lakes.

light is warm and glowing at this time (perfect for photographs) and everyone is out on the verandahs of their homes, down by the water, bathing and washing clothes. Naked children dive-bomb with shrieks from the windows of their family homes, tiny blurs of writhing brown limbs and flashes of grinning white teeth. (They'll splash you if they can get within range, so be careful with your camera.) As you cruise the canals, look for the floating shops, the floating clinics. Everything here is floating. You will undoubtedly be caught in the occasional floating traffic jam if you're here in the late afternoon.

The highlight of a visit to Banjarmasin is a dawn (yes, another one) visit to the city's superlative floating market, **pasar terapung**. Chances are, you will be the only tourists there; everyone else will be paddling in search of bargains on eggs, vegetables and rice. If you're running low on gas, you can stop at the floating gas station. Don't forget to stop off at a floating *warung* for breakfast. Coffee is served along with a selection of rice cakes and pastries, all displayed for you to inspect and choose as you draw up alongside. Breakfasts of this variety, among the *sampans* and canoes, the vendors sheltering from the early morning sun under their wide-brimmed hats, come only once in a lifetime for most of us. Float around for a while and make the most of it (see SOUTH KALIMANTAN in KALIMANTAN, page 260).

The watery world of Banjarmasin's "back streets."

YOUR CHOICE

The Great Outdoors

Indonesia is a vast, mountainous archipelago, much of its lowlands covered in steamy jungle. Environmentalists have long leveled accusing fingers at Indonesia's blithe attitudes to logging; the Indonesian government has responded by establishing over 20 national parks.

One of Indonesia's top national parks, **Ujung Kulon**, can be easily visited on a tour from Jakarta. The park covers more than 750 sq km (270 sq miles) and includes pristine forest, coral reefs and deserted beaches. But most visitors are drawn by the promise of a rare opportunity to glimpse some of Indonesia's native wildlife, notably the near-extinct Javan rhino.

You're more likely to have company (of the human, fellow-traveler variety) at the **Bromo-Tengger-Semeru National Park**, in eastern Java. The attraction is Mt. Bromo, a striking volcanic cone that presides over a hauntingly beautiful lunar landscape. Hiking to the summit of this volcano for the sunrise is a popular activity.

Sumatra's favorite national park getaway is **Gunung Leuser** (*gunung* means mountain). At almost 10,000 sq km (3,500 sq miles), it's a vast place. For most people interest is focused, however, on a small corner of the eastern edge of the park called Bukit Lawang. This is where you will find the **Orangutan Rehabilitation Center**. Those who make it to Sumatra's charming hill resort of Bukittinggi should take a walk in the nearby **Lembah Anai Nature Reserve**, where lucky visitors may clap their eyes on the world's largest flower: the *rafflesia*.

Bali Barat National Park is on the western flank of Bali and is a good place for bird watching, with over 300 species represented, but it doesn't see huge numbers of visitors. Its offshore island, Pulau Menjangan is also noted for great snorkeling and good diving. For most visitors to Bali, the great outdoors is more likely to mean sunning on the beaches or beside a pool, or for the more energetic a hike up Bali's magnificent **Mt. Agung**.

OPPOSITE: Into the dawn by pony at Mt. Bromo. ABOVE: The black sand shore serves as a major footpath in lonely North Bali.

Throughout the scattered islands of Nusa Tenggara the attractions are mostly of the outdoor variety — beaches, more mountains, hikes. On Lombok, Bali's less touristed next door neighbor, hardy trekkers can make their way up to the caldera of **Mt. Rinjani**, where the Segara Anak lake nestles wondrously in a lost world setting. The trek up takes you through the protected forests on Rinjani's slopes. But Nusa Tenggara's most famous national park and attraction is the **Komodo National Park**, where you can watch the world's largest lizards feasting on the prey they have brought down.

Elsewhere around Indonesia, you will find no shortage of outdoor activities and sights. In **Kalimantan** the mighty Kapuas, Barito and Mahakam rivers carry the intrepid into "darkest Borneo," where with the right guides they can embark on jungle treks. The **Tanjung Puting National Park** in Kalimantan is home to Indonesia's other Orangutan Rehabilitation Center and to a host of other wildlife too.

Irian Jaya is emerging as another favored destination for the more adventurous traveler with a love of the great outdoors. The remote **Baliem Valley**, for centuries lost in the clouds and home to the Dani people, can now be reached by airplane. The valley offers splendid hiking opportunities.

Sporting Spree

DIVING AND SNORKELING

With more than 13,600 tropical islands to its name, Indonesia has almost unlimited potential as a diving destination. Whole books have been devoted to the subject, and if you are a serious diver it is to one of these you should turn when planning your itinerary.

Bali is Indonesia's favored diving location. True, Bali may not offer Indonesia's best diving, but the dive shops and schools there are better, making Bali a good place for beginners and for vacationers who have tasted the delights of the submarine world and

would like a second helping. Pro Dive ℂ/FAX (361) 288756, Jalan Sekarwaru, in Sanur, has been in the game for some 25 years and has a wide range of PADI courses to suit all levels of experience, from the true novice to those who fancy themselves as instructors.

Some other reliable dive outfits in Bali include: Baruna Diving Cruising Marine Sports ℂ (361) 753820 FAX (361) 753809, PO Box 3419, Denpasar, Bali; Oceana Dive Center ℂ (361) 288892 FAX (361) 288652, Jalan Bypass Ngurah Rai, Sanur, Bali; and Island Divers ℂ 81-139-6181 FAX (361) 731784, Jalan Dhyana Pura N°5A, Seminyak, Bali.

Currently, Bali's top dive location is Tulamben, which among other drawing cards provides the exciting opportunity to explore the wreck of the USS *Liberty* amongst a plethora of technicolor marine life.

For those who seek to escape the madding crowd, Indonesia is rich in remote and exotic dive sites. But before booking a flight to Sulawesi or Nusa

OPPOSITE: A Treasure Island world awaits divers at Manado. ABOVE: A pufferfish is just one species in an enchanting variety of underwater life found off Indonesia's shores.

Tenggara, consider organizing a dive cruise. Maluku Adventures (415-731-2560 FAX 415-731-2579, PO Box 7625, Menlo Park, CA 94026-7625, USA, offers, among its many diving programs, cruises on the *Pindito*, a Swiss-owned Phinisi Ketch, which sails in luxury comfort around Sulawesi and northwest Irian Jaya, newly emerging and unspoiled dive destinations. Another operator with similar cruises is Poseidon Ventures Dive Tours (714-644-5344 FAX 714-644-5392, 359 San Miguel Drive, Newport Beach, CA 92660, which has the 100-ft MV *Baruna Adventurer* and the MYS *Perentis*, a stylishly converted Bugis schooner with seven en suite cabins. Sulawesi is fast becoming one of the most popular destinations in Indonesia for serious divers. Vantor International Travel (2723-9078 FAX 2724-4903, Room 202, Enterprise Center, 4 Hart Avenue, Tsimshatsui, Kowloon, Hong Kong, has tours to the reefs and underwater valleys of the Bunaken National Park, near Manado (on Sulawesi). Excellent visibility, colorful reefs, wreck diving and abundant marine life — angel fish, turtles, eagleray, tuna, barracuda and dolphins — make this one of Indonesia's most alluring diving

locations. Local dive operators in Sulawesi include: Barracuda Diving Resort ((431) 854279 FAX (431) 864848, Molas Dusun II, Manado, Sulawesi; Murex Manado Dive Resort ((431) 66280 FAX (431) 52116, Jalan Jend. Sudirman N°28, Manado, Sulawesi; and Nusantara Dive Resort ((431) 63988 FAX (431) 60368, Molas Beach, Manado, Sulawesi.

Another diving center is Ambon in Maluku. The Ambon Dive Center (/FAX 911-55685, Pantai Namalatu, Latulahat, Ambon, Maluku, conducts dives out to some 30 world-class sites, where, if you are lucky, you may even catch a glimpse of the rare dugong, the Asian manatee. The night dives off Namalatu Beach receive breathless reports from divers, as do the day dives at Carol's Coral Canyon. Nusa Tenggara also has some good diving sites, though it attracts smaller numbers of divers. In Lombok, Baruna Watersports ((364) 93333 FAX (364) 93140, Sheraton Senggigi Beach Resort, Lombok, can organize dives around the island, where beaches and the diving tend to be better than on its nearby and much more heavily touristed neighbor, Bali. The best diving (and snorkeling) is on Lombok's Gili

Islands, which are rapidly becoming one of Asia's most popular backpacking destinations. Maluku Adventures (see above) have diving tours to other, more remote, destinations in Nusa Tenggara, among them Komodo, an island otherwise famed for its dragons, and the Roti and Alor Islands, near Kupang, West Timor. Don't be surprised if you find yourself puttering out to sea in a traditional *prahu*, though you can be sure that the foreign-run tours meet international safety standards.

Even Sumatra and Kalimantan are emerging as dive centers nowadays. In Sumatra, the Sibolga Marine Resort ((631) 23588 FAX (631) 23338, Sibolga, North Sumatra, conducts dives out to such attractions as Bata Memara (Tower Rock), where you will see clownfish, cardinal fish and blue-spotted stingrays. In Kalimantan, Derawan Island is a world class site, with unique marine life and breathtaking drop-offs.

Snorkeling is an easier and cheaper alternative to diving, and Indonesia is rich in sites. A snorkel, mask and flippers are lightweight additions to your luggage, saving you the trouble of seeking out someone with gear to hire when you find a promising patch of water. The Gili Islands off Lombok have emerged as a popular beach getaway and snorkeling destination amongst budget travelers in recent years.

Waiara, near Maumere in Flores, is another popular place for snorkeling and, above all, diving. **Flores Sao Resort (Sao Wisata)** ((383) 21555 FAX (383) 21666 or bookings in Jakarta at ((21) 370333, extension 78222, is the longest-running dive outfit here. A small bungalow hotel on the shores of the marine reserve, Sao Wisata offers world-class diving and has, indeed, hosted a number of underwater photographic competitions in the past.

SURFING
Surfers are a tight-knit fraternity with their own lingo and their own information networks for finding the best waves. They've descended on the

beaches of Indonesia in a big way. The reasons are simple: great beaches, good surf, and cheap living. Bali is the first stop for most surfers, and on flights from Australia (in particular) airport staff are long-accustomed to dealing with surf boards. You can also buy most of your surfing needs at Kuta — also the best place for more information about surfing around Indonesia. In Kuta, call into Tubes, on Poppies Lane II, a laid-back bar with nightly video screenings (including surf movies); it is a famous surfer hangout and a good source of information. Kuta and Legian have areas where beginners can rent boards and learn about surfing.

Elsewhere around Indonesia, surfing is popular in Lombok, Sumbawa, but most famously at Grajagan, in Java's Alas Purwo National Park (you'll need to join a surfing tour to get here) and on Sumatra's Nias Island. Both of the latter are on the world professional circuit.

OPPOSITE: A lionfish in the waters off Manado, Sulawesi. ABOVE: A surfer catches one of Nias Island's (Sumatra) famous righthanders — one of the archipelago's prime surfing destinations. OVERLEAF: Amongst the orangutans.

HIKING AND CLIMBING

Inevitably, at some point in your Indonesian adventure, you end up puffing up a volcano or a mountain. Perhaps, paraphrasing Mallory on the subject of Everest, it's because they're there.

The primer is **Mt. Bromo** in Java, the hardest part of which is the 4 AM start in order to be there for the sunrise. For a more challenging climb, **Mt. Rinjani**, on Lombok, is popular with hikers; as with many Indonesian hikes and climbs, a guide is essential. **Mt. Agung** in Bali is another popular hike.

Hiking in Indonesia is not all pitting yourself against steep gradients in sulfurous clouds. Parts of the archipelago's lowlands provide superb opportunities to see local wildlife and visit remote villages. Join a guided trek in the **Gunung Leuser National Park** for glimpses of the park's rich wildlife. Tigers, elephants, rhinos and orangutans elusively haunt the jungle depths of the park. The **Toraja** region of Sulawesi, on the other hand, offers the opportunity to hike out to remote villages of a people for whom death and its rites are life's major event. On **Nias Island** (another good surfing destination) in Sumatra, guides will take you out to the megalithic villages of the local people.

THRILLS

Whitewater rafting and bungee jumping, among other adventure sports, are starting to become popular in Indonesia. It's early days yet, and safety standards should be foremost on your mind if you are considering signing up for anything adventurous. Bali is the best place for rafting, simply because the operators have years of experience and employ foreign instructors.

Some rafting agencies in Bali include **Bali Safari Rafting (** (361) 221315 FAX 0361-221316; **Ayung River Rafting (** (361) 238759 FAX 224236; and **Raging Thunder Adventures (** (361) 758822 FAX (361) 758814.

The Open Road

Outside of Bali, where car, four-wheel-drive renting vehicles and motorbikes is popular, you will probably not do any driving in Indonesia; and if you're prudent, you'll spend as little time on the roads as possible. Indonesian highways are seldom ones that travelers break into misty-eyed rapture over.

Even in Bali, where roads remain scant despite the development of the last few decades, the traffic can be heavy at times. And dangerous too. Indonesian drivers tend to hunker down behind the wheel with an air of carefree fatalism that many Western drivers find downright frightening.

A favorite Bali route is from bustling **Denpasar** to the relaxing beach of **Singaraja** on the north coast. It's not wildly scenic, but once you're in Singaraja you might overnight in **Lovina** (just 10 minutes away), which is popular for dolphin-watching, and then take the northern coastal road for an eastwards run all the way to **Amed**, a secluded beach area. Along the way you might stop at **Sangsit**, where there are a couple of temples decorated in relief artwork, and farther around the coast, **Tulamben** with its famous wreck and diving. It may be possible to continue on along this superb stretch of coast, with its views of Lombok on one side and Mt. Agung on the other, to the ruined water-temple at **Ujung**, but it would be a good idea to ask about the condition of the road before you set off. The drive to **Amlapura** is more trouble-free.

Java's most spectacular stretch of road lies between Bogor and Bandung. The 1,500-m (4,900-ft) **Puncak Pass** is a picturesque area of tea plantations and a resort favored by Jakartans as a weekend escape from the heat and the dust of the big city. It's often shrouded in mist, but on clear days it offers breathtaking views of Jakarta on the sweltering plains below.

Lombok on two wheels — just watch out for gravel on the bends.

Backpacking

There are few destinations in the world that can compare with Indonesia as a budget backpacking destination. Travel, accommodation and food are all inexpensive, and with over 17,000 islands and more than 30 ethnic groups scattered the 5,200-km (3,220-mile) length of the archipelago, there's no shortage of interesting adventures, either.

THE BACKPACKING TRAILS

The most popular destinations in Indonesia for backpackers — and for everyone else — are in Java, Sumatra and Bali. For overlanders traveling south from Thailand and Malaysia, there are handy connections from Penang, Kuala Lumpur and Singapore to Medan and the Riau Islands in Sumatra, just off the coast of Singapore. Of course, overlanders from Australia, who may perhaps have traveled the long and arduous route up through the islands of Nusa Tenggara, do the route in reverse.

In Sumatra, the backpacker trail starts in Medan. From there it's a brief hop to the legendary **Lake Toba**, a startling splash of blue in the jungly north of the island that was brought into being by a huge volcanic eruption some 100,000 years ago. Budget accommodation and lively travelers' cafés are a dime a dozen on Samosir Island, which sits in the middle of the lake.

The trail divides at this point. Some travelers head to **Nias Island**, a popular surfing getaway with unspoiled beaches and the added lure of treks into the hills to see the island's megalithic villages. But the vast majority of travelers carry on to **Bukittinggi**, a popular hill station with a host of hiking opportunities in its vicinity.

Tent camping off the beaten track at Sumatra's secluded Lake Maninjan.

From Bukittinggi it's a long haul by bus to Jakarta. It was an ordeal that was once known to travelers as the "Green Hell," a reference to the condition of the roads and the jungle on either side of them. The roads have improved immensely over the last decade, but it's still a long journey (30 hours) that is best broken halfway if you want to preserve your sanity.

The trail divides again in **Jakarta**, which is the transportation hub of all Indonesia. Travelers looking to experience the less touristed delights of more remote islands such as Sulawesi, Maluku or Borneo often jump off from here, traveling onwards either by boat or by plane. Those traveling overland to Bali and onwards generally make a beeline straight for the cultural centers of **Yogyakarta** in central Java. These fascinating cities are rich with historical attractions and cultural pursuits, and also offer a wealth of budget accommodation and food, so that some travelers end up lingering for weeks. From here, **Mt. Bromo** is a standard stopover en route to **Surabaya** and Bali. The old Dutch town of **Malang** is another possible stopover on this route.

Overlanders on their way to Australia must make a decision in Bali: fly direct or island hop down Nusa Tenggara to **Kupang** in Timor, where inexpensive flights go to Darwin. How long it will take you to get from Bali to Timor will depend on your mode of transportation. Roads and boat connections are vastly improved on conditions a decade ago, but it's still a rugged trip. You should figure on spending a couple of weeks doing it, unless you are prepared to speed things up by taking a couple of flights. The most popular en-route stops are **Komodo Island** and the colored lakes of **Mt. Keli Mutu** close to Ende in Flores.

GETTING AROUND

If you're backpacking on a budget you will want to avoid flying whenever possible. It's not just the money. In the traveler's book of rules, flying is a form of cheating: You don't earn the sweet rewards of arrival in the air-conditioned comfort of a quick flight, and you miss out on the scenery too.

Budget travel in Indonesia is essentially buses and boats. Boats are required for interisland (and occasionally upriver) travel; buses are the mainstay of all

overland travel. Safety is a matter for concern on both. If possible use only PELNI-operated boats, and when traveling overland, choose day coaches rather than the night buses (*bis malam*). Indonesian bus drivers are given to suicidal impulses any time of day, but night driving brings out the worst in them.

Indonesian buses come in a variety of forms, but the basic categories are: *ekonomi* (cheap, basic and extremely slow), *patas* (an "express" service that in theory goes from A to B with stops only at designated points), and luxury (usually a Japanese-made monster with on-board movies, toilet and, if you're very unlucky, karaoke). Most luxury services run at night.

PELNI-operated boats offer five classes of travel with wide differences in price and comfort. The temptation, if you're counting your rupiahs, is to plump for *ekonomi*. The drawbacks are threefold: First, sleeping arrangements involve finding a place on the floor (though "mattresses" can usually be rented inexpensively); second, it gets very crowded; and third, the economy-class meals are unpalatable. Going up a bracket to fourth class involves a price

hike of 50%, but it will provide you with an allocated bed in an eight-bunk cabin and access to the first-class restaurant, where you can feast inexpensively on Indonesian cuisine.

WHERE TO STAY

The *losmen*, or homestay, is to Indonesia what the bed and breakfast is to Britain. But in Indonesia you pay a lot less for family hospitality and home cooking than you would in Britain. In fact, if you speak some Indonesian, you can stay in a *penginapan*, which is even cheaper than a *losmen*, but such places are usually unsavory and rarely welcoming to foreigners.

On the well trodden trail from Bali to Sumatra you will find superb value for money on the accommodation front. *Losmen* are abundant in these parts of Indonesia and in popular travel haunts such as Ubud in Bali, Yogyakarta in Java and Lake Toba in Sumatra you will be spoiled for choice. In other parts of the archipelago, you will be less spoiled.

OPPOSITE: A torrent rushes under a rickety bridge in the lost world of Irian Jaya's Baliem Valley.
ABOVE: Solitude by the sea at Pulau Lei Lei, South Sulawesi.

Kalimantan tends to be expensive with the exception of Banjarmasin and Samarinda, as does Irian Jaya.

The cheapest *losmen* will provide a simple room with little more than a bed and perhaps a fan. Washing and toilet facilities will be shared. Bathing in the cheaper Indonesian hotels is done *mandi* style. A *mandi* (which is also the word for "to wash") is a big tub of cold water from which you scoop and shower (never climb into the *mandi* or allow soap or used water to slop back into it). Prices in accommodations with such facilities can be as low as US$2 per night.

When there are no decent *losmen* to be found, ask for a *wisma*, a step up in price and comfort from the *losmen*. When all else fails, most towns will have a couple of Chinese-run budget hotels that have a range of rooms from fan-cooled with shared washing facilities at rates of around US$4 to 5 up to air-conditioned rooms from US$10.

Living It Up

Indonesia is not a wealthy country, but in the major population centers of Java, in the tourist resorts of Bali and in some newly emerging exclusive getaways around the archipelago, visitors will find some opportunities to enjoy the good life Indonesian style. Much of this is owing to the government's realization that tourists are no longer just travelers but beach-loving visitors or city slickers with demanding and, usually, international tastes. To this end, a number of international hotel groups, such as Holiday Inn and Sheraton have pledged to build not just one, but a series of luxury hotels in the country. These are now becoming a reality.

Bali, which has been in the business of catering to foreigners' needs longer than anywhere else in Indonesia does it with more style and grace than anywhere else in the country. But that is not to say that Jakarta, Surabaya, Bandung, Lombok or the Riau Archipelago should be overlooked.

Telephone numbers for the hotels and restaurants mentioned below can be found in the text under the individual place names.

EXCEPTIONAL HOTELS

Bali is where Indonesia comes into its own as a destination for the well-heeled in search of the high life. Bali's best congregates in the southeast of the island, in the tourist districts of Sanur, Nusa Dua, Ubud and Seminyak.

Sanur is favored by expatriates and has many fine hotels and restaurants, along with a few hotel night clubs. Nusa Dua is a five-star tourist enclave, just 15-minute's drive from the lively — and brash — Kuta and Legian tourist areas. The long beach that extends from the airport through Tuban, Kuta, Legian, Seminyak and beyond has something for everybody. From the low-rent hubbub of Kuta's Bemo Corner area to Seminyak's elegant hotels, restaurants and nightlife, it is possible to take a one-night tour that encompasses Bali at its very best and very worst.

For true exclusivity, Bali has three **Aman** resorts: the Amanusa, atop a hill overlooking the golf course at Nusa Dua; the Amandari, just outside Ubud, with its walled bungalows, some replete with private swimming pools; and Amankila, with its stunning clifftop location outside Candi Dasa. Helicopters whiz privileged guests from one resort to the other. For luxury with a hint of adventure, Aman also has an exclusive tented resort Amanwana on Moyo Island, off the island of **Sumbawa** east of Lombok.

In the Legian–Seminyak quarter, the **Legian** and **Oberoi** are justly celebrated. On Jimbaran Beach is the **Four Seasons Resort** with its individual plunge pools, huge villas and ocean vistas. Nusa Dua offers six hotels, but the original **Nusa Dua Beach Hotel**, with its gorgeous gardens, is a study in informal elegance and remains a firm favorite despite the competition. Farther afield on Bukit is the **Bali Cliff (** (361) 771992 FAX (361) 771993 which has perhaps the best prospect on

the island. On Sanur the **Tandjung Sari's** pedigree and standards are guaranteed by its clientele, which reads like a roll call of the rich and famous. **The Bali Hyatt**, another hotel graced by luxurious gardens remains, as ever, one of Bali's best.

Ubud, once the preserve of budget guesthouses, has got into the act nowadays, with a clutch of exclusive resorts and garden hotels. Notable examples include the intimate **Kupu Kupu Barong**, the larger **Ibah Villas**, **Pita Maha** and the new **Four Seasons Resort** in Sayan.

It's a sign of the times that **Lombok**, Bali's island neighbor, is starting to make its own efforts to attract travelers with luxury tastes. The **Oberoi** has 50 villas built in the form of Lombok rice barns (which are worlds removed from the grim image this conjures up) and

OPPOSITE: A luxury cruiseliner awaits off the coast of Komodo Island. BELOW: Another day in paradise at Lombok's Senggigi Beach.

decorated with Asian antiques, while the **Novotel** at Lombok's South Kuta beach is a sublime meeting of Asian and African architectural and design styles. Aerowisata has **Senggigi Beach Hotel** ((364) 93210 FAX (364) 93200 (on the beach of the same name) with a fine **Sheraton** as a neighbor.

In Java there is no shortage of top hotels in the major cities. Even in Surabaya, once a grim destination, you will find branches of the major hotel chains: **Hilton, Sheraton, Shangri-La, Hyatt Regency** and **Westin**. The **Hotel Majapahit** in Surabaya is one of the many old Dutch-era hotels in Indonesia that have been renovated into contemporary five-star luxury and modernity while preserving much of the old charm. In **Bandung**, a city celebrated for its art deco architecture, the **Grand Hotel Preanger**, and the **Savoy Homann** Hotel are renovated colonial structures with exceptionally high standards. In Jakarta the **Grand Hyatt Jakarta** is probably the best, but you can also enjoy your stay swaddled in comfort at the **Hilton**, the **Mandarin Oriental Jakarta**, or the **Shangri-La Jakarta**.

EXCEPTIONAL RESTAURANTS

For excellent cuisine in five-star surroundings the luxury hotels will always indulge you, but you should also get away from the hotel scene if possible. In Jakarta where, along with the tourist areas of Bali, you'll find some of the best restaurants in the country, there are some highly atmospheric restaurants where you can enjoy a night of the high-life at very reasonable prices.

In **Memories** you can dream of colonial Batavia as you feast on that Dutch planter invention, *rijstafel*. **Club Noordwijk** is another restaurant with a colonial ambiance and home style Dutch Indonesian cooking, while **The Oasis** is housed in a Raffles period style building that dates back to 1928. Among other things it distinguishes itself as the only restaurant in Jakarta (and perhaps the world) where a 12-course *rijstafel* is still served by a dozen beautiful maidens.

In Bandung you can sample traditional Sundanese cuisine (which features, but not exclusively, goldfish) at **Babakan Siliwangi**, a place with a delightful ambiance where you get to choose your goldfish from terraced ponds. At **Hanoman's Forest Garden Restaurant**, in Yogyakarta, you can enjoy puppet and Javanese dance performances over an inexpensive, but delicious, Indonesian meal with the added bonus of a delightful garden setting.

On the Balinese dining front the **Lotus** Cafés (in Ubud, Candi Dasa and elsewhere) and **Poppies**, in Kuta, all provide the rare opportunity to eat out beside a lotus pond. The food is good.

The ambiance is great. Another outdoor delight is **La Lucciola** in Seminyak — be there in time for a sundowner before dinner. The **Kafe Warisan** serves high-class French cuisine in a setting that overlooks rice paddies. The **Café Luna** is a chic Italian restaurant that mounts fashion shows and pulls in the late night party crowds who appreciate the alfresco look-at-me seating on the main Seminyak strip.

Sanur is one of the best places in Bali to seek out fine dining. Four of Sanur's best are the Italian restaurant **Mamma Lucia** and the Hyatt-run **Telaga Naga**, a Chinese restaurant set in a picturesque garden that offers both Sichuan and Cantonese dishes. Beachside dining is

again a favorite at Tandjung Sari. The **Kul Kul Restaurant**, allows you to sample that rarest of treats, Balinese cuisine, though only if you order ahead.

In Nusa Dua the best dining is housed in the exclusive hotels and resorts. But for those who want to escape their hotels the Japanese **Matsuri**, the Mexican **Poco Loco**, and the seafood restaurant **Makuwa Pakuwa** all offer ambiance and high standards.

NIGHTLIFE

Indonesian nightlife is rather low key — often not much more than a drink in a bar, a stroll down a dusty main street, or

The bright lights of downtown Jakarta.

a chapter of your book by the light of a 30-watt lamp. However, in some places, it gets better.

Once again, it is Bali that leads the pack when it comes to nightlife. Kuta's **Goa 2001** and **Gado Gado** are among the favorite night haunts. The luxury hotels have discos and some snug little bars.

In Jakarta, nightlife buzzes, though perhaps more so for the locals than tourists. Again, major hotels have good bars and discos while the **Café Batavia** in Fatahillah Square packs in the masses with money to burn and a desire to be seen. The **Jaya Pub**, extraordinarily, still remains after a couple of decades one of the city's best pubs.

Elsewhere in Indonesia, with the exception of major cities with large numbers of expatriates such as Surabaya and Balikpapan (Kalimantan), you will find nightlife options to be mostly of the glitzy karaoke variety beloved by affluent Chinese. Most cities will have a couple of discos that are the haunt of Westernized middle-class Indonesian youth.

CRUISING

If it's the lap of luxury you hanker for, you need not restrict yourself to Indonesia's five-star hotels: Take a cruise.

Pick of the pack is P&O's **Spice Island Cruises (** (361) 286283, Jalan Padang Galak N°25, Sanur. This company offers the *Bali Sea Dancer* which does three- to four-day outings from Bali to Komodo Island, home of the Komodo dragon, to Lombok, celebrated as "Bali 20 Years Ago," and to Badas, the ancient capital of West Sumbawa. It also operates the smaller *Spice Islander* which, with its shallow draft, takes visitors to the more remote Indonesian islands.

Songline Cruises ((361) 286992 FAX (361) 286985, Jalan Danau Tambingan N°64, Sanur, Bali, offer sumptuous cruises around the archipelago on refitted Bugis schooners. The cruises last from three to 11 days, and travel as far afield as Maluku and Irian Jaya. Schooners are also available for charter for groups of 10 or more.

If your time is limited, consider taking a one-day **Bali Hai Cruise (** (361) 720331 FAX (361) 720334, Benoa Harbor, Bali, to Lembongan Island, a watersports paradise.

A large number of other companies offer tours and charters around the waters of Indonesia. They include: **Bali Camar Yacht Charter (** (361) 720591, Benoa Harbor, Bali; **Island Explorer Cruises (** (361) 289856, Jalan Sekar Waru N°9, Sanur, Bali; **Mabua Express (** (361) 721212, Jalan Dermaga II, Benoa Harbor, Bali; **MSY *Perintis* (** (361) 975478, PO Box 7, Ubud Gianyar, Bali; **Phinisi Sea Safari (** (361) 720220, Jalan Sesetan N°210, Denpasar, Bali; and **Wakalouka Cruises (** (361) 723629, Benoa Harbor, Bali.

SPAS AND HEALTH FACILITIES

Lastly, you might like to indulge yourself in a health treatment. A country that has put much faith in massage, manipulation, mud baths and herbal treatments, Indonesia has some great possibilities. Bali has become the capital of inexpensive massage, and not just cheap beach massages; it is also creating a reputation for good therapeutic massage, and beauty treatments with aromatherapy and essential oils.

On a more sophisticated level, the following resorts all provide extensive health facilities and luxurious pampering — at a rather considerable price: **Four Seasons Resort Jimbaran (** (361) 701010 FAX (361) 701022, Jimbaran, Bali; **Four Seasons Resort Sayan (** (361) 701010 FAX (361) 701022, Sayan, Bali; **Bali Nirvana Resort (** (361) 815900 FAX (361) 815901, Tanah Lot, Bali; **Banyan Tree Bintan (** (771) 81347 FAX (771) 81348, Bintan; and **Javana Spa (** (21) 719-8327 in Sukabumi, near Bogor, on Java.

Family Fun

The Indonesian people are great with children. Even so, most of the country is hard work if you have children with you, especially tiny tots. The absence of sidewalks and the helter-skelter traffic mean that you have to keep a vigilant eye on them whenever you leave your hotel, and you'll probably want to avoid bus travel whenever possible.

If you find yourself in Jakarta with children, take them out to **Jaya Ancol**, Indonesia's largest recreation area, where you will find a massive **swimming pool complex**, an **oceanarium**, and the **Dunia Fantasi** fun park, a Disneyland look-a-like. It's the sort of place you can return to for several days in a row and still have things left to see.

The best place in Indonesia for children is Bali. For a start there is the beach, which all children love. Observe a few simple precautions: Watch for that fierce tropical sun, particularly between 11 AM and 3 PM, and cover children with high-factor sunscreen at all times. And, be sure that children are accompanied by an adult when swimming and that they stay within the red and yellow life flags, where lifeguards maintain a constant lookout.

When everyone has had enough of the beach, there is **Waterbom (** (361) 755676 FAX (361) 753517, Jalan Kartika Plaza, Kuta, where pools, artificial rivers and water slides, shimmer and cascade in a beautiful garden setting. Popular with exhausted parents is the supervised children's park where kids can play while you take a rest.

When splashing in the water has lost its shine, you might take the kids to see the dragons. The Komodo dragons, that is. You can see them at the **Indonesia Jaya Crocodile and Reptile Park** and the **Taman Burung Bali (Bird Park)**. At the first your dragons come with a crocodile and snake topping, and at the second it's birds — 250 exotic species of them.

Don't forget **dolphin-watching** at Lovina in the north or the **Monkey Forest** of Ubud. About 20 km (12 miles) from Ubud is the **Sangeh Monkey Forest**, where a cheeky tribe of monkeys will melt the heart of even the most recalcitrant and fed-up child. The **Monkey Temple** at Pulaki in north Bali is another child pleaser.

On a final Bali note, consider — if you can afford it — staying at **Club Mediterranée**, which has a Kid's Club in which all except the very youngest children can participate in planned activities during the daylight hours. The kids have a great time, meet children from other countries, and you get a vacation.

A boy and his fish at Jakarta's Pasar Ikan.
OVERLEAF: Lombok boys take a pause from their seashore pursuits on Kuta Beach.

Cultural Kicks

Indonesia is not without its urban blots on the landscape and provincial backwaters, but organize your trip properly and it will be a cultural smorgasbord. There are few places in the world that offer so much and in such pleasing variety.

MUSEUMS

Jakarta may be the capital of all Indonesia, but in Java you're much better off heading west to **Yogyakarta** for your cultural kicks. Yogyakarta provides easy access to the other cultural attractions of Central Java, but its own attractions are substantial. Yogyakarta has enough museums to keep you busy for a couple of days. Take a look at the chariots used by the sultans of Yogya at the **Museum Kerata Kraton**. Browse through Java's fabulous arts and crafts at the **Sono-Budoyo Museum** — the *kris* knives, *wayang kulit* puppets and batik are highlights, and don't forget to look at the ancient Hindu statuary in the courtyard outside the museum. For the best in modern Yogyakarta's art, visit the **Affandi Museum**, which features the work of the eponymous artist, Indonesia's most celebrated, along with the work of other modern Javanese painters. Another interesting museum excursion is the **Dutch Fort**, Benteng Vredeburg, where the fort architecture is complemented inside by a history of the Indonesian independence.

PERFORMANCES

By night, you have a choice of performances of a *Ramayana* ballet, or *wayang kulit*, Indonesia's fascinating shadow puppet theater. Once every two weeks marathon performances of the latter are held. Yogyakarta is a popular place to study batik and Indonesian language, and it also affords easy access to **Solo**, another cultural center, and to

Borobudur, Indonesia's most splendid Buddhist monument. Yogyakarta and Solo, of course, together are the main centers for Javanese **batik** production, and a stroll around some of the galleries and factories here is a must-do.

Borobudur is so magnificent that it's easy to forget the other temples and statuary in the surrounding countryside. The **Prambanan Temples**, like Borobudur, date back to the ninth century, and the main three are dedicated to the Hindu gods, Shiva, Vishnu and Brahma. They are less overrun by tourists than nearby Borobudur. If you're lucky enough to be in the area on a full-moon night, you can watch an epic performance of the *Ramayana*.

YOUR CHOICE

Once you've put brash party-loving Kuta behind you, you will soon discover that Bali is a cultural extravaganza. And what better place to experience the rhythms of the Balinese cycle of dance and artistic creation than in the village of **Ubud**. Here the week begins with a performance of the Legong dance at the **Ubud Palace**. In the nearby village of **Bona**, Kecak and trance dances are held.

On Tuesday the *Mahabharata* is performed at **Teges Village**, three kilometers (two miles) from Ubud; in Ubud itself the *Ramayana* ballet is held at the Ubud Palace. Both dances perform scenes from the respective Hindu epics.

On Wednesday look for performances of *wayang kulit*, shadow puppets, at **Oka Kartini** and on Thursday the Ubud Palace is host to the Gabor dance. On Friday the Ubud Palace has Barong dance and a Legong dance is held at Peliatan village (two kilometers or one and a quarter miles from Ubud).

The performances continue over the weekend, with another Legong program at the Ubud Palace on Saturday. All this, along with unscheduled performances and festivals means that something is always happening in Ubud. It doesn't

A man in Irian Jaya, clothed only in a penis gourd, stands outside his home with a 300-year-old mummy.

YOUR CHOICE

take visitors long to realize why this small village grew into the major attraction it is today.

MINORITIES AND INDIGENOUS CULTURE

Approximately 25% of Indonesia's 200 million inhabitants belong to one of more than 250 ethnic minorities. Each of these minorities has its own language and traditions, making for an ethnological and cultural diversity matched by almost no other place on the planet.

Java is the seat of mainstream Indonesian society, and most minorities can be found in the more far-flung islands. But even Java is home to some minorities, notably the **Madurese**, who inhabit the island of Madura, just offshore from Surabaya, and who are renowned for their bull races.

Sumatra has a wealth of ethnic groupings. The inhabitants of the **Mentawai Islands**, about 100 km (60 miles) west of Padang, were isolated for centuries. Nowadays a trickle of adventurous travelers are visiting the remote villages of these people. More accessible is the island of **Nias**, which offers the prospect of organized treks into Niassan villages, with their intriguing megalithic architecture and exhibitions of martial jumping exercises. Bukittinggi, a hill station just a couple of hours by road from Padang, is a center for **Minangkabau** culture, a people whose wooden architecture is splendidly elegant in design and execution. The **Bataks**, who inhabit the region around the stunning Lake Toba, are another group with rich cultural traditions and splendid architecture.

Tanatoraja, in southwestern Sulawesi, is home to one of Indonesia's most fascinating ethnic groups: the Toraja people. The **Torajans** inhabit homes with roofs shaped like buffalo horns, and wealthy Torajans will often decorate the entrances to their homes with actual buffalo horns. But it is the funeral traditions of the Torajans that visitors find most fascinating. For the Torajans, death is life's crowning moment, and funerals are celebrated in elaborate rituals that involve feasting, dancing and the sacrifice of buffaloes. The tribes who inhabit the rainforest interior of Kalimantan, Indonesian Borneo, are known collectively as **Dyaks**. In fact the term Dyak is an all-purpose word that covers a variety of different tribes, most of whom inhabit longhouses and formerly practiced head-hunting. For those with the time and the stamina, a journey upriver and a stay in a traditional longhouse is a fascinating glimpse into another world. Don't worry: Head-hunting is a thing of the past; nowadays, drinking and dancing all night are the more immediate threats to your well-being.

Indonesia's greatest ethnic diversity can be found in Irian Jaya, the Indonesian side of Papua New Guinea. Here more than 200 tribes speak more than 500 languages. Many of the tribal areas are inaccessible, but the **Dani** people of the Baliem Valley have become a target for tourism in recent years. The polygamous Dani still dress in penis gourds (men) and grass skirts (women).

Shop till You Drop

If you have a taste for the exotic, Indonesia is the perfect shopping destination. The islands of Indonesia are rich in arts and crafts, with villages of artisans producing everything from stunning batik and woven textiles to woodcarvings and jewelry.

BARGAINING

With the exception of airfares, package tours and restaurant food the price of every commodity or service in Indonesia is subject to negotiation. Even at the top luxury hotels, you

A Sumatran woman — one of more than 250 ethnic minorities — in festive attire.

should always ask for a discount if you aren't on a prepaid tour.

In bargaining, several common sense rules apply. First, never lose your temper or become abusive. The object, after all, is for both you and the merchant to come away from the transaction feeling satisfied. Secondly, always set a price before the service is performed. If you ride in an unmetered taxi without first agreeing on the tariff, prepare to pay whatever the driver demands.

Good bargainers are coy, devious and deceitful. Mask your lust for every new-found treasure with a poker face. If a merchant refuses to bargain, or will come down only 10%, simply walk away.

Still, at some point in the negotiation, one must put the disputed sum in

perspective. If you've spent several thousand dollars to come to Indonesia, it's hardly worth worrying about an additional US$20. Yes, you'll wind up paying more than a local, but the price probably will be a bargain compared to what you would have had to spend for a similar item back home.

ANTIQUES
Antiques are still widely available in Indonesia despite the arrival of large numbers of collectors in recent years. Naturally it pays to do some study before you go if you're serious about what you're buying: you'll come across some very convincing fakes.

Antiques for sale in Indonesia include everything from Dutch era furniture and bric-a-brac to Chinese Ming dynasty porcelain. Local antiques include puppets and carved wooden doors. If you start your travels in Jakarta be sure to visit the capital's famous **Jalan Surabaya**, where you will find examples of the best antiques to be had in shops that take all major credit cards. Don't expect any bargains here, however.

You're more likely to find bargain prices in the antique flea markets of Java. You won't get a valuable Ming for a song, but you may at least find something that you like at a price you can afford. Solo's **Pasar Antik** (antique bazaar) is probably the best for the variety of items on sale.

WOODCARVING
For foreigners, the most famous center for woodcarving in Indonesia is **Mas** in Bali. In fact, woodcarving is carried out the length and breadth of the archipelago, and its scope reaches from exquisitely worked reliefs to simple but bold fertility symbols. But Mas is a good place to start your exploration of Indonesian woodcarving, if only because it offers the unique opportunity to see craftspeople at work. And the locals do produce a great variety of carvings — anything they judge will make money, essentially. Bali, too, is the place to buy **replicas** of traditional and

colonial style furniture and a number of joint venture enterprises have taken root creating good quality furniture for export.

If your travels around the islands will be extensive, there is no end of intriguing woodcarvings that you can look for: the **talismans** of the Bataks in Lake Toba, Sumatra, the "primitive" **fertility symbols** of the Asmats, Irian Jaya, **ancestor statues** from Nias Island in Sumatra, ornately carved furniture in Java. You will need a crate to get it home if you are not careful.

TEXTILES

There is probably nowhere in the world that compares with Indonesia when it comes to handmade textiles. Every region has its own technique, color and design preferences.

Originating in the Javanese word for "to dot" **batik** is Indonesia's most famous textile product. It comes from Java, principally Yogyakarta, Solo and Cirebon, and to this day these are the best places to shop for batik (though you'll find a good selection in the major stores in Jakarta if you are not planning to venture far afield). Designs are

created by the application of wax and successive dips in dye. The results, particularly in the hands of a dedicated batik artist, can be stunning. While simple batik designs are used in material for sarongs, shirts and curtains, the best batik can be hung on a wall, a work of art in itself. The brightest and most colorful batik comes from Pekalongan on the northern coast of Java.

For many repeat visitors to Indonesia, the allure of *ikat*, the archipelago's other textile dyeing tradition, soon begins to eclipse batik. Most commonly found on the islands of Nusa Tenggara, *ikat* designs are produced by dyeing the threads with a prescribed pattern before they are woven into fabric with an even more complex design. Best buys are to be had in Bali, where the gorgeous *ikat* fabrics from Flores, Sumba, Sawu or any of the other islands from the so-called "Cotton Route" are bought up for sale to tourists. These are worth pursuing, for the variety and beauty are exceptional.

OPPOSITE: In Lombok, a boy displays a ceramic mask (top), and a potter (bottom) plies her trade. ABOVE: An artisan painstakingly produces the renowned *ikat* fabrics of Sumba.

And don't miss out on the unusual **bark weaving** from Kalimantan. It sounds rather rustic, but it can be just as beautiful as other textiles. Curio shops in Banjarmasin and Balikpapan are the place to shop for this item.

Short Breaks

Indonesia, vast and sprawling, broken up by sea and divided by mountains and jungles, is not a country that lends itself to short stopovers vacations. Travelers with a short time in Kuala Lumpur or Singapore, for example, might hop over to Medan and from there travel by bus four or five hours to stunning **Lake Toba**, but two days of your trip would be eaten by travel.

Still, this is not to say that it is not worth making the most of an Indonesia stopovers or short trip with an excursion or two. Jakarta is within easy striking distance of a host of fascinating destinations — all you have to do is run the gauntlet of the city's push-and-shove traffic conditions.

One way to beat the traffic is to hop onto a boat. Head down to the Ancol

Marina between 8 or 9 AM any day of the week (though preferably not Sunday) and you are ready to board a boat to the Pulau Seribu, or the **Thousand Islands**. There are not really 1,000 of them, even so, there are enough to keep you busy for weeks. Some have opulent resorts, others are low-key getaways of sun, sand and gently lapping waves. The nearest resort island is **Bidari**, which makes a good base to visit nearby **Onrust Island**, which has the ruins of a Dutch fort. **Ayer** is another resort island slightly farther from Jakarta but still good for a day trip. There are more beach resorts about three hours by car from Jakarta at **Anyer** and **Carita**.

Carita is also the jumping off point for **Krakatau**, the famous volcanic island that shook the world in 1883. It's not feasible to make it a day trip from Jakarta, but if you overnight in Carita you can join a day tour out to the island the next morning and be back in Jakarta at the end of a long day the following evening.

An easy trip out of Jakarta is to **Bogor**, with its magnificent Botanical Gardens; it's less than an hour's drive from the capital via the Jagowari Highway. Those with more time on their hands should continue on to **Bandung** via the stunning **Puncak Pass**. Bandung, the cultural heart of Sundanese West Java and a cool Dutch hill station, requires an overnight stay as you are looking at four hours travel back to Jakarta. An overnight stay will allow visitors an afternoon inspecting some of Bandung's mostly dilapidated art deco architecture and an evening enjoying a performance of traditional Sundanese dance and music.

If you have a short stopovers in Denpasar, Bali, you're in luck; the whole island is within easy access of the international airport. The obvious thing to do is to enjoy a combination of Kuta and Ubud. Both offer fabulous shopping

ABOVE: Sails in the sunset at Jimbaran, Bali. OPPOSITE: In Bali, every day is a festival; pictured here is an annual *odalon*, rededication rite for a temple.

YOUR CHOICE

and inexpensive meals in balmy alfresco restaurants, but other than, despite the short distance between them, they are worlds apart.

Spend a day on the beach at **Kuta**, take in the sunset, enjoy a leisurely meal and a couple of drinks at any of Kuta's countless Indonesian and international style restaurants, and if you're up for it you might sample Kuta's boisterous nightlife, starting perhaps at the Hard Rock Café or Goa 2001 and gravitating later to Double Six. Take the latter course of action, however, and you won't be going anywhere early the next morning.

From Kuta it is a short drive to **Ubud** with a number of fascinating stops en route such as the village of **Batuan**, an artist community with galleries, and **Mas**, a woodcarving village. Ubud is a place to linger for a couple of days, shopping for arts and crafts, enjoying long leisurely lunches, watching dance and puppet performances in the evening.

Even the far north of Bali is easily accessible from Denpasar and the airport, requiring no more than a few hours of travel. If you have time, consider staying over night at **Lovina Beach** in order to be up at dawn to see the dolphins at play. From Lovina, side trips to the **Pulaki Monkey Temple** or to the hot springs at **Banjar** are easily organized. If you're feeling particularly energetic you might even drive up to **Kintamani** , check in at the Lakeview Hotel at Penelokan and climb Mt. Batur the next morning at 3 AM with a guide arranged by the Lakeview, for an incomparable Balinese sunrise.

Festive Flings

The Indonesian year is riotously rich in festivals. No matter when you go, you can be sure that somewhere there will be colorful pageant taking place. All you've got to do is get there.

The only problem is predicting precisely when they are going to fall. Most operate on the lunar calendar, and in Bali traditional festivals are celebrated according to the island's 210-day *pawukon* calendar. This means that annual events often occur twice a year according to the Western calendar, and dates for events always vary from year to year.

Dates, then, for the following list of festivals are approximate only. For precise dates, get in touch with the nearest ITPO, Indonesia Tourist Promotion Office (see TRAVELER'S TIPS, page 282) or inquire at local tourist information centers after you arrive in Indonesia.

ANNUAL HOLIDAYS
New Year's Day (January 1)
Idul Fitri (end of Ramadan)
Nyepi (Balinese New Year)
Good Friday (March or April)

Idul Adha (Feast of the Sacrifice; April or May)
Ascension Day (April or May)
Muharram (Islamic New Year; May)
Waisak Day (Buddha's Birthday; May or June)
Indonesian National Day (17 August)
Christmas Day (25 December)

BALI FESTIVALS

Almost every day is a festival in Bali. For a start, the island is studded with temples, each of which (according to the local 210-day calendar) celebrates its own annual *odalan*, a festive rededication rite.

As already mentioned, predicting dates for Bali's big annual festivals is a near impossibility. Ask at the Badung Government Tourist Office in Denpasar for the dates of Galungan and Kuningan, which are huge island-wide occasions that take place just 10 days apart. During *Galungan* giant *barong* masked figures are paraded through the streets, fluttering *penjors*, or bamboo banners, are placed outside each home and endless dance dramas are performed. It is a time for family and friends, feasting and temple visits.

Kuningan is an altogether quieter event, a purification day associated with the holy spring of Tirta Empul at Tampaksiring.

A traditional dance performance in the village of Kintamani, Bali, captivates onlookers.

If your Bali visit happens to coincide with **Nyepi**, the **Balinese New Year's Day** you will find yourself incarcerated in your hotel or its garden all day. **Nyepi Day** falls on the spring equinox and is observed as a day of complete silence. No fires may be lit, no transport taken, no work done. Flights still operate, however, and specially registered tourist transportation will take you to your hotel.

The night before Nyepi, on the other hand, is one of Bali's most splendid festivals. Giant images, known as *oggi-oggi*, are paraded through the streets on bamboo platforms held aloft by heaving groups of young men. Denpasar is the best place to see this festival. (Note: The festival was banned in 1997, but it is believed it will restart in 1998.)

Another major event is the **Bali Art Festival** (the second week June to the second week July) in Denpasar.

The month-long celebration of traditional arts and culture starts with a huge parade of artists and continues with a fascinating roll-call of disappearing traditions.

JANUARY
FIRST WEEK
Pontianak, West Kalimantan.
Anniversary of West Kalimantan is celebrated with folk performances and art exhibitions.

SECOND TO FOURTH WEEKS
Bondowoso, East Java.
Sapp-Sapp and Tarik Tambang Perahu are performed. Sapp-Sapp is a traditional chicken race in which chickens are released from a boat on the water and directed toward shore. The winner is the one that flies the longest distance. Tarik Tambang Perahu is a tug-of-war between two boats afloat in the middle of the sea.

LAST WEEK
Hila Village, Ambon, Maluku.
Closing New Year celebration. According to Maluku custom, the entire month of January is devoted to celebrating the New Year. This last feast of sago, sweet potatoes and wild game is held in the forest or on the beach, and is accompanied by an all-night sing along.

FEBRUARY
FIRST WEEK
Sidoarjo, East Java.
Celebration of its shrimp chip and batik industries with various attractions.
Selawu, West Java (30 km or 19 miles from Tasikmalaya).
The annual cleansing of heirlooms revives the history of the Suku Naga people.

SECOND WEEK
Siantar, North Sumatra (137 km or 85 miles from Medan).
Rondang Bintang means "full moon." This festival is highlighted by a variety of traditional dances and sporting events. The festival is in the a historical city of the Purba kingdom where old Simalungun houses still stand.
Central Sulawesi
Celebration of Vunja harvest festival.
Parang Kusumo beach south of Yogyakarta.
Coinciding with the birthday of the Sultan of Yogyakarta, offerings are made to appease Nyi Loro Kidul, the goddess of the South Sea. Similar offerings are given at the peaks of the Merapi and Lawu volcanoes.

THIRD WEEK
East Java
The Karo ceremony is staged in the Tosari Pasuruan and Ngadisari Probolinggo areas to commemorate the creation of man by the God Sang Hyang Widi. Lasting two days, the ceremony opens with a Tenggerese dance, the Tari Sodor, performed by adult male dancers.

MARCH
FIRST WEEK
South Lombok in West Nusa Tenggara.
Bagedok harvest festival.
Kudas, Central Java

Elaborate costuming typifies the *barong* in a traditional Balinese dance.

Five-day festival marks the beginning of Ramadan.

Semarang, Central Java.

The Dugderan festival starts one month before the Muslim feasting month of Ramadan and is held in front of the Mesjid Besar. Stalls sell different kinds of food and drink especially for children.

FOURTH WEEK

Pontianak, West Kalimantan.

Decorated boat races and cultural performances celebrate the day the sun is exactly above the equator.

Sarangan, East Java (14.5 km or nine miles from Magetan).

The ceremony of Bersih Desa begins with the burial of a goat's head followed by a week of traditional dances and games

around the Telaga Sarangan resort.

Bandung, West Java.

A marathon commemorates the independence struggle against the Dutch.

APRIL

FIRST WEEK

Majalengka, West Java.

Sugar cane festival.

Muara, North Sumatra.

boat races.

Siborong-borong, North Sumatra.

Batak Horas festival features horse racing.

Pelabuhan Ratu, West Java.

The Sea festival is celebrated by throwing flower petals and a buffalo head into the sea from a colorfully decorated boat. A *wayang golek* puppet show, a *pencak silat* performance and a *ketuk tilu* communal dance are held the night before.

SECOND WEEK

Bitang, North Sulawesi.

Celebrates the city's founding with cultural performances and art exhibitions by different ethnic groups.

THIRD WEEK

Mataram, West Nusa Tenggara.

Celebrates its heritage with parades and exhibitions.

Palu, Central Sulawesi.

Anniversary festival.

FOURTH WEEK

Pontianak, West Kalimantan.

Naik Dago harvest festival.

MAY

Prambanan (outside Yogyakarta).

Ramayana Ballet performed on the open air stage over four nights of the full moon. The four performances are: The Abduction of Sita, Hanoman's Mission, The Death of Kumbokarno and Sita's Trial of Purity.

ABOVE: A colorful Balinese funeral icon. RIGHT: A Balinese girl takes a break from the festivities. OPPOSITE: In Madura, the *kraton* guards (top) wear stern visages, and in Bali's village of Kintamani, festival dancers (bottom) bear offerings to the gods.

FIRST WEEK
Subang (70 km or 43 miles north of Bandung).
Gotong Sisingaan, the traditional art festival and parade with decorated wooden effigies of lions.

THIRD WEEK
Gunung Kunci, Sumedang area of West Java.
Ram fighting.

LAST WEEK
Maumere, Flores, East Nusa Tenggara.
Flores underwater festival.
Surabaya, East Java.
Taman Surya, Anniversary of Surabaya celebrated with *wayang kulit* shadow plays and popular folk comedies.

JUNE
Prambanan (outside Yogyakarta).
Ramayana Ballet. As the performance takes place four nights during full moon, the dates are variable.

FIRST WEEK
Cibubur, Jakarta.
Floriculture exhibition and festival at the Wiladatika Botanical Gardens.

SECOND WEEK
Jakarta
Dragonboat races at Ancol marina.

THIRD WEEK
Pandaan (45 km or 28 miles south of Surabaya).
Javanese ballet. The East Java classical ballet festival held at the Chandra Wilwatikita. Staged against a back drop of distant volcanoes, the performances are based on the East Javanese Majapahit and Kahuripan eras, as well as the traditional Hindu epics, the *Mahabharata* and the *Ramayana*.
Yogyakarta
Tumplak Wajik ceremony takes place in the main pavilion of the city's *kraton* when huge mounds of rice are decorated with vegetables, eggs and cakes so they can be blessed and distributed to the poor. The making of the mounds is

accompanied by rhythmic chanting and playing of instruments to ward off evil spirits.

FOURTH WEEK
Jakarta
The anniversary of the city is celebrated with an all night party at Ancol Dreamland Park.

JULY
Prambanan (outside Yogyakarta).
Ramayana Ballet at Prambanan. As the performance takes place four nights during full moon, the dates are variable.

JULY THROUGH OCTOBER
Tanatoraja, South Sulawesi
The Rambu Solo religious ceremony is held to insure that the dead will be accepted by God. A buffalo is killed, then bodies are carried to their ultimate resting places in niches on the hanging rock cliffs.

ABOVE: Javanese orchestras can be seen every afternoon in Yogyakarta's leading hotels.
OPPOSITE: The hypnotic sound of the gamelan can induce a trance-like state in some dancers.

South-central Java coast.
Asyura Javanese New Year. A ceremony held to appease Nyi Loro Kidul, the goddess of the South Sea. Pilgrims swim in the Sedudo waterfall 24 km (15 miles) from Nganjuk in the belief the water will keep them young. Ceremonial meals are held in the village of Menang.
Solo (Surakarta) Central Java.
Kirab Pusaka Kraton is the ceremony observed by the two ruling courts of Surakarta, the Kasunanan and the Mangkunegaran, to celebrate the Javanese New Year. Heirlooms are displayed in a procession of court attendants dressed in traditional costume.
Pager Rejo village, Kretek, Yogyakarta.
Suran is an ancient event at Pager Rego on the first day of the Javanese New Year. A black goat and two cocks are paraded about the village and then slaughtered at noon. The four legs of the goat are planted at the corners of the village with its head in the center to prevent future disasters.

END OF JULY
Ambon
Yacht Race from Ambon to Darwin begins.
Padang province, West Sumatra.
Tabot: A festival held throughout Padang province to commemorate the death of Mohammed's grandchildren Hassan and Husein. Effigies of Bouraq, the winged horse with a woman's head who saved the souls of the two boys, are carried in a procession before being thrown into the sea.

AUGUST
Prambanan (outside Yogyakarta).
Ramayana Ballet. As the performance takes place four nights during full moon, the dates are variable.

FIRST WEEK
Baruppu Tanatoraja village, South Sulawesi.
Ma'nene festival to change the shroud on the corpse of Tau-tau. Taken down from its hillside nook for one night, the newly shrouded statue serves as a center piece for dancing. The following day it is returned to its normal perch.
Rancakalong, Sumedang, West Java.
Ngalaksa Rice festival accompanied by night of *jentreng* dancing.

SECOND WEEK
Bandung
Pawai Pembangunan. Independence parade followed by outdoor cultural performances.
Muncar, East Java.
Petik Laut Muncar. Fishermen fill a boat with a goat's heads and other offerings which they then throw into the sea. After the ceremony, there are canoe and sailboat races plus fishing competitions and Gandrung dancers.
Yogyakarta
Turtledove Contest. Song birds compete in southern square of the Sultan's palace for trophy.

THIRD WEEK
Pandaan (45 km or 28 miles south of Surabaya).
East Java ballet festival at the Candra Wilwatika open-air theater.

Situbondo, East Java.
Sapp-Sapp and *Tarik Tambang Perahu* festivities on Pasir Putih Beach.
Palembang, South Sumatra.
Canoe races celebrate Independence Day. Canoes used on the Musi river are shaped like animals.
Cianjur, West Java.
Arak-Arakan Kuda Kosong horse procession has decorated horses escorted by incense-bearing guards.

FOURTH WEEK
Yogyakarta
Saparan Gamping ceremony Five kilometers (three miles) west of Yogyakarta there is a limestone hill outside Ambarketawang Gamping village thought to be 50 million years old that has been quarried for centuries. To protect the limestone workers once a year a life-size statues of a bride and bridegroom are made out of glutinous rice and filled with brown sugar syrup representing human blood. The statues are then sacrificed to so that villagers can remain safe for another year.

LAST WEEK
Jatinom, Central Java.
Yaqowiyu festival honors former Muslim sage. *Apem* pancakes made of rice and corn flour are eaten for good luck.

SEPTEMBER
Prambanan (outside Yogyakarta) — *Ramayana Ballet*. As the performance takes place four nights during full moon, the dates are variable.

FIRST WEEK
Ambon
The anniversary of the city is celebrated with Maluku dances and feasting.
Madura island
Karapan Sapi bull race championship.

THIRD WEEK
Manado, North Sulawesi.
Anniversary of North Sulawesi is celebrated with cultural performances, bull races and fashion shows.

LAST WEEK
Tenggarong, East Kalimantan.
Erau festival culminates when a mock dragon is thrown in the Mahakam river.

OCTOBER
FIRST WEEK
Cirebon, Kasepuhan and **Kanoman**.
Muludan Panjang Jimat. Cleaning and blessing of the heirlooms of these princely courts.

SECOND WEEK
Pamekasan, Madura, East Java.
Bull racing championship.

THIRD WEEK
Pandaan (45 km or 28 miles south of Surabaya).
East Java classical ballet festival.

NOVEMBER
FIRST WEEK
North Sulawesi.
Anniversary of the founding of the Minahasa regency is celebrated with traditional cultural ceremonies.

OPPOSITE and ABOVE: Balinese dancing requires the limber torso of a teenager.

THIRD WEEK
Pontianak
Trans Equator Marathon.

LAST WEEK
Malang, East Java.
Anniversary of Malang.

DECEMBER
FIRST WEEK
Mataram, West Nusa Tenggara.
Ketupat War. Farmers from the town
throw *ketupat* (steamed rice wrapped in
palm leaves) at each other in hopes that
they will be prosperous.
Tasikmalaya, West Java.
A sea festival. West Javan thanksgiving
festival in which a buffalo is sacrificed
prior to singing and canoe races.
Kesodo, Nusa Tenggara.
At dawn on the fourteenth day of the
twelfth month of the Tenggerese year
priests of the Tenggerese Buddha
Dharma offer fruit, flowers and rice to
the God of Bromo who lives in the
Mt. Bromo volcano crater.
Bondowoso, East Java
Bull fighting.

Galloping Gourmets

Indonesians do not live to eat in the
way the Thais or the Chinese do. This
does not mean you can't have a good meal
with great service in Jakarta. Indeed, the
city has some very fine restaurants. But
don't expect gourmet dining every night.

Indonesian food is a regional, rather
than national, cuisine. When Jakartans
consider their dining possibilities they
think of Sundanese food from West Java,
Central Java's *gudeg* or West Sumatra's
Padang cuisine. Sundanese specialize in
grilled freshwater fish, accompanied by
an assortment of raw vegetables and
sambal, the chili relish found throughout
the country. *Gudeg* is comparatively
sweet, and Padang, somewhat like the
Dutch *rijstafel*, is served in a series of side
dishes from which you can choose and be
charged on the basis of only what and
how much you eat.

A taste for Padang food is a useful
addition to your dining repertoire
because this popular cuisine is found all
over Indonesia. Padang restaurants can
be off-putting because of the way the
dishes are arrayed in the window. Where
business is brisk, however, freshness and
hygiene are generally good. The most
famous Padang dish is the delicious
rendang, a beef curry simmered in
coconut milk until the latter achieves the
consistency of a paste and the meat
becomes melt-in-your-mouth tender.

Originally, Indonesian food was eaten
off a banana leaf with the right hand.
Today, *warung* (sidewalk food stalls),
rumah makan (small cafés) and *restoran*
(restaurants) serve it on a plate with a
spoon and fork. Anything with the word
nasi in it means it's served with rice; *nasi
goreng* (fried rice) is a standard; *nasi
campur* is an inexpensive and filling
sampler of vegetables, soup and meat
with rice and can be found all over
Indonesia; *nasi putih* is plain boiled or
steamed rice. Other standard dishes that
you will find yourself wolfing down
while traveling across the archipelago are
mie goreng (fried noodles), *gado gado*, the
ubiquitous side dish served alongside ·
satay — essentially a vegetable salad
with peanut sauce.

Indonesian food goes best with tea,
soft drinks or beer. It never was intended
to be accompanied by wine, assuming
you can find an Indonesian restaurant
that has wine. In truth, wine probably
should be avoided entirely while in
Indonesia since what little there is
available largely consists (for reasons
stemming from import monopolies) of
inferior Australian jug wine, and even
that is heavily taxed as though it were
bottled in French château.

RIJSTAFEL
The term *rijstafel* dates back centuries
and translates literally as "rice table."
No one is certain exactly how the term
originated, but everyone agrees that the

Market traders TOP — here in Lombok — rarely
wanting for a ready smile. An abundance of exotic
fruits BOTTOM are available for a song in Indonesia.

YOUR CHOICE

dinner itself was a creation of Dutch planters.

Indonesian people traditionally eat rice with fish or meat, perhaps a vegetable dish, and a spicy sambal made from fresh red chilies. This rather simple meal was not enough for Dutch planters, however, who labored from dawn till dusk in an unforgiving climate alien to their upbringing. They added more and more dishes — curried beef, fried chicken, turmeric pickles — until the various courses, arrayed around a steaming serving bowl of white rice, covered the entire table.

In the beginning, this type of meal was served only on plantations and at home parties where domestic labor was cheap. But before long fancy hotels such as the Hotel Des Indes in Batavia were going the planters one better by having each of the *rijstafel's* 12 courses served by a different beautiful maiden.

World War II ended this elaborate method of presentation. Flushed with revolutionary ardor, formerly obsequious Indonesian maidens no longer wanted to serve plates of fish steamed in coconut milk to *tuan blanda* (colonial Dutch). Today those passions have cooled and the *rijstafel* is making a comeback.

A *rijstafel* banquet can contain an infinite variety of courses, but it usually begins with chicken soup followed by spicy hard boiled eggs, pan-fried red snapper and a beef stew. After those dishes are empty, chicken in coconut milk, lamb satay, fried grated coconut with peanuts and braised mixed vegetables arrive. Still hungry? That's good since you'll need room for shrimp crackers, pickles and fried bananas before the coffee arrives.

Special Interests

LEARNING

The obvious thing to study in Indonesia is Bahasa Indonesia, the national language of 200 million people. You can study the language formally in Jakarta, Yogyakarta, and best of all in Bali.

The **Center for Foreign Languages** ((361) 234256, Jalan Abimanyu N°17A, Denpasar, has courses in Bahasa Indonesia for both groups and individuals. Another place to study in Bali is the **Bali Language Training and Cultural Center** ((361) 239331, Jalan Tukad Pakerisan N°80, Panjejr, Denpasar.

For very serious students, Jakarta is the place to study. The **Indonesian Australian Language Foundation** ((21) 521-2230, Jalan Rasuna Said, Kav C6, Jakarta is one of the best, though it is definitely not the place to get a budget run-down of useful greetings.

For less formal courses, Yogyakarta, where you will find large numbers of young Westerners with an interest in things Indonesian, is probably the best place to go. Along with inexpensive pay-as-you-go language courses, Yogya also has popular courses in making batik.

MEDITATION

Meditation is usually associated with Buddhism, a religion that has long been eclipsed by Islam in Indonesia, and the meditational types generally restrict their explorations to Thailand and the sub-continent. The exception to this rule is Solo in Central Java, which attracts small numbers of Europeans for its meditation retreats.

Getting to the bottom of just what the meditation schools of Solo are about is no easy matter, but presumably this is why some people take the courses. Sometimes referred to by the term *kabatinan*, which translates unhelpfully as "mysticism," Solo spiritualism draws on Hinduism and Buddhism, filtering them through the prism of Javanese sensibilities. Those with a keen interest in Buddhism should bear in mind that Solo is far removed from the main currents of the faith.

The best way to get information about meditation courses in Solo is to go there and ask around at the budget

In the house of the artist Antonio Blanco, Ubud, Bali. No aspect of Balinese life is without some sign of hope and joy.

guesthouses. Well-known teachers who are popular with Western students include Pak Hardjanto and Pak Suyono.

TATTOOING

As designer tattooing becomes ever more popular, more and more people are looking to the tattoo artists of Bali for their inventive and meticulous designs. Often working out of small premises on inconspicuous side streets, they attract a surprisingly large number of Western "canvases," ensuring their work gets a worldwide audience.

Some of Bali's better known artists and workshops include **Alit's Tattoo** ((361) 483527, just outside Denpasar (at Jalan Imam Bonjol N°198), which has quite a reputation — the needle rattles and jumps as the traffic roars past the windows; **Made Bugik's Demon Art Tattoo**, on Jalan Double Six, which has thousands of designs to choose from; and Agung Wah's ("Tonto") place, **Tattoo Body Art Design**, on Jalan Benesan in Kuta (on the side street that runs towards the sea almost opposite the Matahari cinemas on Jalan Legian).

Taking a Tour

Don't underestimate the size of Indonesia. Some of the most fascinating destinations can take days to get to after you've touched down in Jakarta. And getting there is not always easy if you don't speak at least some Indonesian. Some people — and it's not a bad idea if time is against you or your interests are specialized — choose to take a tour rather than tackle the place on their own.

Think carefully about what you want out of your trip before you sign up. If you just want a general Indonesia sampler, a highlights tour that coddles you in the comfort of luxury hotels, feeds you on the best of Indonesian cuisine, and shows you the country at its most splendid, go for one of the large,

The verdant foothills of Mt. Bromo give no hint of the lunar landscape that awaits at higher altitudes.

established operators. **Garuda Airlines**
(800) 247-8380 TOLL-FREE in the United
States, for example, offers a number of
Garuda Orient vacation packages for
people traveling from North America.
Call for a brochure containing detailed
price information.

Other established tour operators in
the United States that specialize in
Indonesia include: **Vayatours** ((818)
287-9906 FAX (818) 287-6769 at 110W
Las Tunas Drive, Suite B, San Gabriel,
CA 91776 and **Mountain Travel Sobek**
((510) 525-8100 FAX (510) 525-7710, 6420
Fairmount Avenue, El Cerrito, CA 94530.
Mountain Travel Sobek are also in
Europe, at High Wycombe, England
((01494) 448901 FAX (01494) 465526 and
in Sydney, Australia ((02) 9264-465526
FAX (02) 9267-3047.

Sobek Expeditions specializes in
adventure travel. Its packages often
touch down only briefly in Jakarta before
heading to Irian Jaya's Baliem Valley or
Sumatra's riverine jungles.

Another successful Indonesia
adventure tour operator is **Bolder
Adventures** (800) 397-5917 TOLL-FREE at
PO Box 1279, Boulder, CO 80306, which
offers specialist wildlife tours and tours
led by veteran Indonesia guidebook
writer, Bill Dalton.

P.T. Tomaco ((21) 320087 is in the
Jakarta Theater Building at Jalan M.H.
Thamrin N°9, and puts together jungle
river trips that head into the heart of
the Borneo rainforest. **East Indies
Expeditions** ((21) 754-2703, Jalan
Merak II/10, Griya Cinere I, is
another Jakarta-based agency that
leads adventurous tours to remote
parts of the archipelago.

Diving coral reefs, climbing volcanoes
and sailing the Celebes Sea in Bugis
schooners can be arranged through
agencies that specialize in each activity.
The Department of Tourism (see
TRAVELERS' TIPS, page 286) or the
Indonesian Tourist Promotion Office, the
ITPO (see TRAVELERS' TIPS, page 282) can
direct you to the appropriate company.

Those interested in exploring the
seldom visited islands of Nusa Tenggara

should call **Spice Islands Cruises** ((21)
593401-2 FAX (21) 593403, Jalan Jend.
S. Parman N°78, Jakarta Barat. Spice
Islands' 40-m (130-ft) *Island Explorer* or
the *Bali Sea Dancer* will take passengers
on fabulous cruises such as a 12-day trip
around the Sawu Sea to Flores, Timor,
Sawu, Sumba and Komodo.

Jakarta has numerous travel agencies,
many of them located on the third floor
of the Borobudur Hotel. All of them offer
three standard city tours: a morning tour
that goes to Old Batavia, the National
Museum, the National Monument
(MONAS) and the Art Market (Pasar Seni)
at Ancol Park; an afternoon tour that
visits Jalan Surabaya, MONAS monument,
Ancol Park and the Oceanarium; and the
evening excursion to Ancol with dinner
included. Frankly, the best investment,
both in time and money, is to shop
around in front of the major hotels for a
taxi driver with a bit of English and rent
your own car.

Satriavi Tours ((21) 380-3944, at Jalan
Prapatan N°32, can arrange a variety of
guided tours throughout the archipelago.
Though it has a thick brochure full of
standardized tours, it will gladly
personalize individual vacations.

For something more adventurous,
Tread Ventures ((403) 286-1095 FAX (403)
286-3171, 7703 68th Avenue NW, Calgary,
offer cycling tours of Indonesia that take
you off the beaten trail.

BIRD WATCHING SAFARIS

Indonesia is a heaven-on-earth for bird
watching. One-sixth of the world's birds,
some 1,500 species, live on the country's
13,667 islands. Roughly half of these
birds are found nowhere else on earth.

More than a century ago British
naturalist Alfred Russel Wallace
described Indonesia's king bird of
paradise as a "gem of cinnabar red
plumage with a gloss like spun silk."
Wherever Wallace traveled in the islands
he found golden orioles, numerous
species of hornbills and "the gorgeous
little minivet fly-catcher which looks like
a flame of fire as it flutters among the
bushes."

Today, although less than 10% of the original habitat on Java and Bali remains, bird watchers can visit several impressive national parks and reserves. Some, such as the bird sanctuary on Rambut Island in Jakarta Bay, offer easy access. Others, such as Ujung Kulon National Park on the southwestern tip of Java, require a more daring spirit.

The islands of Sulawesi, Makulu and Nusa Tenggara have 246 endemic species. Sulawesi alone has 70 birds that are found nowhere else. This group includes two hornbills, five mynas, six kingfishers and an unusual maleo which buries its eggs in hot black sand and then abandons them to hatch on their own.

Anyone interested in bird-watching vacations should write to *Kukila*, the Bulletin of the Indonesian Ornithological Society, at PO Box 4087, Jakarta 4087. The **Birding in Indonesia** WEB SITE www.xs4all.nl/~rolivier/ is a good source of information. Look, too, for *Birding Indonesia* (see RECOMMENDED READING, page 297) a useful travel guide devoted entirely to bird watching; for serious bird-watchers it is an essential purchase before heading to Indonesia.

White water thrills in West Java.

Welcome
to
Indonesia

FOR HUNDREDS OF YEARS the islands of Indonesia have fired the imaginations of foreigners. Hindu traders in the second century were astonished by the variety of foods, the profusion of spices and the gentleness of natives such as those on Bali, who now refer to their home as the Isle of the Gods. Already possessing everything they needed, the Spice Islanders proved to be difficult trading partners. Finally, the Chinese, desperate for the islands' pepper, nutmeg and cloves, agreed to pay in gold, and used Song dynasty porcelain as supplemental ballast on the long trip south from the Center of the World.

The infusion of riches only added to the islands' exotic allure. Marco Polo, who swung through the archipelago in the thirteenth century on his return voyage to Italy, described the region as the wealthiest place on earth. "The quantity of gold collected there exceeds all calculation and belief," he noted. Arabs arriving two centuries earlier had planted the seed of Islam at the northern tip of Sumatra, then proceeded to ship spices back to Damascus. Competition among the European nations to secure a portion of the lucrative spice trade prompted the inadvertent discovery of the New World by Columbus in 1492. In his 1939 travel classic, *Inside Asia*, John Gunther's impressions of the country were remarkably similar to those of Marco Polo seven centuries before. "The dominant fact about the islands is that, like Croesus and John D. Rockefeller, they are rich," he wrote. "They are the Big Loot of Asia."

The days of sailing galleons into Indonesia and filling them with loot are over. Today adventurers come to explore the ruins of lost civilizations, or hike through stone age villages where pigs are the principal medium of exchange or watch maidens in gold-embroidered bodices seductively dance in front of elaborately carved temples beneath the full moon.

Today Indonesia has 192 million people, making it the world's fourth most populous country. Its 13,667 islands stretch more than 5,160 km (3,200 miles) along the equator, a distance equal to that from San Francisco to Bermuda. Half of New Guinea, the world's second largest island (after Greenland) belongs to Indonesia, as does three-quarters of Borneo, the world's third largest island.

Sumatra, which ranks sixth in size, is as big as California.

Yet for all its size and wealth, vast areas of Indonesia remain largely undeveloped wilderness. More than 1,600 of the world's 9,000 species of birds are native to Indonesia. At least 40,000 species of plants and trees, 10% of all those existing in the world, are found here. There are 3,000 kinds of trees in the rainforests of Sumatra and Kalimantan (the Indonesian name for its portion of Borneo), which alone boasts twice as many species of trees as found in all of Africa. There

are more than 300 nature reserves, national parks and protected forest areas. Indeed, 6.5 percent of the country's total land area (of over two million square kilometers or 780,000 sq miles) must remain pristine by law.

Indonesia is a land of volcanoes: towering, jungle-covered peaks that both enrich and destroy. Of the 500 volcanoes in Indonesia, 128 remain active. Yet the overriding rhythm of the nation is set by wind and water, not rock and fire. From November to March the west monsoon brings torrential rain to

OPPOSITE: Island hideaways — Fida Daru Island, near Flores TOP and No Man's Island, Batam, BOTTOM. ABOVE: Palms bend with the trade winds at Aceh Beach in North Sumatra. .

Sumatra, Java and the Lesser Sunda Islands. For the remainder of the year the eastern monsoon buffets the country with dry air parched by the heat of the Australian deserts.

EARLY KINGDOMS

The first great Indonesian kingdom, Srivijaya, rose to prominence in the seventh century in South Sumatra. A Buddhist kingdom in which nobles were taught Indian Pallava script by monks invited from India, Srivijaya's power resulted from its location on the Malacca Strait. Srivijaya's rulers were expansionist by inclination, and soon their realm included ports along the Malay Peninsula and parts of modern Thailand. By the tenth century an impressive triangle trade linked Sumatra with India and China. Gold, porcelain and silk would be traded by the emperor of China for rhinoceros horn, cloves, cardamom and camphorwood. To India and beyond Srivijaya kings would dispatch cloves, aloe, ivory and sandalwood.

As Srivijaya prospered, it ran up against the equally powerful Hindu kingdom of **Mataram** on the plains of Central Java near present day Yogyakarta. The leaders of Mataram were not worldly sophisticates like their peers from the Sumatran coast. Their kingdom was inland and agricultural.

The Mataram empire eventually fell when the Buddhist **Sailendra dynasty** allied itself with Srivijaya's remaining rulers. The new Buddhist empire celebrated its power in 850 with the construction of Borobudur in Central Java. Yet within a few years of the completion of the world's greatest Buddhist temple, the Sailendra princes were overthrown by survivors of the Hindu kingdom of Mataram, who commemorated their triumph with the Prambanan temple complex.

By the end of the thirteenth century the Hindu–Buddhist empires of Central Java, and the crumbling remnants of Srivijaya on the Sumatran coast, were gradually being replaced by the **Majapahit kingdom**. Founded in East Java in 1293 the Majapahit empire only lasted one hundred years, but many Indonesian historians consider it to be their country's greatest epoch because of the kingdom's enlightened leadership. Majapahit leaders such as Gajah Mada and

Hayam Wuruk sought to extend their influence through the force of art and ideas, not violent conquest. The Majapahit's greatest legacy was, undoubtedly, its incorporation of Hindu thoughts, words and symbols into a unified Indonesian culture.

ARRIVAL OF ISLAM

Arab traders began arriving in Sumatra even before the birth of Mohammed in 570 AD. As trade between India, Melaka and China grew, so did their influence. By the end of the fifteenth century most of the area around modern Bandar Aceh had converted to Islam and proselytizing imams were hard at work in Java and Sulawesi. With the Portuguese capture of Melaka in 1511, Islamic trad-

ers began moving to Indonesia in even larger numbers. In 1477, the people of Demak accepted Islam en masse. Cirebon and other Javanese cities quickly followed.

Though rajahs and sultans had great power over the life of the people, from the outset Islam was considered an egalitarian religion, a faith in which all people were equal before Allah and his prophet Mohammed. Islam not only allowed Indonesians to escape the Hindu caste system but also provided a unifying force against Christian colonialists.

As the spice trade increased, so did the spread of Islam. Yet, never was it proffered at the point of a sword. Animist Dyaks who rejected the religion because of its prohibition against their favorite food, pork, sur-

vived unchanged after the wave of Islam passed. Ironically, the greatest change probably occurred to Islam itself, which gained millions of converts by pragmatically adapting itself to the disparate cultures and beliefs of the archipelago.

PRECURSORS OF COLONIALISM

In most parts of the world the advance of European civilization was preceded by the cross and the sword. In Southeast Asia, Europe's advance guard was financed not by the church or the crown but by merchant trading houses anxious, nay desperate, to monopolize the lucrative trade in spices. It

Stone sentinels loom over Borobudur on the island of Java.

is no exaggeration to assert that everything which transpired in the archipelago from the sixteenth to the eighteenth centuries stemmed from the scramble for cloves, nutmeg, cinnamon and pepper.

The first European (after Marco Polo) to arrive in Indonesia was Alfonso d'Albuquerque. A Portuguese adventurer fresh from his victory over Melaka, Albuquerque's goal was to locate the Moluccas and then organize the spice trade out of the islands of Tidore and Ternate.

Unlike the French with their *mission civilitresse* or the English, who were determined that Britannia should rule the waves, the Portuguese did not try to subjugate alien societies. Their goal was simply to establish defensible trading bases — colonies similar to Melaka, Macao and Goa — through which natural resources and trade wares could be funneled back to Lisbon.

Because they did not attempt to hold large amounts of territory or install their own officialdom, the Portuguese were often dismissed as a relatively harmless force, no better or worse that the usual sort of brigands that roamed the South China Sea. In 1570, however, the Portuguese decided to venture outside their armed fort and play palace games of intrigue. Imagining they would receive better terms from his successor, they assassinated the sultan of Ternate. Too late, the overextended and woefully outnumbered Portuguese garrison realized their miscalculation. Instead of meekly accepting the fait accompli, the people of Ternate violently rose up and threw the Portuguese off the island.

The Portuguese may have proven themselves inept colonialists, but they hung on in Indonesia longer than any other European nation. It was not until 1975 when the Indonesian army invaded and forcibly annexed the colony of East Timor that Lisbon's flag was finally officially lowered.

By the beginning of the seventeenth century Portugal's presence was waning rapidly, but Holland's control of the islands was by no means certain. For a time it appeared that it might be the British who would eventually get the upper hand. Wherever the Dutch East India Company had a trading post, so did the British East India Company.

The Dutch finally succeeded in pushing the British back to Malaya, but in 1811, when Holland was occupied by France in the Napoleonic Wars, Britain returned in the person of Sir Stamford Raffles.

The renowned father of Singapore immediately set to work and within five years he had started a trading post at Bengkulu, unearthed the overgrown temple of Borobudur, chronicled the cannibalistic proclivities of Lake Toba's Batak tribesmen and discovered an enormous insect-eating flower 100 cm (40 in) in diameter that a delighted London Zoological Society named *rafflesia* in his honor.

Impressed by Indonesia's natural resources, Raffles urged Whitehall to hang on to the archipelago, but in 1816 he was overruled and eight years later Britain, in return for Dutch possessions in Malaya and India, formally recognized Dutch sovereignty over the East Indies.

COLONIALISM UNDER THE DUTCH

Three and a half centuries of Dutch colonial rule began inauspiciously in 1596 when Dutch captain Cornelius de Houtman limped into the West Java port of Banten. For Houtman it had been an arduous voyage in which more than half of his 250 man crew had died. That he had found Java at all was something of an accomplishment. The location of the East Indies was a secret. Portuguese were the only Europeans who knew how to sail to the fabled Spice Islands, and they jealously guarded their charts and rudders. Houtman's dismay vanished when after returning home he discovered that his cargo of pepper and cloves brought a handsome profit.

To maximize their effort and prevent needless competition among themselves, Dutch merchant companies joined together in 1602 to form the Dutch East India Company (VOC). The VOC had extraordinary powers and functioned as an independent government that raised an army, signed foreign treaties and administered justice on behalf of the Netherlands government.

The commander of the VOC in the Indies was Jan Pieterszoon Coen, and under his direction "Jan Compagnie" quickly set about monopolizing the spice trade. In 1607, after defeating the Portuguese at Tidore, the VOC obtained exclusive rights to all the cloves on Ternate. By the end of the decade Coen had exterminated most of the people on Banda and controlled nutmeg as well.

From its base in Batavia (today's Jakarta), the VOC expanded its sphere of influence, capturing Melaka (1641), Makassar (1667) and south Sumatra. By the end of the seventeenth century the VOC had eliminated the threat from the Portuguese, Spanish and British and had established a trade route extending half way round the world.

Because the VOC goal was high commodity prices, not increased productivity, it often burned existing plantations and destroyed surplus amounts of cloves, nutmeg and cinnamon. The policy caused tremendous human suffering, but revolts were kept to a minimum because of the VOC's adroit manipulation of competing sultanates. The culmination of Holland's "divide and conquer" policy came in 1755 when the VOC divided the old Mataram kingdom so that the sultans of Yogyakarta and Solo could scheme among themselves instead of uniting to oust the Dutch.

Despite its initial success, the VOC found itself in trouble by the middle of the eighteenth century. Unsuccessful wars and the increase in British sea power brought an end to monopolies and secure trade routes. As the VOC became more isolated, corruption increased. Import duties and local production taxes were diverted by company employees. In 1799 the VOC declared bankruptcy and was taken over by the Dutch colonial service.

Dutch civil servants sent to Batavia quickly learned that the vast VOC empire was not what it seemed. Beyond Java, Makassar and selected Sumatran enclaves, the Indies were mostly in the hands of Indonesians. Not only were the islands not producing revenue, they actually were a drain on the Netherlands, which itself was fast approaching bankruptcy following the partition of Belgium in 1830.

The response to the demand for more revenue was the Culture System in which all of Java and Sumatra, save for the ungov-

ernable northern tip around Aceh, were turned into state-owned plantations. Instead of growing rice to feed the population, Indonesia's most fertile land was used to grow cash crops such as coffee, cotton and indigo that would bring good prices in Europe. Along with increased taxes the Culture System made colonialism profitable again, but the abuses so enraged Dutch liberals that they began to push in parliament for a series of reforms known as the Ethical Policy.

Essentially, the Ethical Policy aimed at creating a system that was both humane and

profitable. After two centuries of neglect, Dutch politicians reasoned that if they improved the economic well-being of Indonesians, the Indonesians themselves would become an enormous market. For the first time, starting in about 1910, Indonesian children were brought to Holland for advanced education. But the Ethical Policy was too little too late. Many children of the elite who were brought to Holland and exposed to the ideas of Karl Marx became revolutionaries. As for the great bulk of people, little changed. At the start of the war, only 630 Indonesians out of a population of 68 million had graduated from high school.

A sultan's guard at Yogyakarta.

THE RISE OF NATIONALISM

Despite three centuries of rule, the Dutch never fully subdued Indonesia. More than 15,000 Dutch soldiers died putting down a Central Java rebellion by Mataram Prince Diponegoro in 1825. The Acehnese fought the Dutch to a stand-off in a bitter *perang sabil* (holy war) that lasted 40 years. The Bugis battled the Dutch on and off for nearly 200 years. Indeed, it wasn't until 1905 that peace finally came to South Sulawesi.

By the early decades of the twentieth century it was clear that, despite Holland's Ethical Policy, colonialism couldn't last forever in Indonesia. In 1909 the Islamic Organization (Sarekat Islam) provided a forum where Indonesians both urban and rural found common cause against the Dutch. In 1914 the Perserikatan Kommunist Indonesia began to organize quietly. Begun in Bandung in 1927, the Indonesian Nationalist Party (PNI) soon became the largest and most outspoken voice for independence primarily because of its leader, a young engineer named Soekarno. Soekarno (whose name is sometimes spelled Sukarno) saw himself as the Gandhi of Indonesia, a man who would gain full independence for his country through the use of civil disobedience.

Unfortunately for Soekarno, the rise of the PNI coincided with the world-wide depression of the 1930s. With commodity prices falling the Dutch refused to consider reform and responded to the nationalist sentiment by sending the main leaders into internal exile.

World War II

In the beginning Batavia had no part in World War II, but in January 1942 Japanese troops landed on Borneo and the Celebes. The following month they invaded Sumatra. By mid-March Batavia had fallen and the retreat was on. Unable to contain the onslaught, Dutch soldiers, planters, civilian officials and families boarded transports bound for safer harbors.

Initially, Indonesians welcomed the Japanese as fellow Asian liberators and in the early months the Japanese military supported nationalist movements and talked of granting independence. But before long Tokyo's true intentions became clear. In fervently Islamic Aceh, people were forced to begin the day by bowing east toward Tokyo instead of west toward Mecca.

Resentment against the Japanese was kept to a minimum, however, by nationalists such as Soekarno and Mohammed Hatta, who were allowed to carry on their political activities and form groups such as the Volunteer Army of Defenders, a civil defense militia that provided a foundation for the independence struggle to come.

In the waning months of the war the Japanese gave their consent to a conference in which Soekarno outlined his vision for the new Indonesia. In addition to the island groups historically considered part of the country, Soekarno's boundaries encompassed Netherlands New Guinea, Sarawak, Brunei and North Borneo plus the entire Malay Peninsula. The Japanese, who had no power to further Soekarno's ambitions or prevent their own collapse, demurred, as did the British and Australian military leaders who temporarily occupied the country at the end of the war.

THE STRUGGLE FOR INDEPENDENCE

In 1946 Dutch troops began to filter back into Indonesia, but the country to which they returned was not the one they had left in 1942. Medan and Palembang on Sumatra had to be bombed before they could be reoccupied. Nationalists in Bandung burned most of the city rather than turn it back to the Dutch intact. Heavy fighting destroyed much of Surabaya, and Yogyakarta was strafed by Dutch fighters to make it safe for troops to enter. Dutch troops eventually regained control of all major towns, but the rural byways and paddy fields remained in the hands of nationalists who rallied the peasantry with cries of "merdeka" (freedom).

The cries may have fallen on deaf ears in the Hague, but at the United Nations and in Washington the combination of Dutch intransigence and Indonesian persistence became an annoying embarrassment. Disturbed that the amount Holland was spending on the war was approaching the sum it was receiving from the United States under the Marshall Plan, Washington threatened to curtail aid and join the Netherlands' adversaries in the

United Nations. Confronted with a war they did not have the means to win, the Dutch finally capitulated and on December 27, 1949 Indonesia proclaimed its independence.

CHAOS AND DEMOCRACY

The new nation of Indonesia began to unravel within weeks of its declaration of Independence. The Minahasans of North Sulawesi wanted nothing to do with the new country. Neither did the Ambonese, who had fought alongside the Dutch. Despite Soekarno's

Soekarno's audacity offended Western leaders. Soekarno kept mistresses openly and bragged about his sexual prowess. He even had portraits of his amorous conquests hung in the Hotel Indonesia (where they continue to decorate guestrooms to this day). The West could laugh at Soekarno's peccadilloes, but it could not forgive his flirtation with Maoism, and in 1965, following a botched communist coup, it stood by silently as the Indonesian army methodically eliminated hundreds of thousands of suspected communists and Soekarno supporters.

guiding concept of *pancasila*, under which democracy would be forged from Islam, tribal *adat* (custom) and patriotic nationalism, communists, radical Muslims and disgruntled minorities all wanted their regions to secede.

Soekarno's response was an oxymoronic concept called "guided democracy" in which the country's democratically-elected parliament was suspended in 1956 and decision-making power was given to administrators picked by Soekarno.

In 1958 armed rebellions against Soekarno's centralized administration flared briefly in West Sumatra and North Sulawesi. Troops crushed the rebels, then, in 1962, fulfilled Soekarno's lust for *lebensraum* by annexing Netherlands New Guinea.

General Suharto led the 1965 anti-communist purge, and was carried to power by hopes of stability and prosperity. He ran the country with a tight grip for 32 years, his corrupt and repressive regime impervious to public participation. His rule did bring growth, improving the lot of the people such that Indonesia was touted as a model of poor-country development. Chaos returned in 1998 with an economic crisis and rampant inflation; subsequent riots and protests led to Suharto's resignation. The country's new leaders struggle with the challenges of economic restructuring and a public demand for a cleaner, more democratic government.

Spirits of Dutch planters silently wander the nutmeg groves surrounding Fort Belgica on Banda Neira.

Java

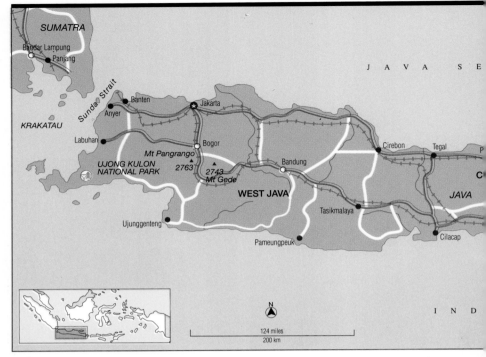

JAVA IS THE CRADLE of Indonesian civilization. Though it comprises only seven percent of the country's total land area, it leads the way for every other part of the country — the "outer islands" — politically, economically and socially. Bali may have become Indonesia's leading tourist destination, but the nation's heart and soul, along with 65% of the total population, reside in Java.

Though Java contains Indonesia's most modern and prosperous cities, the island is a study in contrasts. It is, beyond question, the most fertile stretch of earth of this planet, yet its population lives on the brink of Malthusian calamity. It is 80% rural, yet still manages to be one of the most densely populated places in Asia. It is the center of power for the world's largest Islamic nation, yet people value Buddhist tranquillity and spend long tropical nights retelling epic Hindu legends.

Though all of the residents of the Island respond to the term "Javanese," the island actually is home to five distinct sociological groups, three of which have a significant impact on the culture. Traditional Javanese

live in the central and eastern portions of the island and constitute the bulk of the population. Heirs to an extremely sophisticated culture and language, they continue to prize the Brahman refinements introduced centuries ago by Hindu mystics. For Javanese, the *kratons* (Sultans' palaces) of Yogyakarta and Solo are not dusty anachronisms, but a reflection of the values still cherished by society.

West Java is home to the island's Sundanese, the island's second-largest group which practices a purer form of Islam. The island of Madura, along with an adjoining slice of Java north of Surabaya is populated by Madurese. Unlike the Javanese, who consider displays of emotion uncivilized, the less-prosperous Madurese are hot-tempered practitioners of *pencak silat*, a particularly lethal form of hand-to-hand combat.

Though each group exhibits a distinct personality and approach to Islam, all perceive themselves to be part of a social hierarchy that values courtesy, self control and the wisdom that comes with age. Deference and good manners are essential on Java since there's scarcely any room to run

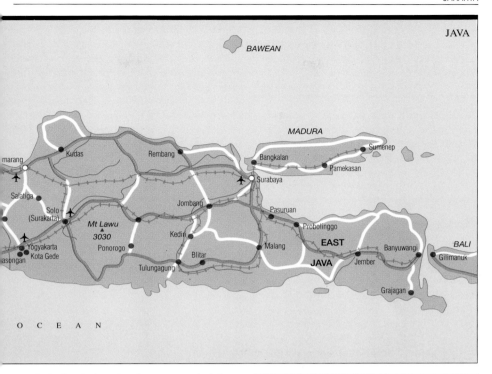

amok. Indeed, the island is so crowded that each year thousands of impoverished peasants voluntarily petition for resettlement under the *transmigrasi* program started by the Dutch.

Two-thirds of the world's active volcanoes are located on Java, but the tumultuous natural forces at work on the island have not inhibited a refined appreciation of the arts and music. In Central Java, *wayang kulit* shadow puppet plays are repeatedly presented in every *kampung* (village), while in the west, Sundanese gather to see *wayang golek* puppets perform similar stories. As a result, travelers who venture beyond Jakarta are never far from the exotic chime of gamelan orchestras whose music has been described as the sound of "moonlight and flowing water."

The delights of Java are tempered of course by the archipelago's most serious social problems. But despite the poverty, noise and traffic, Java remains a sensual delight — a place where the smell of cloves, the wonder of ancient temples and the caress of a batik sarong converge to create an unforgettable impression.

JAKARTA

For many travelers a vacation to Indonesia begins in Jakarta, a sprawling metropolis of around nine million that covers two and a half times the entire land area of Singapore or the Isle of Wight.

After several decades of tremendous growth, Indonesia's capital can seem overpowering. The streets meander like those in a rural village, constantly changing names and numbering systems. The traffic is unrelenting, especially at rush hour. Some visitors closet themselves in resort hotels, surrounded by tennis courts, jogging paths, nightly barbecues and shopping arcades. But they miss discovering a city that has modern skyscrapers, excellent museums and more colonial architecture than any other capital in the region.

Before you begin your explorations, consider that even Indonesians barely tolerate the heat and noise of the city: Nobody walks. And, no one rides buses if they can afford a taxi. It's simply too hot. Make a list of sights, rent an air-conditioned car (chauffeur-driven) or taxi by the day or hour and go touring. Because Indonesia is an OPEC oil producer, transportation here is very inexpensive. Find a good driver, bargain for a fair price and begin an adventure that can't be equaled anywhere else in Asia.

BACKGROUND

Early in the seventeenth century, Dutch and British merchants peacefully established outposts along the Java Sea coast. The situation changed radically a few years later in 1629 when Sultan Agung of the Mataram

named Weltevreden was built at the end of the eighteenth century to house the more affluent citizens. As Batavia grew its canals turned out to be a mixed blessing. They were ideal for social and commercial transportation, but also served as a refuse dump for the city's waste. Accordingly, they stank, and from 1730 to 1830 frequent outbursts of malarial plague gave Batavia the reputation of being "the graveyard of the Orient."

Building construction during the early nineteenth century under the direction of Dutch Governor Daendals centered on Welte-

dynasty in Yogyakarta attacked Dutch fortifications protecting the garrison they called Batavia. Dutch governor general Jan Pieterszoon Coen arrived from the Moluccas the following year. He routed Agung, burned the city the Javanese called Jayakarta and established a system of colonial administration that would endure for the next three centuries.

Under the determined and occasionally ruthless leadership of Coen, the Dutch set out to build an "Amsterdam of the tropics." A geometric matrix of streets and canals named after Dutch cities and provinces was laid out. Houses, warehouses, churches, a court and the Stadhuis were built. As business expanded, so did the city. A suburb

vreden. Konigsplein, now Merdeka Square, was completed in 1818; Waterlooplein, now Lapangan Banten Square opposite the Borobudur Hotel, in 1826. In 1839 the Immanuel Church in front of the Gambir Railway Station went up. It was followed in 1848 by the Supreme Court, now the Ceramics Museum. During this same period a new Dutch Governor's residence was built that today serves as the National Palace or Istana Negara. The opening of the Suez Canal in 1883 prompted the construction of a new port at Tanjung Priok.

By the early twentieth century the hub of the city was the Konigsplein. All of the stolid white government buildings and museums along today's Jalan Medan Merdeka Barat and Medan Merdeka Utara once housed departments of the Dutch East Indies. In the decades between the wars, the city expanded south along Jalan Thamrin.

The effect of all the building around the Weltevreden area was to move the heart of the city away from Old Batavia, today referred to as Jakarta Kota.

GENERAL INFORMATION

For general information about Indonesia, the head office of the Department of Tourism ((21) 383-8217 at Jalan Merdeka Barat N°16–19 is the place to go. The Jakarta Tourist Information Office ((21) 314-2067, Jalan Thamrin, Jakarta Theater Building, is the place for information on Jakarta its and surroundings.

Travel agents, particularly the ones in the budget Jalan Jaksa area are also good for independent information. While you obviously can't rely on the airlines for objective information, you may need to visit either Garuda or Merpati. There are a number of Garuda Indonesia offices in the city. The two most convenient are in the Hotel Indonesia ((21) 320-0568 and in the Hotel Borobudur Inter-Continental ((21) 231-1991. Merpati Nusantara Airlines ((21) 654-0690 is at Jalan Angkasa N°B-15, Kav 2, Jakarta.

WHAT TO SEE AND DO

Jakarta's size and traffic congestion make it vital to plan sightseeing in advance.

Fortunately, this is easily done since the city is divided into sectors. Just about everything a visitor to Jakarta will want to see is located along a north–south axis extending from Sunda Kelapa on the Java Sea to Taman Mini Indonesia and the highway to Bogor in the south.

Secondary points of reference are provided by the Indonesian capital's many statues. President Soekarno used to say that "only a great nation honors its heroes." With the help of Soviet artists, who during the 1950s were actively exporting "Socialist Heroism" statuary, Soekarno sprinkled monuments throughout Jakarta. Today, they have become points of reference — "Jalan Blora is two blocks south of the Welcome

Statue" — that not only help people pinpoint destinations, but also commemorate revolutionary martyrs, historical events and Javanese mythology. Hanoman, the King of Monkeys from the *Ramayana*, is incarnated as **God of the Wind** atop a curving pedestal in the traffic circle on Jalan Gatot Subroto. Several monuments honor the fight for independence. The large figure of a man breaking his chains in Lapangan Banteng in front of the Borobudur Hotel commemorates the **Liberation of Irian Jaya**. The statue of a woman giving rice to a peasant soldier at

Menteng Prapatan in front of the Hyatt Aryaduta is known as the **Farmer Statue**.

In the center of Merdeka Square is MONAS, or the Monumen Nasional, a 137-m (400-ft)-tall marble column. The **Welcome Statue** in front of the Hotel Indonesia was built for the 1962 Asian Games. It shows a young boy and girl extending their arms in a gesture of greeting. Located in a traffic circle at the entrance to Kebayoran district at the end of Jalan Jend. Sudirman is the **Youth Spirit Monument** which shows a muscular young man carrying the "torch of development."

OPPOSITE: An old Batavia drawbridge spanning the Kali Besar still serves modern commuters. ABOVE: For a bird's-eye view of the Dutch mansions around Medan Merdeka, ride the elevator to the top of the National Monument.

Because of their foreign style and grandiosity, Soekarno monuments are subject to spoofing. The Youth Spirit Monument is sometimes referred to as "pizza man" or "the mad waiter" since the torch of development resembles a pizza *flambé*. The Welcome Statue is known as "Hansel and Gretel."

Jakarta Kota

Old Batavia, known as Jakarta Kota, is the logical place to begin exploring Indonesia's capital since Jakarta was born along the banks of the Ciliwung River. Sunda Kelapa, where

the Ciliwung enters the Java Sea, was the main port for the Hindu kingdom of Sunda, the capital of which was near Bogor. The Muslim leader Fatahillah Khan captured Kelapa in 1527, forced the population to accept Islam and renamed the city Jayakarta, which means "Complete Victory." In 1619 the newly-appointed Dutch Governor General Jan Pieterszoon Coen marshaled his forces, destroyed Jayakarta and claimed what remained for the Dutch East India Company (VOC). Ten years later he had to fight again for this land that he had wrested from Fatahillah's followers and finally after battling, and defeating, Sultan Agung in 1629, established a settlement which grew into the prosperous town of Batavia.

Java

The area settled by Coen begins at the end of Jalan Pintu Besar Selatan, itself an extension of Jalan Gajah Mada, and extends northward to the sea. Heading north, Jalan Pintu Besar Selatan turns into Jalan Pintu Besar Utara. It passes the **Kota Railway Station** on the right and the **Bank Exspor Impor Indonesia** on the left, one of the area's best examples of restored early colonial architecture.

Within a block or so past the bank is **Taman Fatahillah** the VOC's administrative center that ironically is named after another foreign

conqueror, Fatahillah Khan. In the center of the cobblestone square is a polluted fountain that two centuries ago was the area's main source of clean water. Before being executed prisoners kept in the basement dungeons of the stadhuis were allowed a final drink from the fountain.

Built in 1627, today the Stadhuis is the **Jakarta Museum**, but the building is in appalling condition and is nearly devoid of furniture. It nevertheless is worth visiting to see the Soekarno-era murals that show porcine Dutch colonials hobnobbing at a *rijstafel* with posturing Javanese nobles. Before

A watchtower built by the Dutch East India Company and elaborate Portuguese graves bespeak Java's colonial heritage.

leaving be sure to crawl inside one of the dungeon cells where Javanese revolutionaries were kept chained. The museum is open from 9 AM to 3 PM; Friday it closes at 2:30 PM; Saturday at 12:30 PM; it is closed Monday.

On the opposite side of the square sits the old Portuguese cannon **Si Jagur**. Local folklore claims that sitting on its barrel will restore fertility to women.

On the west side of the square is the **Wayang Museum**, an old Dutch Church (Jan Pieterszoon Coen is buried here) that now houses Indonesia's best collection of pup-

pets. *Wayang* puppet shows were used to arouse Indonesian peasants against the Dutch during the revolution. Every Sunday at 10 AM a free puppet show complete with gamelan orchestra is presented on the second floor of the museum. Opening hours are the same as for the Jakarta Museum.

Directly across from the Wayang Museum on the east side of the plaza is the **Fine Arts Museum**. The collection of paintings housed in this, the old Raad van Justitie, is limited, but interesting. Don't miss the wing housing the Adam Malik collection of Chinese ceramics on the second floor up a spiral, wrought iron staircase. His collection includes rare Ming and Song dynasty celadon. Opening hours are the same as the Jakarta Museum.

After inspecting Taman Fatahillah's three museums, head back to Jalan Pintu Besar Utara, then go north to the old bridge over the Kali Besar (Grand Canal). This point was originally the mouth of the Ciliwung River and where Jan Pieterszoon Coen built the first Dutch fort, Kasteel Batavia. The fort is long

gone, but the **watchtower** on Jalan Ikan remains, just as it was in the days when the Dutch military used it to guard against invaders.

From the watchtower of the old fort you'll see a large number of sail-powered schooners called *pinisi* that still ply the archipelago's shallow-draught ports. To get a closer look at the boats you'll need to visit the dock, which you can do by way of the **Maritime Museum**; it's a short distance northwest along Pasar Ikan.

The museum is housed in an old VOC warehouse that dates back to the mid-seventeenth century. Displays comprise maritime exhibits (boats and so on) from all over the archipelago. Open from 9 AM to 2 PM, closed Monday.

From the docks of the **Sunda Kelapa Harbor** it is possible to arrange a sampan ride amongst the *pinisi*, most of which bring timber from Kalimantan and return with rice, cement and consumer goods. The going price for a harbor sampan ride, after some spirited bargaining, is around US$2. The trip will take you around the original warehouses, where the Dutch stored pepper, to the breakwater where locals fish.

Ancol Park

After a long morning in Old Batavia the best place for lunch, and a radical change of pace, is to head west to **Ancol Park** on the shore of the Java Sea. The park is huge, composed of a Disneyland-type theme park called **Dunia Fantasi**, an art market called **Pasar Seni**, and other attractions such as a **Seaworld** and a **Waterworld** complete with a wave pool and waterslides. Entry into the park is around US$1 or $2 per person. Pasar Seni has several outdoor restaurants.

To see it in its entirety, Dunia Fantasi requires a full day. It's composed of a variety of thematic areas, such as the Wild West section representing North America, and an the English Tudor house symbolizing Great Britain.

Central Jakarta

Merdeka Square, the old Dutch Konigsplein, is the center of modern Jakarta. Most of the major government ministries, the office of President Suharto, the national oil company

Pertamina and the National Museum are located in this area.

MONAS, also called the **National Monument**, is here — a marble obelisk which "burns" with an eternal flame made of bronze that is gilded with 35 kg (80 lbs) of gold. A one-minute elevator ride to the top of MONAS brings you to the observation deck and a spectacular view of the city, the mountains rising in the south and the 1,000 Islands extending far to the north across the Java Sea. A small fee is charged to climb MONAS. At the base of the monument is the **Museum of**

Behind Merdeka Palace on Jalan Veteran is the slightly older Presidential Palace, the **Istana Negara**, built for a Dutch businessman. This is a separate palace in which state functions are often held. Between the two palaces is the State Guesthouse, **Wisma Negara**, where foreign dignitaries stay.

Founded 200 years ago as the Batavia Society for Arts and Sciences, the **National Museum**, Jalan Merdeka Barat, has five sections, including a Hindu–Buddhist wing with stonecarvings from the seventh through fifteenth centuries, a pre-history room with

National History that traces Indonesia's revolutionary struggle in 48 dioramas. The museum and observation deck are open daily from 9 AM to 5 PM. If you find yourself at MONAS during lunch time, stop at the **Sari Krung** across the street, an open-air Sundanese restaurant.

Completed in 1879 for Dutch Governors General, who considered the adjacent Istana Negara too small, Merdeka Palace, a white colonial building on Jalan Merdeka Utara was originally known as Konigsplein Palace. It was seldom used by the Dutch governors, who preferred the climate in Bogor. President Suharto also prefers to live and work elsewhere, but uses the Palace for important state occasions.

skulls, weapons and cooking utensils and an ethnographic department with displays from each of the archipelago's island groups. There is also a ceramics room featuring Chinese, Thai and Vietnamese porcelain and a heavily-guarded treasure room with jeweled statues, solid gold *krises* and gilded amulets. Open Tuesday to Sunday from 8:30 AM to 2:30 PM. On Friday the museum closes at 11:30 AM.

JAVA MAN

One of the National Museum's most valued treasures is the skull of Java Man. In 1890

OPPOSITE: The Kota Railway Station, Jakarta's largest, is a scene of perpetual activity.
ABOVE: Jakarta's sprawling expanse makes it one of Asia's largest cities.

Dutch military physician Eugene Dubois, an amateur paleoanthropologist assigned to Central Java, discovered the fossilized jawbone of a primate possessing definite human characteristics. Could it be the "missing link" between apes and *Homo erectus* written about by Charles Darwin? Christian groups opposed to the theory of evolution denounced Dubois, arguing that there was no link to discover. But similar fossils discovered outside Peking in 1921 vindicated Dubois' "Java Man."

Several museums claim to have the skull unearthed by Dubois. There is a Java Man here at the National Museum. Another rests at the Sangiran site outside Solo (Surakarta) where Dubois' dig was located. The Geological Museum in Bandung also claims to have the original.

Memory Lane

Walking in Jakarta can be unpleasant because of the heat, humidity and general traffic noise. But there are two tree-lined avenues—jalans Imam Bonjol and Diponegoro — that can only be appreciated from the unhurried perspective of a pedestrian. Heading in an easterly direction from the Welcome Statue, Imam Bonjol (which quickly changes names to Diponegoro) cuts through the trendy residential section of Batavia the Dutch developed between the two world wars. The homes are textbook examples of Dutch colonial architecture that now serve as diplomatic residences.

Jakarta Selatan

The southern portion of Jakarta is the newest part of the city. Much of the area consists of upscale residential and shopping in Kebayoran and Blok M. Although there are few historical points of interest, there are two locations relatively close together that can fill an interesting day.

Military history buffs should visit the **Armed Forces Museum** (Satria Mandala) on Jalan Gatot Subroto N°14, which was originally the family mansion of Dewi Soekarno, wife of Indonesia's first President. Scores of dioramas focus on the military struggle for independence from 1945 to 1949. Entire floors are devoted to displays of small arms. Outside there are field artillery, tanks and fighter planes parked about landscaped gardens. Open Tuesday to Sunday from 9 AM to 3:30 PM.

Taman Mini Indonesia

About 19 km (12 miles) south of the center of Jakarta, just off the toll expressway to Bogor, is Taman Mini (Indonesia in Miniature) recreation park built by President Suharto's wife, Madam Tien. At Taman Mini you can see, and enter, traditional housing from each of Indonesia's 27 provinces such as the Redang longhouses of the Kalimantan Dyaks and the saddle-shaped Toraja houses of South Sulawesi. There are miniature replicas of Central Java's Borobudur and Prambanan, plus a bird park and orchid garden. There is even a building built in the shape of a Komodo Dragon. Open daily from 8 AM to 5 PM. The best way to get to the park is by taxi.

WHERE TO STAY

Jakarta has the full complement of accommodation, ranging from inexpensive dorm beds in the Jalan Jaksa area to five-star standards around the Welcome Statue. All midrange to luxury hotels are subject to a 15.5% government tax and service charge.

Luxury

Some of Jakarta's best hotels are conveniently clustered together on the Welcome Statue roundabout. This puts you on Jalan M.H. Thamrin in the center of Jakarta's business and financial district, close to the massive Plaza Indonesia shopping center, the IBM and Unilever headquarters, and the British, German and Japanese embassies. Perhaps the best of them is the **Grand Hyatt Jakarta** ((21) 390-1234 FAX (21) 390-6426. All rooms are spacious and well-appointed, and the recreation deck includes three hectares (seven acres) of gardens, tennis and squash courts, an 800-m jogging track, a Jacuzzi and a 43-m pool with a swim-up bar. Eateries and bars, with entertainment, beckon at every level of the four floor atrium.

Also on the Welcome Statue roundabout is the 27-story **Mandarin Oriental Jakarta** ((21) 314-1307 FAX (21) 314-8680, another ultra-luxurious hotel with fine service and top-notch restaurants.

North of this area in the vicinity of the Liberation of Irian Monument is the **Borobudur Inter-Continental** ((21) 380-4444 FAX (21) 380-5555. Located on nine hectares (23 acres) in the heart of Jakarta, on Jalan Lapangan Banteng the Borobudur's greatest asset is its garden, which contains an Olympic-size swimming pool, eight tennis courts (two of them inside), eight squash and badminton courts, a jogging trail and miniature golf course plus a track for roller skating. The **Jakarta Hilton** ((21) 570-3600 FAX (21) 573-3089, Jalan Jend. Gatot Subroto is a self-contained city. Fifty gardeners manicure its 14 hectares (35 acres). More than 40 ball boys man the 14 tennis courts. One jungle path leads to a pizzeria, another ends up at a Japanese restaurant. The Hilton's shopping arcade has 20 shops built to resemble a Balinese village nestled around a man-made lake. Guests enjoy access to the Executive Club, a members-only sports and social club frequented by some of the capital's most prominent citizens. Special facilities exist for women travelers, and handicapped visitors are well catered for.

The city has many other luxury hotels. Should you find the above fully booked (which happens during holidays, trade fairs and conferences), one of the luxury hotels listed below may be the answer:

Shangri-La Jakarta ((21) 570-3530 FAX (21) 570-7440, Kota BNI City Complex, Jakarta 10220;; **Holiday Inn Crowne Plaza Jakarta** ((21) 526-8833 FAX (21) 526-8831, Jalan Gatot Subroto Kav 2-3, Jakarta 12930; **Hotel Atlet Century Park Jakarta** ((21) 571-2041 FAX (21) 571-2191, Jalan Pintu Satu Senayan, Jakarta 10270; **Dusit Mangga Dua** ((21) 612-8811 FAX (21) 612-8822, Jalan Mangga Dua Raya, Jakarta 11043; **Hotel Kristal** ((21) 750-7050 FAX (21) 750-7110, Jalan Tarogong Raya Cilandak Barat, Jakarta; **Omni Batavia** ((21) 690-4118 FAX (21) 690-4092, Jalan Kali Besar Barat N°44-46, Jakarta 11230; **Jayakarta Tower Hotel** ((21) 629-4408 FAX (21) 629-3000, Jalan Hayam Wuruk N°126, Jakarta 11180.

Moderate

With rates of over US$120 for the cheapest standard doubles, the **Hotel Indonesia** ((21) 314-0008 FAX (21) 314-1508, Jalan M.H.

Thamrin, is very much in the top-end of the mid-range bracket. It's overpriced. Stay here only if you want the *frisson* of imagining yourself in 1965, Indonesia's *Year of Living Dangerously*, when the Hotel Indonesia was the top place in town and was the eye of the storm from which journalists filed on the rioting then sweeping the city.

The Jalan Jaksa area, directly south of Merdeka Square, which was until five years ago almost exclusively the domain of backpackers, is now home to some good-value mid-range hotels. The **Hotel Arcadia** ((21) 230-0050 FAX (21) 230-0995, is recommended. It's a small but friendly hotel with very tastefully appointed rooms at Jalan Wahid Hasyim N°114. The nearby **Hotel Le Margot** ((21) 391-3830, at N°15 Jalan Jaksa, is another small place with very reasonable prices given the facilities (business center, bar and restaurant) and the spotless, comfortable rooms.

The **Cikini Sofyan** ((21) 314-0695 FAX (21) 310-0432, Jalan Cikini Raya N°79, is a clean, casual hotel of 115 rooms within walking distance of dozens of antique stores on jalans Surabaya, Kebon Sirah and Cikini Raya. Prices are reasonable, though take a look at your room before checking in as some of them are on small. Don't worry about walking around this part of Jakarta at night. Because President Suharto's home nearby, there's no shortage of police patrols.

Inexpensive

Backpackers congregate in the Jalan Jaksa area, and with good reason. The neighborhood is central, has dozens of inexpensive homestays and restaurants, and is also a good place to make onward travel bookings. The cheapest places in this area, however, tend to be depressingly gloomy and cramped, and it's worth paying a little extra for a better class of homestay.

The **Djody Hotel** ((21) 315-1404 is at Jalan Jaksa N°35 and has a wide range of rooms (including rooms at the next door hostel under the same management). They'll do your laundry cheaply and help with organizing tickets. Along with the inexpensive fan-cooled rooms, some air-conditioned rooms are also available.

Close by, at Jalan Kebon Sirih Barat N°35, is the **Borneo Hostel** ((21) 314-0095, which has a popular café at street level — a good place to meet other travelers. Some rooms are very basic indeed, but the larger ones with attached bath are a good value.

The **Karya II Hotel** ((21) 325078, 310-1380, on Jalan Raden Saleh N°37, over in the Cikini area southeast of Jalan Jaksa, is a step up from the rock-bottom budget rooms of backpacker land, with air-conditioned rooms with attached bath from around US$25. Take a look too at the **Yannie International Guesthouse** ((21) 314-0012, which is next door at N°35. It has long been a feature on the Jakarta budget hotel scene, and is popular for its clean rooms and friendly service.

WHERE TO EAT

Diners in Jakarta are spoiled for choices when it comes to eating out. Not only does the capital have the best Indonesian food in the archipelago, it also has the greatest variety of foreign cuisine.

Don't restrict your dining to the air-conditioned restaurants and the food courts of the five-star hotels. Be adventurous and sample some street food. If you're new to Indonesia, however, the hustle and bustle of *warung* style street stalls may be intimidating. A good alternative is the **Sarinah Department Store** on Jalan Thamrin. Here you'll find more than two dozen food stores serving Jakarta street food in air-conditioned and hygienic surroundings. There's a branch of the **Hard Rock Café** in the same building if that's more your style. The **Hotel Indonesia** has a fine Indonesian buffet that provides a good sampler of local cuisine.

Bakmi Gajah Mada ((21) 310-2258 and 310-2259, Jalan M.H. Thamrin N°21, is part of a successful chain of Indonesian restaurants and is another good place to start your Indonesian culinary adventure. Two other Gajah Mada restaurants, at Jalan Gajah Mada N°92, and Jalan Melawai Raya N°3, cater to Jakarta's craving for noodles. All three are always packed, and reservations and credit cards are not accepted. All three Bakmi Gajah Madas are open for lunch from 10 AM to 3 PM, and at night from 4:30 PM to 10:30 PM.

When Jakartans are in the mood for fried chicken they head to the Kebayoran area of Jakarta Selatan, where two of Java's most

famous restaurateurs, **Ibu Umi** and **Nyonya Suharti**, provide simple yet tasty meals a economical prices. Chicken comes in whol or half portions, with delicious side dishe that cost next to nothing. Ibu Umi is at Jalan Supomo Manggarai N°14. Suharti is at Jalan Kapt. Tendean N°13 in Jakarta Selatan. Both are open daily 10 AM to 10 PM. No reserva tions; no credit cards.

Memories (251-0402 in the Wisma Indocement building on Jalan Jend, Sudir man, Kav N°70–71 makes you feel as if you've arrived in colonial Batavia. The Baruna bar

where you can knock back an *oude genever* resembles a gentleman's bar aboard an old Holland-America cruise ship. The menu which features a nightly *rijstafel*, is heavy with Dutch dishes such as Belgian endives with ham, cheese sauce and mashed potatoes Don't expect a budget night out, but for a treat, Memories is a unique experience. The Indonesian antiques and bric-a-brac on display are often for sale. Salad fans, should avai themselves of Memories' salad bar, which is among the city's best. Dinner is served daily from 7 to 11 PM; lunch is served Monday to Saturday from noon to 3 PM.

Tucked away on busy Jalan A.H. Agus Salim, **Natrabu** is one of the best places in Jakarta to try Padang food. The moment you sit down 12 dishes, along with rice, are brought to your table by waiters dressed in traditional Sumatran clothes. The spinach-like dish consists of young tapioca leaves; that wrinkled slice of beef is cow lung. Try a bit of everything (and pay for every dish) or stick to dishes such as shrimp satay and beef simmered in coconut cream. Even if you try every dish expect to pay under US$10.

Club Noordwijk ((21) 353909 at Jalan Juanda N°5A, offers home style Dutch Indonesian cooking in a tranquil Old Batavia

dining room is decorated with gold-embroidered sarongs from Sumatra. The adjacent Topeng Bar is enlivened by colorful Balinese masks and Javanese paintings. The menu is studded with items such as Beluga caviar and tournedos Rossini, but more moderately priced fare is available. Dishes such as the ginger-flavored frog leg fillets seasoned with peppercorns and the fresh marinated tuna steak cost less than US$10. The Oasis is the only restaurant in Jakarta (and perhaps the world) where a 12-course *rijstafel* is still served by a dozen beautiful maidens.

setting. There is Dutch street organ music and dancing nightly, and as you might expect you pay international prices for all these touches. It's open daily except Sundays. Lunch is served from noon to 3 PM, dinner from 6 to 11 PM.

In 1928 **The Oasis** ((21) 315-0646, Jalan Raden Saleh Raya N°47 was built as a private residence in Raffles period style by a Dutch millionaire. During World War II the last Governor General of the Dutch East Indies made the house his unofficial residence when Japanese bombing made him feel uneasy in Konigsplein Palace. After the war the building became the residence of the United States Naval attaché, who gave the annual Marine Ball in the garden. The main

It's open daily for lunch and dinner, and reservations are essential.

Tony Roma's, the American ribs specialist is at two locations: the Panin Bank Center, Ground Floor, Jalan Jend. Sudirman Kav ((21) 720-2738; and Jalan KH Wahid Hasyim N°49-51 ((21) 384-5511. **Le Bistro** ((21) 390-9249, Jalan KH Wahid Hasyim N°75, was Jakarta's pioneering French restaurant, and 15 years on it's still going strong. The menu is not adventurous, but what it does, it does well. **Planet Hollywood** ((21) 526-7827, Jalan Gatot Subroto, Kav N°16, is a new arrival in

Exotic savory snacks at affordable prices OPPOSITE and colorful fruit and beverage hawkers ABOVE make Indonesia's outdoor markets extremely popular.

Jakarta but one that should be familiar to most overseas visitors. It's a good place to take the children.

Summer Palace ((21) 314-2970, Gedung Tedja Buana Lot 7, Jalan Menteng Raya N°29, is a Chinese restaurant devoted to that spiciest of Chinese cuisines, Sichuan. It's a big place, in the Chinese style, with ambiance in its own way for those who enjoy the bright lights and noisy bustle of Chinese dining.

Near the Horison Hotel and Ancol Park, the **Phinisi (** (21) 690-0947 is a floating seafood restaurant at Pantai Marina in the Java Sea that is a popular fixture on the Jakarta dining scene. Enjoy grilled fish on the top deck or go below for Chinese and Thai food. Prices are moderate and opening hours are from 11 AM until 2:30 PM and from 5:30 to 10:30 PM.

An outdoor garden restaurant on Jalan Silang Monas Tenggara with artificial waterfalls serving typical Sundanese food, **Sari Kuring** serves mainly grilled fish (that you eat with your right hand) but there are other items on the menu such as shrimp satay skewered on a stick and grilled lobster. End the meal with young coconut meat with ice or a peanut milkshake. Also try a glass of *markisa* (grenadilla or passionfruit) juice from North Sumatra. Open daily for lunch and dinner.

Feast for hours on excellent food and pay only pennies at the **Satay House Senayan** at Jalan Kebon Sirih N°31A. The menu features favorites such as Madurese beef soup, *gado gado* salad, *nasi goreng* and satay. It's open daily 10 AM to 10 PM.

SHOPPING

There are three types of shopping areas in Jakarta. The first are air-conditioned shopping plazas where original and fake designer collections are mixed with ready-to-wear batik and *wayang golek* puppets. Here prices are fixed and major credit cards are accepted.

The second category consists of *pasars* where gold can be bought by the gram, fabrics by the meter and where curios compete for space with everything from baby prams to electric fans. Though many items bear price tags, discounts are granted if you are the least bit insistent.

Travelers with a sense of adventure will want to head straight for the city's antique shops where bargaining is *de rigueur*. These shops are scattered about the city near enclaves of expatriate homes and in hotels. Here travelers checks are accepted only grudgingly and the use of a credit card depends on the amount of the purchase. Prices drop dramatically at the merest hint of hard cash.

Women staying in Jakarta for more than several days should stop by the **American Women's Association** on Jalan Sinabung N°11–20 in Kebayoran Baru to purchase a

copy of the organization's hefty *Shopper's Guide*. The book has locations, hours of operation and helpful comments on just about everything one can do, see or buy in Jakarta. The AWA also sells a fact-filled book called *Introducing Indonesia* that provides excellent background on Indonesian customs, history and culture. The book is intended for expatriate wives planning to settle in Jakarta, but its travel section has succinct descriptions of hotels, restaurants and shopping areas throughout the country you may find interesting.

Shopping in Style

Jakarta's ritziest shopping center is the **Plaza Indonesia** at the Grand Hyatt. But if you've seen one luxury shopping center you have seen them all; shop here for designer fashions in a thoroughly import-only culture.

The **Keris Gallery** on Jalan Cokroaminoto is an excellent destination for shoppers interested in jewelry since the various stores offer a variety of designer, costume and traditional native styles. There is also a generous selection of designer batik stores, some of which sponsor midday fashion shows.

Two **Sarinah Department Stores** on Jalan Thamrin and in Kebayoran Baru are priority stops since each offers a good selection of

are higher now that Indonesia enforces anti-piracy laws.

Just east of the old Portuguese Church and across the street from Jakarta's Kota Station railway yard is the **Manga Dua Shopping Center** on Jalan Manga Dua Raya. Most of the merchandise here consists of Chinese lanterns, basic kitchenware and other domestic necessities. Go on Sunday, if you dare, to take in the scene of thousands of Jakartans out enjoying their middle class buying power or simply *cuci mata* (window shopping). Composed of numerous blocks, sections and

handicrafts and batik at reasonable prices. Both stores have batik boutiques with original creations by famous batik designers such as Irwin Tirta and Poppy Dharsono. This is an excellent place to begin your comparison shopping since prices charged by Sarinah are the standard by which competing outlets set their prices.

Bargain Centers

Glodok Plaza in the middle of Chinatown is difficult to get to because of the traffic clogging jalans Gajah Mada and Hayam Wuruk, but the wait is worth it if you're in the market for computer or electrical products. Bargaining is essential here, but don't be too insistent when it comes to computer software. Prices

floors, Manga Dua is an easy place to get lost or separated from your group with its hundreds of shops lining a maze of crowded aisles.

Antiques

For hundreds of years Indonesia has been a crossroads for traders from throughout Asia. Indians, Turks and Chinese all brought treasures to trade for spices. Portuguese, Dutch and British who came as colonists brought household goods. Once settled in the archipelago, they commissioned the building of

OPPOSITE: Curios from throughout the archipelago are on sale in Jakarta. ABOVE: Some of the best antiques can be found in the stalls along Jakarta's Jalan Surabaya.

houses full of furniture. Today, everything they left behind (and imitations of it) is for sale side by side with native handicrafts.

Jalan Surabaya in Menteng is the first stop for any antique hunter. On this street, open-front antique shops extend for more than a half mile. Each store has its specialty. Some offer Buddha heads in bronze or sandstone, Dyak artwork, Russian samovars or Dutch hanging lamps. Others sell maritime navigational instruments, Japanese swords, old coins or porcelain from sunken ships. Bargaining is essential and all transactions are

Chinese porcelain. Chinese ceramics were brought to Java during the height of the spice trade. Much of what one finds today is "kitchen Ming," roughly made porcelain that was used as ballast for ships carrying tea, coffee and other spices. Open Monday to Saturday 9 AM to 6 PM.

Buyung Art at Jalan Kebon Sirih Timur N°20 has a wide selection of primitive art as does **New Ganesha** at Jalan Kebon Sirih Timur N°5A and **Uji Dornis Art & Curio** at Jalan Kebon Sirih Timur N°20A. Primitive art does not necessarily mean old, of course.

in cash. If you're still easing into bargaining protocol, remember to maintain a smile, compare prices and aim to bring the asking price down by about 30 to 40%.

After exploring Jalan Surabaya, move on to Jalan Kebon Sirih Timur. **Amadeus**, Jalan Kebon Sirih Timur N°50, specializes in primitive art from Irian Jaya and the Lake Toba area of Sumatra. There are also stores on Jalan Majapahit.

Bahni Art Shop Jalan Kebon Sirih Timur N°6, has an eclectic assortment of merchandise ranging from German clocks to antique telephones. Most of the store is given over to

Much of what is available is of recent vintage, items produced by the country's stone age tribes.

Ndalem, Jalan Kebon Sirih Timur N°8, sells aged batik and stonecarvings. Its Buddha figures range from US$500 to US$5,000. Open daily from 9 AM to 6 PM.

Sriwijaya at Jalan Kebon Sirih Timur N°158, has a large assortment of Dutch lamps and antique terracotta roof tiles from Palembang, South Sumatra. There are also Batak-carved buffalo horns from North Sumatra.

Jalan Bangka Raya, **Jalan Kemang Bangka** and **Jalan Ciputat Raya** also have their share of antique stores due largely to the nearby expatriate housing in Menteng. Be on the lookout for Huanghuali rosewood

Wayang golek puppets (left) dressed in colorful batik are carved in Western Java. *Wayang kulit* shadow puppets (right) are a Central Java favorite.

chairs from China. Ming dynasty furniture is rapidly appreciating in value because the Huanghuali species of hardwood is extinct.

Art

Jakarta has hundreds of art galleries featuring traditional and batik painting. One of the nicest places to browse is **Pasar Seni** in Ancol Park. Built atop a reclaimed swamp, this immaculately clean park allows artists, restaurateurs and strolling musicians to mingle under the stars beside the Java Sea. **Gita Ramayana** features batik paintings that can be paid for by credit card. **Sanggar Bali** has Balinese paintings and woodcarvings produced in Ubud and Mas.

Batik

Central Java offers the best buys on batik, but if Jakarta is your only stop, **Batik Berdikari**, Jalan Mesjid Pal VII N°7B, Palmerah, is a worthwhile stop. Here you can see the creative process unfold and purchase handmade silk and cotton garments. Be sure to bring a camera to photograph the 40 employees waxing, dying and washing fabric. Located in West Jakarta, the factory is open daily from 9 AM to 5 PM.

Handicrafts

Jakarta Handicraft Center, Jalan Pekalongan N°12A, has a variety of woodcarvings, rattan baskets, brass and copper artifacts and Sumatran textiles. Open 9 AM to 6:30 PM, Sunday 10 AM to 4 PM.

NIGHTLIFE

With everything from local cultural performances to London-beat clubs, Jakarta has Indonesia's most sophisticated and varied nightlife scene. Perhaps it has something to do with the hot tropical sun, but this is not an early-to-bed town. Discos don't really begin to fill until after 10:30 PM. Many sidewalk food vendors around the National Monument stay busy serving *nasi goreng* and *satay* long past midnight to Jakartans enjoying the (relatively) cool night air.

The reason Jakartans can literally burn the midnight oil and still make it to work the next morning is because they pace themselves throughout the hot tropical day, and

take a brief nap after returning home from work. Resting from 5 PM to 6:30 PM is a good idea for you, too, if you hope to enjoy most of the attractions listed below.

Cultural Performances

Though Yogyakarta is considered the center of Javanese culture, Jakarta has much to offer in the way of classical dancing and puppet shows. For *wayang orang* and *ketoprak* (Javanese dance dramas), visit the **Bhatara Theater**, Jalan Kalilio N°15, where performances are staged nightly (except Saturday) from 8:15 PM to midnight.

There is always something happening at **Taman Ismail Marzuki** (TIM), Jakarta's largest cultural center. For the daily listing of events look at the "Around Town" part of the *Indonesian Observer* or the "What's on in Jakarta Today" section of the *Indonesian Times*.

Another venue with changing performances is the **Gedung Kesenian Jakarta**, Jalan Gudung Kesenian N°1. Not all shows here are Indonesian, however. Check with the newspapers above or with one of the tourist offices for details of the current program.

Miss Titjih's Theater, Jalan Kabel Pendek, presents a nightly Sundanese folk drama performance at 7 PM and 9 PM. It's well worth seeing.

Bars

As is the case elsewhere in Asia, there has been an explosion of Western style bars over the last few years in Jakarta. The Irish theme is popular, and here it is represented by **O'Reilly's** at the Grand Hyatt. The general air of conviviality and the live Irish music on weekends make up for the international-standard prices. **Chequers**, at the Mandarin Oriental, operates along similar lines and at similar prices. The **Hard Rock Café**, on the first floor of the Sarinah Department Store on Jalan Thamrin, provides their recognizable mix of rock and roll memorabilia, loud music and hamburgers.

Café Batavia at Fatahillah Square is the latest in designer chic, and is a popular spot to be seen exchanging the contents of your wallet for a cocktail with an exotic name. Still, it provides a fascinating glimpse of the highlife Jakarta style.

The **Tavern Pub**, in the Aryaduta Hotel, is one of Jakarta's older establishments, but it still pulls in the crowds. Another long-runner is the **George and Dragon**, Jalan Teluk Betung N°32, next to the Kartika Plaza hotel. Directly across Jalan Thamrin from the Kartika Plaza is a small lane, awash in neon, called Jalan Blora. The jumble of country-western bars and Chinese nightclubs make it seem an exciting place, but the interior of these bars belies the promise outside, and it's best to avoid the entire street.

Jaya Pub is a Jakarta institution. It's an upstairs bar behind the Jaya Building at Jalan M.H. Thamrin N°12. Live music is sometimes featured, and late on weekends it can get very lively here.

Live Music

Jakarta has its own **Blue Note**, Atria Square, Lower Ground, Jalan Jend. Sudirman Kav, the prestigious jazz chain, as sure a sign as any that Jakarta is emerging as a cosmopolitan, international city. Another jazz venue is **Jamz**, at Blok M. Check out **BATS** at the Shangri-La Hotel on Jalan Sudirman, one of the hippest spots in town and a spot for live music.

Discos

Dance venues come and go in popularity; any of the pubs listed above will be good places to ask around for the latest hot spots. Nowhere gets started much before 11 PM.

Terminal 1, at Godok Plaza, is very much a local scene, but one worth taking a look at. Essentially it brings together dancing, kara-oke, live music and straight drinking in a three-floor extravaganza—a format that has proved popular throughout Asia.

For a look at the clubbing scene, stop by **Big Fire**, at the Plaza Indonesia, which attracts a young bopping crowd to its sleek interior and hi-tech sound system.

Tanamur, at Jalan Tanah Abang Timur N°14, is "old school" but is notable for its highly mixed clientele — you won't feel out of place here as a foreigner, and you are guaranteed to meet people.

HOW TO GET THERE AND AWAY

All international flights coming into and leaving from Jakarta use the Soekarno–Hatta International Airport. All departing flights, whether international or inside Indonesia, require that a departure tax be paid in rupiah (see HOW TO GET THERE in TRAVELERS' TIPS, page 279).

Some internal flights continue to leave from Jakarta's two secondary airports, Kemayoran and Halim (see HOW TO GET THERE in TRAVELERS' TIPS, page 279).

WEST JAVA

The province of West Java is surprisingly beautiful and easily accessible because of modern, divided highways built over the past 15 years. Only minutes outside Jakarta the roads begin to climb and the foothills of the highlands emerge. Bamboo forests and tea plantations accent miles of terraced ricefields.

ALONG THE COAST

Along the western and southern coastlines, West Java has excellent beaches that look out on the Sunda Strait and the massive volcano **Krakatau** which shook the world when it erupted in August 1883 (see VISIT THE SON OF KRAKATOA in TOP SPOTS, page 16). The actual volcano was destroyed in the explosion, but a new crater known as **Anak Krakatau** (Son of Krakatau) can be visited by boat. Before setting out, make sure the volcano is safe to visit since from time to time it still emits dangerous fumes. This area also has West Java's **Ujung Kulon Nature Reserve**, the last refuge of the near-extinct one-horned Java rhino. Both attractions can be reached from the beach resorts of **Anyer** and **Carita** (see below).

The best way to visit Ujung Kulon Nature Reserve, which is one of Indonesia's two United Nations World Heritage sites (the other is Komodo Island), is to join a tour in Carita. Costs start at around US$150 for three nights in the park, all-inclusive. Doing it solo involves organizing a permit and guides in the town of Labuan (close to Carita). Although the reserve offers fantastic jungle walks and rich wildlife, you should bear in mind that rhino sightings are extremely rare. Hunted to near extinction, numbers of this rare beast hover at around 60.

Visitors to Krakatau are advised not to seek bargains when chartering a boat. The crossing is often rough and many boats that locals charter out are not safe. The **Mambruk Quality Resort** (see below) in Anyer has reliable boats that do the crossing, as do some of the more luxury hotel outfits in Carita.

Where to Stay

The **Anyer Beach Hometel and Resort (** (254) 629224 FAX (254) 629500, Jalan Raya Karang Bolong is a luxury choice with mid-range

popular beach resort in Java. Swimming is only safe in the southwestern section of this peninsula; but the shortage of safe beaches does not keep the crowds at bay. Pangandaran is a good spot to relax, sunbathe and tuck in to some inexpensive seafood. It is also near a second excellent game reserve, the **Pananjung Pangandaran** where a variety of civet cats, monkeys, pythons and deer can be seen within a teak forest. Hiking tours of the game reserve are widely advertised in Pangandaran and can be organized at short notice.

prices. It has a swimming pool, a good beach and spacious air-conditioned bungalows. A step up in price is the **Mambruk Quality Resort (** (254) 601602 FAX (254) 81723, which has luxurious villas with lanais right on the beach next to a grass volleyball court, tennis courts, swimming pool and soccer field.

Carita, to the south of Anyer, is a resort area that caters to vacationing Jakartans. The **Resort Lippo Carita (** (254) 61180 is a sprawling place that commands a good stretch of beach. Room rates are mid-range and up.

SOUTH COAST

In the southeast corner of Barat province is **Pangandaran**, a fishing village and the most

West Java's southern coastline is cloaked in mystery and superstition. It is the home of the mythical goddess Nyi Loro Kidul, the Queen of the South Seas. The south coast's major resort, the Samudra Beach Hotel, keeps room N°318 permanently empty for the goddess' occasional visits. The room attracts pilgrims from throughout the country who believe Nyi Loro Kidul's blessing can protect them on crossings of her treacherous seas.

Where to Stay '

Most of the hotels and *losmen* are on the west beach since the beaches are poor and the

---

Southwest Java's Ujung Kulon Nature Reserve ABOVE and OVERLEAF boasts a variety of jungle wildlife.

Indian totem poles, Rambo and 007 style façades (including one with a taxi crashing through a roof) is a fascinating spectacle (see also SHOPPING, below).

Where to Stay

LUXURY

The hotel situation in Bandung has improved immensely over the last few years because of a construction boom. Nevertheless, make a reservation if you're heading up to Bandung on a weekend, since this is when many Jakartans drive up to for the cooler temperatures.

When Dutch architect A.F. Albers was commissioned to take down the old Homann Hotel and put up a new modern one in 1939, he designed a pleasure palace meant to remind colonial plantation owners and visiting bureaucrats of what was in those days the epitome of good living — a luxury cruise ship. In so doing, Albers built what art historians say is a tropical art deco masterpiece, the **Savoy Homann** ((22) 432244 or (22) 430083 FAX (22) 431583, Jalan Asia Afrika N°112. The long building, with its central bridge and rising funnel, has corridors that resemble the deck of a ship. Clever step-backs or recessions in the façade provide the building with a unique rhythm as if it were rising and falling over ocean waves. Zhou Enlai, Norodom Sihanouk and Jawaharlal Nehru stayed here while attending the 1955

A villa in Bandung typifies the city's fascinating legacy of tropical art deco.

Asia-Africa conference (that became the non-aligned movement) across the street. Charlie Chaplin and Mary Pickford also hung out at the Homann during the 1920s.

The Homann's rooms have balconies and are well maintained. Sixteen of the old Dutch suites have been preserved in their original condition with teak wainscoting, ceilings and Dutch glass doors dividing the bedroom from the sitting room. It is easily the most interesting hotel in town.

The **Grand Hotel Preanger** ((22) 431631 FAX (22) 430034, Jalan Asia Afrika N°81, was originally a 53-room art deco hotel dating back to 1928. It has been enlarged and modernized with the addition of a 157-room high-rise and is the best hotel in Bandung. The architect tried to duplicate the atmosphere of the original building; to capture the feel of pre-war Bandung, ask for one of the old rooms in the Asia Afrika wing.

Luxury in a relaxing countryside setting can be experienced several kilometers north of town at the **Chedi Hotel** ((22) 230333 FAX (22) 230633, Jalan Renca Bantang N°56–58. With 50 rooms, it offers a stylish intimacy along with international-class amenities. Its only drawback is that it places you rather far from the city center.

MODERATE

At the top of the middle bracket is the **Panghegar Hotel** ((22) 432286 FAX (22) 431583, Jalan Merdeka N°2, which is nowadays looking slightly tired and is more memorable for the sunset views from its Panyawangan Revolving Restaurant. Some of the deluxe rooms with north-facing views are not bad, but in all there are probably better deals to be had around town.

The **Mutiara Hotel** ((22) 420-0333 FAX (22) 420-4961, Jalan Kebon Kewung N°60, has nothing in the way of art deco ambiance, but has a good central location near the train station and offers excellent mid-range standards in its clean and spacious rooms.

The **Hotel Braga** ((22) 420-4685 at Jalan Braga N°8, is a rambling old Dutch hotel with a renovated wing. The latter is the place to stay, as standards in the older rooms veer erratically from faded to neglected. Still, there's no denying the place has character. It has a central location too.

INEXPENSIVE

The **Hotel Surabaya** ((22) 436739, Jalan Kebonjati N°71, is yet another rambling old colonial monster sinking into decrepitude. On the budget front, however, this hotel has some good deals — take a look at a range of rooms before making a choice. It has a good location up the road from the train station.

As is the case at other popular Indonesian destinations, finding a homestay is no problem if you want to economize in an intimate family setting. **Le Yossie Homestay** ((22) 420-5453, Jalan Kebonjati, is representative, offering a choice of dormitory accommodation and private rooms with shared washing facilities for less than US$5. Another popular homestay, and a good place to meet other travelers, is the **Losmen Sakadarna** ((22) 439897, Jalan Kebonjati N°34. Again, accommodation is basic, but the friendly atmosphere and low prices make up for the lack of amenities.

Where to Eat

Less spicy than most Indonesian fare, Sunda food relies on fresh vegetables, fruit and fish. *Ikan mas* (goldfish) is a popular Sunda specialty that is served fried (*ikan mas goreng*), or steamed with spices (*ikan mas pepes*), and served with a sour vegetable soup (*sayur asam*).

Babakan Siliwangi, Jalan Siliwangi N°7, specializes in goldfish which diners can select from terraced ponds. Covered by a roof but otherwise open to the elements, tables look out beyond the fish ponds to a vest-pocket rice field. Left-overs get tossed to the goldfish, which can fight like piranhas when scraps are at stake. Open daily 9 AM to 10 PM.

Just around the corner from the Savoy Homann and the Grand Hotel Preanger, the **Braga**, Jalan Braga N°58, is a brasserie with a pastry chef who began his apprenticeship when Indonesia still belonged to the Dutch. This bakery and restaurant is one of the city's oldest and finest restaurants. It has a large menu brimming with European and Sichuan dishes. Open daily from 9 AM to 11 PM.

Bandung's best Chinese restaurant is the **Queen International** on Jalan Dalem Kaum N°79. Open daily from 10 AM to 11 PM, it specializes in Cantonese food. For a traditional *rijstafel* dinner, duck into the restaurant at the **Savoy Homann**. The **Pondok Kapau**, Jalan Asia Afrika N°43, is a good place to try Padang cuisine—it's very popular with locals.

Shopping

A large fashion industry has developed in Bandung, which produces 60% of Indonesia's textiles. Jeans and denim accessories along with T-shirts and belts are sold at bargain prices along a colorful street known as **Cihampelas**, or **Jeans Street** (see also WHAT TO SEE AND DO, above). There are plenty of bargains to be had here, though you should always check carefully for quality. Stores are open from 10 AM to 9 PM.

Shoes are also a bargain in Bandung. **Jalan Cibaduyut**, seven kilometers (four miles) south of the railroad track, has more than 50 open-front shops full of leather, snakeskin and crocodile shoes. The variety here is tremendous and the prices are low. If you like a style that's not in your size and are able to wait three or four days, the stores will have shoes made to order. Handmade men's shoes are US$50 a pair, women's shoes cost US$11.

For modern sterling silver jewelry visit **Runa Jewelry workshop** on Jalan Gegerkalong Hilir N°64. Runa also sells pottery from the nearby village of Plered, batik and *wayang golek* puppets.

For *wayang golek* puppets it's possible, in Bandung, to go to the source. Aming Sutisna, the best puppet maker in West Java, lives at Jalan Moh. Ramdan N°4. It takes six days to make a puppet, the time about equally divided between carving and painting the soft *albassia* wood. For the Sutisna family, puppets are literally a cottage industry. Aming's workshop is the kitchen, his wife, Aos Utari, makes the puppets' clothing. Sutisna's puppets start at US$40, more than Jakarta's Sarinah department store charges, but the carving is much more detailed. Open daily; cash transactions only.

Bandung has a good selection of art galleries where purchases can be made. The **Braga Gallery**, Jalan Braga N°68, is a good place to start looking. It's open 9 AM to 7:30 PM, closed Sunday.

Nightlife

The Sundanese are known for their music made with the *angklung*, a percussion instrument made of bamboo pipes which when shaken produce a mellow tone similar to that of a xylophone. *Angklung* concerts are performed at several places around Bandung, the most famous of which is **Pak Ujo's Angklung Show** in the village of Padasuka. Here, every afternoon at 3:30 PM, 30 local children play Javanese and Western tunes.

The **Rumentang Siang**, Jalan Baranangsiang N°1, is a performing arts center that hosts regular *wayang golek* puppet performances and other local cultural events. Check with the Visitor Information Center for schedules.

For performances of Sundanese dance, the Panghegar Hotel (see above) has dinner performances on Wednesday and Saturday night starting at 7:30 PM in the **Pasundan Dining Room**.

For a few drinks in an environment conducive to meeting locals — expatriate and otherwise — wander down to Jalan Braga, where you will find the **North Sea Bar** near the intersection of Jalan Lembong and farther south, near the intersection of Jalan Naripan, the **Braga Pub**. If you're looking for some late night action, locals in either of these bars should be able to fill you in on the latest happening spots around town. **La Dream Palace** ((22) 433970, is a disco on the second floor of the Asia Afrika Plaza next to the post office. One of this disco's two dance floors is on springs, a situation which tests your balance as well as your rhythm. Open nightly 9 PM to 2 AM.

Golf

Bandung has three excellent golf courses, while nearby in Lembang — at an altitude twice that of Bandung — there's a fourth. In Bandung, the 18-hole **Dago Golf Course**, at the top end of Jalan Juanda, is beautifully laid out in hilly countryside. The **Bandung Giri Gahana Golf and Country Club**, at Jatinangor some 40 minutes from Bandung, is unanimously considered the best in Indonesia. The nine-hole **Panorama Panghegar Golf Course** near Lembang is probably the most beautiful course in the country.

How to Get There and Away

There are regular flights to Bandung with Merpati, Bouraq and Sempati airlines from Jakarta and from many other Indonesian destinations. The cheapest way to get to the city is by 48/48 Taxi, which is not a taxi at all but an inexpensive minibus service that makes the trip between Jakarta and Bandung in around four hours. The minibuses leave Jakarta approximately every five minutes from their depot next to the Satriavi Tours office on Jalan Prapatan.

Rail travel between Jakarta and Bandung is fast and convenient. The *Parahyangan* train has approximately half-hour departures from before daybreak until around 8:30 PM. First- and executive-class coaches are air-conditioned. Trains stop at each of Jakarta's three stations: Gambir, Kota and Jatinegara. There is also an express train to Cirebon called the *Gunung Jati* that leaves Jakarta Kota Station thrice daily.

In Bandung, regular metered cabs operate as do those in Jakarta. Bandung taxis can be hired for US$4 an hour for service inside the city.

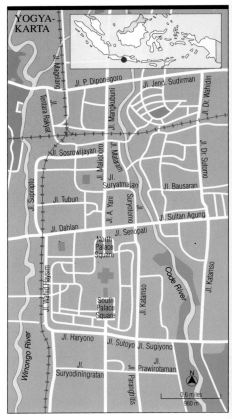

YOGYAKARTA

Central Java is the cultural cradle of Indonesia. Together with the special administrative area of Yogyakarta, it accounts for more than 30% of Java's population. Most of the region's creative energy radiates from the Yogyakarta–Surakarta (more commonly known as Solo) corridor where earlier civilizations flourished on the rich volcanic soil. Indeed, the history of Indonesia, from the coming of Islam to the arrival of Independence, turns largely on actions taken by the sultans and kings of Central Java.

In no other Indonesian city does the past so intimately overlap the present as it does in Yogyakarta, a "special autonomous region" of 2,945 sq km (1,137 sq miles) with a population of around three million, though the city itself has a population of just 500,000. The sultan's palace, or *kraton*, is still the heart of the city, and comes alive every Sunday when a gamelan orchestra and Javanese dancers perform. The Shivaistic temple complex of Prambanan and Buddhist Borobudur, acclaimed as one of the seven wonders of the world, are as impressive today as they were back in the tenth and ninth centuries, when each embodied the grandeur and sophistication of the Mataram and Sailendra dynasties. These and other temple complexes reflect the vitality of Central Java's modern culture which makes Yogya second only to Bali as a tourist destination.

GENERAL INFORMATION

The Tourist Information Office is in central Yogyakarta at Jalan Malioboro N°14-16 ((274) 566000; it's open weekdays from 8 AM to 7 PM and on Saturday from 8 AM to noon.

WHAT TO SEE AND DO

Borobudur is about an hour's drive northwest of town. The best time to visit is at sunrise or late in the day, since the massive stone

Yogyakarta's Taman Sari "Water Castle" west of the *kraton* evokes an image of bygone splendor.

temple absorbs the midday heat. **Prambanan** lies northeast of Yogya on the highway to Solo, and can be accomplished as afternoon trip, following a morning at Borobudur and lunch back in Yogya. Alternatively, you can stop at Prambanan on the way to Solo.

Borobudur and Environs

After uncovering the ruins of Borobudur in 1814, Stamford Raffles wrote: "The interior of Java contains temples that, as works of labor and art, dwarf to nothing all our wonders and admiration at the pyramids of Egypt." Raffles might be even more impressed today now that Borobudur has been rebuilt with the aid of US$60 million in UNESCO funds (see also A SYMPHONY IN STONE, page 10 in TOP SPOTS).

The largest Buddhist shrine in the world, Borobudur was built between 778 and 856 AD, 300 years before Angkor Wat in Cambodia and 200 years before Notre Dame in Paris. Seen from the air, the temple forms a mandala; from the ground it is laid out like a bell-shaped dome or stupa, and covers the top of a steep hill like a mantle. The elaborately-carved galleries ascend in 10 levels, corresponding to the divisions within the Mahayana Buddhist universe. The first visible level (the temple's original base is no longer visible) depicts the delights of human life and the punishments that await sinners. Then come five levels of diminishing size that are surmounted by three more circular and concentric terraces that support 72 miniature, perforated stupas, each of which contains a meditating Buddha. A total of 2,700 carved stone panels on the balustrades about the monument relate the Buddha's teaching and depict scenes from his life, so that climbing Borobudur is a religious journey. Borobudur is open daily from 6 AM to 5 PM.

If time permits, visit **Candi Mendut**, located about one kilometer (just over half a mile) east of Borobudur. The intricately carved reliefs at this temple, the largest in any Indonesian temple, are breathtaking in their beauty and show everything from child-eating ogres to mythological money trees.

Built four centuries before the great cathedrals at Chartres and Rheims, Borobudur is the world's most imposing Buddhist monument.

only a few stops. The *Bima* has air-conditioned first-class compartments that contain pull-down beds with linens. The night train that links Bandung with Surabaya via Yogya is called the *Mutiara*. The only day-time train between Jakarta and Yogya worth taking is the *Fajar Utama*. All of the others are uncomfortably crowded and excruciatingly slow.

Night buses travel to all of the above destinations, but are considered dangerous — even by Indonesians used to the vagaries of bus travel on the archipelago — because of the likelihood of accidents.

price. The Ambarrukmo is also the best place to shop for a package tour. Ida's Tours, Jatayu Mulya, Matahari Tours, Milangkori, Natrabu, Pacto, Paradise Bali Indah, Rama Royal Holiday, Satriavi, Sri Rama, Tunas Indonesia and Vaya Tours all have small offices along the arcade off the lobby. For the comparison shopper, this place is paradise.

Most of the companies offer city tours that center on a visit to the *kraton*. This tour should be avoided. The *kraton* has a staff of official guides who provide free tours on request,

Yogya's in-town transport runs the gamut from horse-drawn *andong* carriages to hotel rental cars. Because Yogya is relatively flat, the most popular way to get about the city is on pedal-powered *becaks*. A dollar will take you almost anywhere in Yogya on a *becak*, though as a tourist this may require some determined but friendly haggling. Private cars available for rent outside the main hotels and shouldn't cost much more than US$4 an hour for travel inside the city.

The most efficient and inexpensive way to get about Central Java is to go to the front of the Ambarrukmo Palace hotel and talk with the drivers. Find one who speaks English and then bargain for his best price. The more days you require, the lower the

though a small tip is appreciated. The "Art and Handicraft" tours offered by Satriavi and Pacto are well worth the time, however, since both include trips to villages outside the city.

CENTRAL JAVA

Beyond the special autonomous region of Yogyakarta and the neighboring ruins of kingdoms past, lie the rich paddy lands of Central Java, the spiritual center of the real Indonesia. It was here the ancient Sailendra and Mataram kingdoms flourished a

Sun-dried earthenware from Kasongan comes in a variety of shapes and colors.

millennium ago. Here, too, the Majapahit empire spread the Hindu philosophy throughout Java and Bali. And it was here, from the second Mataram empire's capital of Kota Gede, near Yogyakarta, that the island's most accomplished warrior, Sultan Agung, extended his rule across the Java Sea to Borneo, Sumatra and the Celebes.

Convinced of his spiritual alliance with Nyi Loro Kidul, the Goddess of the South Seas, the Sultan believed he could carry Islam's banner throughout the archipelago. His failure to take the Dutch stronghold of Batavia led to his demise and the eventual spread of Dutch colonial rule.

Successors to Sultan Agung remained loyal to the South Seas Goddess, but she continued to be a fickle mistress. Though the Mataram kingdom endured into the mid-nineteenth century, it was controlled by the Dutch who used it to their own ends, pitting Yogyakarta against Surakarta (Solo) in a series of petty aristocratic wars.

SOLO

In 1745 King Pakubuwono II chose the tiny village of Solo as the location of his new palace, the Surakarta Hadiningrat. The king quickly put an end to all local rebellions, making Solo the official capital of Javanese culture and classical arts for the next 200 years. Today, the two names, Solo and Surakarta, are interchangeable though it's Solo you hear most often.

Solo's primacy in Central Java ended following World War II when its sultan displayed an ambivalent attitude toward independence while Yogyakarta was becoming a center for revolutionary struggle. Today, Solo's role is less central than nearby Yogyakarta, and it's an altogether quieter city. But as many locals will point out, Solo is more distinctly Javanese and those who bypass the city miss a great deal, for Solo's history is fully as rich as that of its more touristed neighbor.

General Information

The **Solo Tourist Office** ((271) 711435, Jalan Slamet Riyadi N°275, is open daily from 8 AM to 5 PM and is a good place to pick up local maps and get the low-down on upcoming events.

What to See and Do

The *kraton*, which received US$3.8 million in repairs following a disastrous fire in 1985, is much like Yogya's in that a thick outer wall encloses a grid of lanes and alleyways. A soothing marble performance pavilion used for coronations leads to an interior courtyard surrounded by 77 Ming dynasty porcelain vases. The 31-m (97-ft)-high Royal Meditation Tower on one side is the tallest building in Solo, and resembles a Dutch windmill without the arms.

According to legend, the Goddess of the South Seas, Nyi Loro Kidul, is the spiritual wife of the sultan of Solo, and she demands periodic visits in the tower. The *kraton* is open every day except Friday from 8:30 AM to 1:30 PM. There is classical Javanese dancing every Sunday from 10 AM to 2 PM.

Nearly a kilometer (half a mile) northwest of the main *kraton* is **Pura Mangkunegaran**, a smaller palace built by an offshoot of Surakarta's royal family. Completed in 1866, the outer pavilion was built of solid teak without the use of a single nail. Behind the Pendopo is a ceremonial hall full of antiques that belonged to Prince Mankunegara IV. Be sure to see the ninth century male and female chastity belts. Open Monday through Saturday from 9 AM to 2 PM, Sunday from 9 AM to 1 PM.

East of Solo, Mt. Lawu rises over 3,000 m (9,940 ft) from the paddy fields into swirling clouds of white mist. Motorists headed for Surabaya skirt the mountain, but you may want to take the Kemuning village road to **Candi Sukuh**, a fifteenth century Majapahit shrine 40 km (25 miles) east of Solo, erected by a fertility cult. The temple is known for its erotic carvings, but the genitalia depicted seems more anatomical than pornographic. What makes the temple mysterious is its location in a secluded pine forest and the fact it has a flat-topped Mayan appearance.

Before leaving Solo you should consider trying a *jamu*, the traditional herbal medicine Javanese have used for hundreds of years. There are two kinds of *jamu*: dried herbs and leaves that must be boiled in water before being drunk, and powders which are commercially produced and available in

Women play traditional game in Solo's Mangkunagaran Palace

Islam during the twilight of the crumbling Majapahit kingdom. One of the anchors from Cheng Ho's ships is on display, but the real attraction of the temple is its atmosphere. Swirling with incense, the various shrines are packed with worshippers and fortune-tellers who divine the future with bamboo sticks or small birds.

From the Sam Po Kong Temple it is only a short *becak* ride to Semarang's Chinatown which has its own temple, the garishly painted **Tay Kak Sie**. The small lanes leading off Jalan Pekojan have a number of Chinese medicine and spice shops.

Those who have been sufficiently adventurous to try a *jamu* on their journey through Java may wish to visit the two factories where nearly all of them are made. **Jamu Jago (** (24) 285533, Jalan Setia Budi, will assign a guide to explain how herbs are turned into medicine; an appointment is necessary. The other *jamu* factory, **Jamu Nyonya Meneer (** (24) 285732, Jalan Raya Kaligawe, is farther out of town, but it has a herbal medicine museum that helps explain *jamus* better than most guides do.

Where to Stay

Semarang may be slightly off the beaten track, but it has no shortage of places to stay.

Down on Simpang Lima (Five Ways) Square, the **Hotel Ciputra (** (24) 413115 FAX (24) 413113 is a new luxury addition to Semarang's hotel scene. It's a modern place, with all the amenities you'd expect of a hotel that is striving for a five-star rating. The nearby **Hotel Graha Santika (** (24) 449888, Jalan Pandanaran N°116, is another luxury hotel, with little to differentiate it from the Ciputra except that it is marginally less expensive.

The **Holiday Inn Semarang (** (240) 416222 FAX (24) 449717, Jalan Sisingamangaraja N°16, Semarang is the third of the new luxury hotels and offers the standard Holiday Inn facilities.

The **Metro Grand Park Hotel (** (24) 547371, Jalan H Agus Salim N°2, once the best hotel in town, has become somewhat run down. It does, however, have a central location. The **Queen Hotel (** (24) 547063, nearby on Jalan Gajah Mada N°44–52, is a better value mid-range hotel.

Where to Eat

There are several Chinese restaurants scattered around the city, and many of them serve Cantonese *dim sum* for breakfast and lunch. In the evening, there are dozens of food stalls and small cafés, *warungs*, at the Pasar Ya'ik night market. The only truly distinctive restaurant in town is **Toko Oen**, an enormous old-fashioned tea room with a South Seas ambiance. Located at Jalan Permuda N°52, the Toko Oen's waiters look as if they might have been around long enough to have started their careers with the Dutch, but they move smartly enough, no matter whether the order is a milk shake, or a gin and tonic. If you're in town on a Thursday or Friday, try one of their sumptuous lunch buffets.

How to Get There and Away

Semarang has surprisingly good air connections with the rest of Indonesia. Merpati has numerous non-stop flights from Jakarta, as well from Bandung and Surabaya. Bouraq and Mandala also link Semarang with Jakarta and even with Banjarmasin in Kalimantan. Sempati has direct flights from Jakarta and Surabaya.

Semarang is on the rail line that links Jakarta with Cirebon and Surabaya. For the most comfortable ride from Jakarta, take the first-class *Mutiara Utara*.

There is a PELNI office **(** (24) 555156 in Semarang at Jalan Tantular N°25. Regular PELNI boats sail to various destinations in Kalimantan.

EAST JAVA

If the world's most densely-populated island can be said to have a hinterland, then East Java is the hinterland. Outside of industrialized Surabaya, this activities in this region are exclusively agricultural. Most travelers to Indonesia skip over East Java in their rush to get to Bali. Those who linger for a while will discover the fertile plains that were home to the powerful Majapahit Hindu kingdom.

The main attraction of this area is the volcanic peak of Mt. Bromo, whose summit has become a beckoning call for most travelers who pass though the region.

SURABAYA

Surabaya, the provincial capital and Indonesia's second largest city, is an industrial town that lacks Yogya's charm and Jakarta's history. Long a destination of schooners from Makassar, Surabaya finally fell to the Mataram empire in 1625, but its history really began in 1945 when its resistance forces began Indonesia's war of independence by battling the British who had landed to secure Java for the soon-to-return Dutch.

With a population well over 3.6 million, Surabaya has prospered since independence. In addition to being the seat of the provincial government, it is home to the Indonesian navy and much of Java's heavy industry. Most tourist attractions, with the exception of the Surabaya Zoo, are outside the city.

General Information

The Tourist Information Center ((31) 524499, Jalan Permuda N°118, does its best to be of assistance to the odd soul who passes through.

What to See and Do

Built in 1836, the **Rakhmat** and **Sunan Bungkul mosques** constitute the religious heart of fundamentalist East Java. A more popular attraction for tourists, however, is the **Red Bridge**, or Jembatan Merah, which once was the center of Dutch Surabaya. Old office buildings, warehouses and banks with their high ceilings testify to the lengths the Dutch went to capture a cool breeze. They also serve as evidence of the quality that went into the construction of colonial buildings. Formerly the home of the Dutch governor, the **Grahadi** on Jalan Permuda today serves as the home of the Indonesian governor of East Java. Also worth visiting is the **Majapahit Hotel**, the Dutch colonial hotel that served as Japanese officers' quarters during World War II.

The **Surabaya Zoo**, on Jalan Diponegoro near the Joyoboyo bus station, is Southeast Asia's largest zoological park. Because of the heat and humidity, the zoo does not have many mammals. Its space is devoted to exotic tropical birds, nocturnal animals, Komodo dragons and fish. It's open from 7 AM to 4 PM.

Across the road from the zoo, the **MPU Tantular Museum** has an assortment of Mesolithic farming implements and some stone artifacts from the Majapahit period. Open Tuesday through Sunday from 8 AM to 1 PM.

If you happen to be passing through Surabaya in the summer, don't miss the East Java Ballet Festival at **Candra Wilwatika**, an open-air amphitheater 42 km (26 miles) south of Surabaya on the road to Malang. Here Javanese classical dances are performed beneath the Gunung Penanggungan volcano on the first and third Saturday nights between May and October. Unlike the Prambanan Ballet Festival in Yogyakarta which presents a single version of the *Ramayana*, the Candra Wilwatika performances include indigenous East Javan stories in addition to the *Ramayana*. Buses to **Pandaan** take about an hour, and from the bus station it is fairly easy to get a Colt minivan to Candra Wilwatika.

Where to Stay

LUXURY

If you haven't already made reservations, it's worth inquiring about discounts at Surabaya's luxury hotels. The city has a surfeit of them, and low occupancy rates ensure brisk competition.

The **Hyatt Regency Surabaya** ((31) 511234 FAX (31) 512038, Jalan Basuki Rahmat N°124–128, is one of a number of hotels that vie for the distinction of being acclaimed Surabaya's best. Built around a swimming pool, its rooms sport panoramic views of the city. Substantial discounts are available for the asking.

The **Patra Surabaya Hilton International** ((31) 582703-6 FAX (31) 574504, is one of seven new top-class hotels (amongst them a new Sheraton Hotel and Towers, and a Holiday Inn) that have come to Surabaya. If during your stay you require in-house movies, a business center, golf, tennis and an outdoor pool, this is the place for you.

For the ultimate in colonial appeal, stay at the **Majapahit** ((31) 43351 FAX (31) 43599, Jalan Tunjungan N°65. Built in 1910 around a pleasant flower garden, the hotel today has been beautifully restored and is one of Surabaya's finest accommodations.

MODERATE

Located in the city center, the **Garden Hotel** ((31) 47000 FAX (31) 516111, Jalan Permuda N°21, has a sauna, swimming pool and a rooftop restaurant. It's an older hotel and at the upper end of the mid-range category.

The **Tanjung Hotel** ((31) 534-4031 FAX (31) 512290, Jalan Panglima Sudirman N°43–45, is a step down both in comfort and in price, but if you're looking for basic mid-range accommodation that doesn't make a dent in your budget, this is a good choice.

Occupying the middle ground between these two hotels, is the well managed **Cendana Hotel** ((31) 545-5333 FAX (31) 514367, Jalan Kombes Pol M Doeryat N°6. Ask for a discount.

INEXPENSIVE

Unlike Yogyakarta and Solo, Surabaya doesn't have a great deal of budget accommodation. The **Hotel Paviljoen** ((31) 534-3449, Jalan Genteng Basar N°94, is an old unrenovated Dutch colonial hotel. If you decide to stay here, it's worth casting your eye over several rooms before making a choice, as some are much more salubrious than others. Both fan-cooled and air-conditioned rooms are available.

The standard backpacker hotel, which has been running as long as anyone can remember, is the **Bamboe Denn** ((31) 534-0333, Jalan Ketabang Kali N°6A. There's an attached English school where you might well end up giving an impromptu lesson. The rooms are as basic as they get, but you'll find yourself in convivial company.

Where to Eat

Everything from local specialties to Japanese and Chinese cuisine can be found at the air-conditioned food stalls at **Tunjungan Plaza**, Jalan Tunjungan opposite the Bank Duta, and **Surabaya Plaza**, Jalan Permuda, close to the Tourist Information Center. Tunjungan Plaza in particular is a good place to seek out a bite to eat. Along with the usual American fast-food barns, you'll find the **New Singapore**, an excellent Chinese restaurant.

Café Venezia, Jalan Ambengan N°16, is deservedly popular, both for its delightful setting in an old villa and for its wide-ranging and inexpensive menu. Along with standards such as steak and French fries, it does Japanese *teppanyaki* and some Korean dishes. On the same street, at N°3, is **Ambengan Soto**, a locally renowned soup restaurant where you can feast on Indonesian cuisine at inexpensive prices.

One of the more trendy spots in town is the **News Café**, Jalan Panglima Sudirman N°47. It's as much bar as restaurant, but the international fare is of high standard. Later in the evening live bands perform here.

For night market food, the best area is along Jalan Pasar Genteng. Many *warungs* come to life here in the evenings, serving a wide variety of Indonesian specialties at rock-bottom prices.

How to Get There and Away

Surabaya is a major transit hub, with daily flights from every corner of the country. Traveling to and from Surabaya, the challenge is not finding a flight, but deciding which offered by four competing airlines is the cheapest. You can let a travel agent do this for you, or if you are a determined do-it-yourselfer, ring around to Garuda ((31) 534-5886, Merpati ((31) 588111, Bouraq ((31) 545-2918 and Sempati ((31) 532-1612. Fly Garuda whenever possible — they're probably safest.

There are three train stations in Surabaya. Westbound trains from Jakarta via Solo and Yogyakarta arrive at the Gubeng station. Trains coming from Jakarta via Semarang arrive at the Pasar Turi railway complex. Commuter trains from Malang arrive at either the Kota or Gubeng stations.

The cheapest way to move about East Java, or across the island for that matter, is by overnight bus. But the margin of cost savings offered by the bus is not worth the danger associated with traveling Java's narrow, traffic-clogged highways. Scarcely a month passes without some bus careening off a highway with substantial loss of life. Ask at your hotel about the minibus services which run to most major Javanese destinations and travel by day rather than by night.

As befits the home port of the Indonesian navy, Surabaya is well served by all manner of ocean going vessels. PELNI boats arrive from here on a regular basis from Sulawesi and Kalimantan. The PELNI office is at Jalan Pahlawan N°112 and is open weekdays from 9 AM to 1:30 PM.

MADURA

Thirty minutes by ferry from Surabaya is the sparsely populated and spectacular island of Madura. Largely ignored by tour groups, Madura initially seems a rather imposing place. The north coast is arid, rocky and treeless, a desolate cattle breeding area where goats browse on tufts of weedy scrub. The fertile south coast, however, more than compensates. Covered with tobacco plantations, orchards and edged with golden beaches, the south coast is home to most of the population and the location of the island's most famous attraction: *kerapan sapi,* bull racing.

Background

Reputed to be the fiercest people in the archipelago, the wiry, hot-tempered Madurese were incorporated into the Mataram empire in 1624 by Sultan Agung. The Madurese were not content to become vassals, however, and eventually, through intermarriage, succeeded in achieving hegemony over the eastern half of Java. But Madura was no match for the Dutch, who exiled the Madurese warrior-prince to South Africa, despite his

assistance in helping the Dutch subdue the sultans of Central Java.

What to See and Do

Madura's famed *kerapan sapi* bull races are staged from the middle of August until the end of October. The races, which originated long ago when farmers began racing their plow animals across the fields, are run on an elimination basis. Small villages hold the first races in August and the winners go on to stiffer competition in larger district towns. The grand finale in Madura's capital of

Pamekasan takes place in October when as many as 100 flower-bedecked bulls parade through town in preparation for several days of 100-m races (refer to SEE THE RUNNING OF THE BULLS in TOP SPOTS, page 14).

Events in Pamekasan make Pamplona's running of the bulls seem like a walk in the park. Bulls are roused to fever pitch with frenzied gamelan music, then given a jolt of arak wine to insure fire-in-the-belly competitiveness. Shorn of ribbons and flowers, they are lashed to heavy wooden sledges atop which drivers, who also have partaken of the arak, drive the bulls toward the finish line with whips and piercing cries. Entry into the stadium outside Pamekasan is inexpensive, but you may wish to sign up for a tour organized by Surabaya's Orient Express ((31) 43315, Jalan Basuki Rachmat N°78, as they offer seats roped off from the general madness.

OPPOSITE: Despite rich soil and intensive cultivation of rice, Java must import food to feed its growing population. ABOVE: Indonesians have worshipped in mosques similar to this one at Sumenep on the island of Madura for nearly 500 years.

Where to Stay

Pamekasan's main hotel is the **Garuda** ((324) 22589, a rambling central city establishment on Jalan Mesigit N°1. Basic fan-cooled double rooms are very affordable, but better-quality air-conditioned rooms can be had too. A smaller, quieter alternative is the **Hotel Trunojoyo** ((324) 22181, located in an alley just off Jalan Trunojoyo. Breakfast is included in the price of the rooms, which range from inexpensive to lower mid-range depending on whether or not they have air conditioning.

How to Get There and Away

Ferries leave the Surabaya port of Tanjung Perak approximately every 15 minutes for the brief 30-minute crossing to Kamal on the southwest tip of Madura. At Kamal, Colt minibuses wait to take passengers to villages throughout the island.

MALANG

Malang is a pleasant mountain town with broad streets, well tended parks and an abundance of colonial architecture. A carefully planned coffee plantation market town on the banks of the Brantas River, Malang was founded a century ago. Dozens of old Dutch villas still line jalans Ijen, Kawi and Semeru, and Dutch is still spoken by older Indonesians.

General Information

There's a small Tourist Office ((341) 366216, Jalan Semeru N°4; it's a good place to pick up local information and a map.

What to See and Do

At the **Pasar Besar** several blocks south of the main square, you'll find a large clothing market and an antique section full of Dutch and Chinese items. Not too far from the Pasar, at N°Jalan Ijen N°25, is the **Brawijaya Army Museum**, an artillery packed arsenal that chronicles the history of the locally based Brawijaya Division of the Indonesian Army.

East Java has its share of temples, but unlike those in Central Java you'll need some travel time to get to them. **Candi Singosari**, **Candi Jago**, **Candi Kidal** and **Candi Penataran** are impressive temple complexes dating back to 1200 AD. All four are difficult to get to; tours are the best way to go.

A large number of agencies in Malang offer temple tours. One of the most popular agencies, and highly recommended, is the tour run out of the Toko Oen restaurant, **Toko Oen's Tour and Information Service** ((341) 64052, Jalan Basuki Rakhmat N°5. It leads individual, customized and group tours at prices that work out much cheaper than the deals available in Surabaya.

Where to Stay

Guests at the **Tugu Park Hotel** ((341) 363891 FAX (341) 362747, Jalan Tugu N°3, all agree that it is a real find in a place where you'd least expect it. Modern but with class and style, the suites, furnished in various Asian themes, are particularly worth spending a little extra for. Rates are at the lower end of the luxury scale.

In the mid-range bracket, another excellent lodging is the **Hotel Graha Santika** ((341) 324989, Jalan Cerme N°16. Its great asset is its art deco architecture which has been given a thoughtful renovation. Facilities include a swimming pool.

The venerable **Hotel Pelangi** ((341) 365156, Jalan Merdeka Selatan N°3, catered to the *tuan blanda* (Dutch overseers) in the heyday of Dutch rule and still exudes an air of fusty colonialism. The large, air-conditioned rooms still have operating ceiling fans and wicker recliners that imperiously survey the town square that Dutch engineers laid out a century ago.

The **Splendid Inn** ((341) 366860 FAX (341) 363618, Jalan Mohopahit N°2–4, is a smaller hotel with an ambiance similar to the Pelangi. The inn is an old Dutch mansion that has been divided into bright and airy rooms, each with its own bath. Even if you stay elsewhere stop by the Splendid Inn's informal bar for a sundown libation.

The popular place amongst backpackers is the **Hotel Helios** ((341) 362741, Jalan Pattimura N°37, a small hotel where the simple rooms overlook the courtyard garden. It's a

There is no questioning who are the stars at Madura's bull races. Before the competition begins, bulls are shorn of ribbons and flowers.

good place to meet other travelers and get information on trips farther afield.

Where to Eat

There are a couple of splendidly atmospheric restaurants in Malang. The **Melati Restaurant** at the Hotel Pelangi is atmospherically the best, but the food is better at the **Toko Oen Restaurant**, Jalan Basuki Rakhmat N°5, where starched waiters hover at your table while you lounge in wicker furniture. In both restaurants you'll find a good mix of Western and local dishes.

The restaurant at the **Splendid Inn** has a reasonably priced Western menu. In the mood for alfresco dining? Then spend the evening at **Pasar Senggol**, a colorful assortment of *warungs* near Jalan Majapahit. For more food stall dining, but in less raucous surroundings, try the **Food Center**, next to the Mitra Department Store on Jalan Agus Salim.

How to Get There and Away

The only flights to Malang are from Jakarta with Merpati every day. More than a half dozen trains make the three-hour journey from Surabaya every day. Buses take around two hours from Surabaya, but it's worth spending a bit extra, particularly if you are traveling in a group, to charter an air-conditioned minibus and make the trip in relative comfort.

MT. BROMO

Mt. Bromo (2,392 m or 7,848 ft) is a wildly popular attraction, a brooding volcanic presence in the heart of the Bromo-Tengger-Semeru National Park. In the early hours each morning, before the sun has touched the sky with color, travelers can be seen strung out across the floor of the spectacular Tengger crater climbing to the peak of Bromo for the sunrise. Climbing up Mt. Bromo has become one of Java's must-dos, particularly for backpacking travelers.

There are numerous approaches to Mt. Bromo, but the usual one is via the town of Probolinggo. Don't overnight in Probolinggo, as it's a miserable place with nothing to recommend it. Once in Probolinggo, rent a jeep or jump in a minibus and head up

to Cemoro Lemang, where there is budget accommodation on the lip of the volcanic crater (the perfect place from which to start your early morning climb), or if you require more comfort, repair to the **Hotel Raya Bromo**, which is six kilometers (four miles) short of Cemoro Lemang. You'll need to organize transport to the lip of the crater in the morning if you take the latter option.

Climbers staying in Cemoro Lemang rise at 4:30 AM (you'll need some warm clothes) for the three-kilometer (two-mile) hike down into the crater and across that eerie landscape called the "sea of sand." The trail is clear, but you should carry a flashlight or hire a local guide. The climb, even to the top of Bromo, is not particularly demanding for anyone in reasonably good shape,

and the entire walk takes not much more than an hour.

The great attraction is the sunrise. In the right conditions the sun ascends through a sea of clouds that roil at your feet. But you may be unlucky enough to find yourself in the clouds, a faint taste of sulfur on your tongue, with little to see. The best months for visibility are from April to November.

Where to Stay

The **Hotel Raya Bromo** ((335) 711802, uphill from the village of Sukapura, is the luxury option at Bromo. Most people, however, stay at Cemoro Lawang, where there is a good selection of hotels, hostels and *losmen*. The **Hotel Bromo Permai** ((335) 23459, is the best choice.

How to Get There and Away

The town of Probolinggo is easily accessible from Surabaya or from Malang by minibus or rent car, taking two to two and half hours from either. Mt. Bromo tours are widely advertised in Malang and prices are generally very reasonable.

Steaming fissures, bubbling mud, jagged lava and a swirling sea of sand give Mt. Bromo an otherworldly appearance.

Bali

Option two is renting a van by the hour or for the day. The *bemo* corners in Kuta and Legian are packed with drivers of Mitsubishi vans who yell "Transport!" the moment a foreigner approaches. Rates are usually reasonable after some haggling, and you leave the hassles of parking and dealing with foreign road rules to the driver.

DENPASAR

Few people have anything nice to say about Denpasar. Before you're even out of the air-

port the taxi drivers will explain that Singaraja was supposed to be the island's capital. "Denpasar was just a market town," they scowl, searching for an appropriate explanation, "that just grew." It is worthwhile, however, to pause briefly and see a couple of sights before you continue north to more colorful locales.

GENERAL INFORMATION

Denpasar has two tourism offices. The **Badung Government Tourist Office (** (361) 234569 or 223602, Merdeka Building, Jalan Surapati N°7, provides maps, lists of festivals (valuable as these go by the Balinese calendar and so vary from year to year) and

details of dance and other performances. Open Tuesday to Sunday from 7 AM to 2 PM; open Friday until 11 PM.

The **Bali Government Tourist Office (** (361) 222387 FAX 226313, by contrast, is difficult to find, being located in a complex of government buildings, and not oriented to the needs of the individual inquirer.

The **Immigration Office (Kantor Imigrasi) (** (361) 227828, is in the Renon Complex, Niti Mandala. Open Monday to Saturday from 7 AM to 1 PM; open Friday until 11 PM, Saturday until noon.

WHAT TO SEE AND DO

The **Bali Museum**, across from Puputan Badung Park, consists of several buildings and pavilions that serve as good examples of palace and temple architecture. The large structure with the verandah in the second courtyard is an example of the type of royal building in which rajahs would hold audiences. With so much of cultural interest around the island, it's arguable whether a visit to the museum is worthwhile unless you have plenty of time for Bali alone. The museum is open from 8 AM to 3 PM daily, and closed all day on Mondays.

Follow the course of the Badung River several blocks and you'll arrive at **Pasar Badung**, the morning market. Across a narrow bridge is the **Kumba Sari** shopping center.. The morning market has three floors that contain, from top to bottom, clothing, spices and fruit. Floors one and two are great for picture taking. Be sure to save film for **Pura Melanting**, a small temple in front of the Pasar. This is one of the most active temples in Bali, a place swirling with incense, full of women in sarongs offering fruit and flowers to the gods. If the prayer here seems particularly fervent it's because the women are Pasar Badung merchants praying for a profitable day.

Along Gajah Mada, Denpasar's main street, there are several curio stores. The best antique store in Denpasar, **Arts of Asia Gallery** is a few blocks away at Jalan Thamrin 27–37, Blok C5. All the items on sale here have been personally collected by Verra Darwiko,

Ritual dances begin with the arrival of a gamelan orchestra.

the English-speaking owner of the store whose love of things beautiful is evident. Much of the pottery and woodcarving here is of museum quality.

There is a six-week long annual Bali Arts Festival between mid-June and the end of July at the **Werdi Budaya Arts Center**, on Jalan Nusa Indah.

KUTA BEACH

Once Bali's poorest district, Kuta is now the most Westernized (perhaps more accurately, Australianized) part of the island. A fascinating collision of bars, beach hotels, curio shops and simple inns called *losmen*, Kuta has given itself over almost entirely to tourism. But don't write it off. Despite the touts and traffic, it still has the best beach in Bali, accommodation that is both excellent and affordable and some of the best nightlife entertainment in Indonesia.

The main difference between Kuta and the more exclusive resorts to the east is that Kuta sees more interaction between locals and visitors. Many Kuta businesses, particularly hotels, are still in local hands. Large hotels have, of course, moved in too, but this simply serves to lend the area an interestingly democratic air: All tastes and all bank balances are catered for.

The day on the beach follows a regular cycle. The Surf Rescue take up their positions at 6 AM and even then there are the early morning joggers and before-breakfast swimmers. By nine the beach is filling up with suntan zealots, souvenir hawkers, drink vendors, masseurs and itinerant vendors of sun hats and beach mats. By midday the glare and heat has driven all but the most hardy sun-worshippers into the shade. By three or four the shadows are lengthening, and by 5:30 PM the crowds are beginning to arrive for the daily ritual of watching the sunset. Kuta's famed sunsets may not come off to the crowd's satisfaction every evening, but at their best they're a miracle of kaleidoscopic color that will linger in your memory for years.

On a cautionary note, beachgoers should beware of the dangerous undertows that can drag even a strong swimmer out to sea. Swim only in the areas marked out by the **Surf Rescue**, which is run by the Badung Government Tourist Office in Denpasar. It maintains four stations along the beach, at Kuta, Half-Legian, Legian and at the Kuta Palace Hotel. Known officially as Badung Surf Life Saving Bali, the service was set up in 1972 in response to the increased use of Kuta Beach for surfing and the number of lives being lost there. The Bali Oberoi has a private surf rescue service.

WHERE TO STAY

Kuta accommodation is spread over a large area, but most of it — and there are hundreds of places to choose from — is concentrated in the Kuta-Legian area, which is where you will find the beach, restaurants and all the nightlife. If you're going to stay in Kuta you may as well be in the thick of it. Quieter accommodation is available in Seminyak to the north, while upmarket rooms and cottages can be found in Sanur to the east.

Kuta is one of the few places in Indonesia that caters successfully to the full range of travelers — from budget backpackers to five-star high-flyers. Bear in mind that the budget recommendations below are guidelines only — the scene is constantly changing.

Luxury
South of Kuta, in the area close to the airport known as Tuban, is the **Holiday Inn Bali Hai** ((361) 753035 FAX (361) 754548, and the large **Kartika Plaza** ((361) 751067 FAX (361) 752475. Both are on the sea, although the best strip of beach is a 10-minute walk away.

The Holiday Inn sports a pleasant Balinese ambiance, and includes such features as IDD telephones, minibars, tea and coffee making facilities, satellite television, as well as non-smoking rooms and rooms with features to assist handicapped travelers. Restaurants include the Indonesian style **Ratna Satay Terrace** and home-away-from-home crowd pleasers such as **O'Brian's Pub**.

The Kartika Plaza is set in attractive tropical gardens, and the ocean-facing bungalows are particularly recommended. Other features include two swimming pools, paddling

Balinese life is by no means all temple ritual — TOP: A vendor of non-traditional masks in Denpasar. BOTTOM: Massage at Kuta Beach. Note the numbered sun hats. All masseurs must have a license. Half an hour's massage costs under $US1.

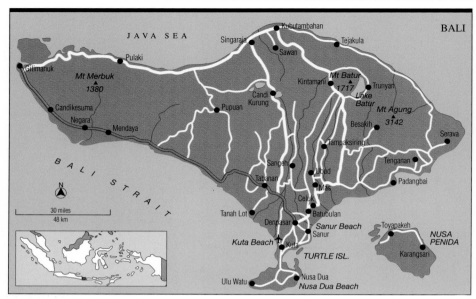

pools and a playground, tennis and squash courts, and even a miniature golf course. Restaurants include the **Melati** for Indonesian fare and the **Segara** for Italian cuisine.

The **Villa Lalu** ((361) 731051 FAX (361) 731052, in Seminyak, just north of Legian, is a unique alternative for those who find international style hotels too big and impersonal for their tastes. Twelve fully-furnished, thatched-roofed, two-story villas give the guest the feeling of having settled into a traditional village. Also in Seminyak is the **Bali Oberoi** ((361) 730361 FAX (361) 730954, one of Bali's truly luxurious retreats, offering privacy in an intimate and well-managed setting. Accommodation is in villas surrounded by lush gardens.

If you are traveling in a small group, the **Villa Pantai Biru** ((361) 732093 FAX (361) 732094, is a possibility. This is another cozy getaway with villa style accommodation. Guests can take a full villa, with five air-conditioned bedrooms, or a half-share with two bedrooms, for a minimum stay of two nights.

Moderate

Accommodation in Kuta is arguably at its best in the mid-range category. Out of season, excellent discounts are usually available. It's worth making a booking for you first night and then shopping around for the best deal after you arrive, particularly

if you are going to be spending some time in Kuta.

Well located on Legian's best stretch of beach is the **Legian Beach Hotel** ((361) 751711 FAX (361) 752651. With a large and beautiful garden, a swimming pool and access directly onto the sand, this three-star hotel is an excellent choice — consider paying a little extra for a bungalow. Hawkers are prohibited in the area around the sun chairs immediately in front of the hotel.

For those who want to be in the heart of Kuta on the lane where it all started, **Poppies Cottages** ((361) 751059 FAX (361) 752364 is right in the center of Poppies Lane. It achieved fame as one of the pioneering luxury outfits, and its thatched bungalow rooms in a garden setting have become a standard Kuta, indeed Balinese, pattern. It's highly recommended. Self-catering facilities, and babysitters, are available on request. Book well in advance.

Aneka Beach Bungalows ((361) 752067 FAX (361) 752892 is, as the name suggests, a collection of bungalows beside the beach. Prices are very reasonable, particularly given that staying here puts you next to Kuta Beach and a short stroll from Kuta Square and countless restaurants and bars. The stunning swimming pool area and the tastefully appointed rooms make this hotel look pricier than it is.

Inexpensive

Agung Beach Bungalow ((361) 751264 FAX (361) 753752 is a five-minute walk from the ocean. Agung has 70 rooms with either air conditioning or fans, the latter being the budget option at around US$18 for a double. It comes with a swimming pool and a restaurant, and is a popular place.

Rates are similar at **Matahari Bungalows** ((361) 751616 FAX (361) 751761 where all rooms have balcony areas, and where you are conveniently located between Legian and Kuta (walking distance to either). Rooms are available either in air-conditioned or in cheaper fan-cooled varieties.

The charming **Yulia Beach Inn** ((361) 751616 FAX (361) 751761, is another centrally located budget option. Again the cheaper rooms are fan-cooled, but more luxurious air-conditioned versions are also available.

WHERE TO EAT

You could spend several months eating out in Kuta without exhausting its possibilities. Standards are not uniformly high, but the best places are often surprisingly good, and prices are always reasonable.

Made's Warung ((361) 755397, Jalan Pantai, is a Kuta institution. It started doing Western cuisine 25 years ago, and today it remains a good place to eat — the range of food is vast, from strawberries to roast beef, with some Indonesian and Chinese treats, too. The menu overflows onto the very walls; the atmosphere is come-as-you-are chic. If it's all too down-at-heel for you, wander over to **Made's Warung II** ((361) 732130, which is in the Paris end of Kuta — Seminyak — and gets a smarter class of customer than its parent does in Kuta.

Poppies Lane I ((361) 751059 is another long-runner, and was for many years universally acclaimed the best restaurant in Kuta. The meals here are still good, but top prize goes to the alfresco setting, which is a tropical bower of horticultural delights. The tuna fish steak is recommended. For desert try the black rice pudding, a Balinese favorite sweetened with palm sugar and coconut milk. Open daily 8 AM to 11 PM.

First timers tend to be skeptical: a Mexican restaurant in Kuta? But those who know their way around Mexican cuisine swear by the authenticity of **TJ's** ((361) 751093. As at Poppies, which is just around the corner, the atmosphere is a soothing combination of dappled greenery and ambient sounds.

Northerners who long for potatoes and home-made sausages will find the land of their heart's desire at the **Swiss Restaurant** ((361) 751735, on Jalan Pura Bagus Taruna. Bratwurst, *wiener kartoffelsalat* and *apfelstrudel* rub shoulders with *fondue bourguignonne*. The owner is, in addition, the Swiss consul.

For French food at a very reasonable price try **The French Restaurant** at **Topi Kopi** ((361) 754243, a few yards along from Swiss Restaurant. French food can also be found at **Le Bistro** ((361) 730973, Jalan Legian. Far and away the classiest place for dining French style is the **Kafe Warisan** ((361) 731175 overlooking rice paddies not far from the Bali Oberoi.

Probably the best Italian cuisine is at **Café Luna** ((361) 730805 opposite Goa 2001 in Seminyak. Fresh pasta is made every day on the premises. It's an elegant establishment that mounts fashion shows in a large and beautiful hall behind the main restaurant space at 11 PM every Friday. It's particularly popular with the nightlife set.

Farther afield, and just north of the Oberoi at Seminyak is fashionable **La Lucciola** a wonderful beachside restaurant that combines inventive Italian-Australian cuisine with dynamic sunset views and inspired cocktails.

Two kilometers (one-and-a-half miles) north of *Bemo* Corner on Jalan Legian, the **Glory Bar and Restaurant** ((361) 51091 is the place to go for Indonesian and Balinese food. It's open daily from 8 AM to midnight, but the big attraction is the Wednesday night Balinese buffet with *babi guleng,* suckling pig.

Back towards Kuta, the **SC Restaurant** ((361) 753769, Jalan Legian, is one of the best places in Kuta for grilled seafood. The day's catch is displayed on a bed of shaved ice. Pick out what you want, order a beer and in minutes you'll be enjoying tasty shrimp, fish or lobster.

OVERLEAF: Balinese *prahu* on the beach at Sanur, where crossings are launched to Jungutbatu on Nusa Lembongan.

NIGHTLIFE

Every night is party night in Kuta. As is the case elsewhere around Indonesia, however, things don't get rolling until late. Some of the more popular clubs with dancing may be near deserted before midnight. Still, if you're happy with a quiet drink, there are always places to go early in the evening.

In Kuta itself there is no shortage of bars. Go take a look at **Tubes**, an atmospheric surfer's hangout where stylish Japanese women can always be seen on the arms of their Balinese boyfriends watching surfing movies on the big screen. The **Hard Rock Café** has the now familiar formula of hamburgers, expensive drinks and loud music — there are often long lines to get in. **Peanuts II** has been running for as long as anyone can remember, sponsoring pub crawls with dubious catch-cries such as "avoid hangovers, stay drunk."

It's the Seminyak end of Kuta that sees the most late night action. **Goa 2001** is as good a place as any to start the evening. From here, follow the crowds to the happening spot for that night. It may be **Gado Gado** or **Taj Mahal** or **Warung Tapas**, or **66** (pronounced "double six"). The latter is right next to the well-known A.J. Hackett bungee jumping outfit, and patrons have been known to dance, jump and return to the dance floor exhilarated and refreshed.

SHOPPING

When it comes to arts and crafts and clothing few tourist destinations in Asia offer Kuta's range and competitive pricing. Visitors staying in upmarket hotels in Nusa Dua and Sanur invariably come to Kuta on shopping sprees. Shops selling high quality goods are plentiful, mixed in with those offering tourist souvenirs.

For vacation reading matter, look for the second hand bookshops in Poppies Lane, and in the other lanes that run between Jalan Legian and Jalan Pantai. Particularly recommended, both for the range and quality of its stock, is the **Kertai Bookshop**, Jalan Pantai, on the left as you walk toward the beach. New and secondhand books are available and

can be traded in at half-price when you have finished with them.

The farther you go up Jalan Legian towards Seminyak the classier things become, and eventually it's all boutiques where a tiny number of exquisite things are sold in resplendent surroundings. Look for designer sunglasses at **Sol** ((361) 755072, on Kuta Square, Australian sports fashions at **Dreamland** ((361) 755159, also on Kuta Square, and surfing accessories at **Aloha Surf Station** ((361) 758286, at the Kuta end of Jalan Legian. **Irie Collection** is the place for fabrics, while bizarre candlesticks are a specialty at **Titien Collection** ((361) 730448, in Seminyak. Custom-made picture frames are the specialty of **Toko Kaca Taman Sari** ((361) 730424, and at **Ulu Watu** ((361) 753428 (Jalan Bakungsari branch), the specialty is Balinese lace.

For sarongs, take a walk along Jalan Double Six, which is brimming with fabric shops.

Locally produced furniture is popular. **Setya Budi Art** ((361) 730560, Jalan Tunjung Mekar, is a good place to compare prices. More furniture and *objets d'art* are on sale in Seminyak at **Warisan** ((361) 730710.

Back in Kuta, the island's biggest department store is **Matahari** on Kuta Square (not to be confused with the smaller Matahari building containing Kuta's cinemas on Jalan Legian). And a new Kuta shopping complex focusing on the arts is **Bali Plaza**, close to Waterbom park, Jalan Kartika Plaza.

For those with the time to shop around, a trip out to one of the "crafts villages" around Bali is recommended. Balinese artisans produce woodcarvings in the village of Mas, stonecarvings in Batubulan and paintings in Ubud. All the of crafts in these villages are reasonably priced and of the highest quality. If you have a couple of weeks in Bali, a sensible course of action is to shop around in Kuta, decide what you like, and then leave your shopping for later when you've seen what's on offer elsewhere around the island. It may be that some of things you saw at the beginning of you trip will have lost their luster by the time you've been to Mas or Ubud.

SANUR BEACH

An upmarket alternative to Kuta, Sanur offers a more orderly environment and a beach conducive to swimming because of a protective offshore reef. Sanur, along with Ubud, was one of the first Balinese villages to be "discovered" by European artists such as the Belgian Le Mayeur. Le Mayeur's house next to the Bali Beach hotel has been turned into the **Museum Le Mayeur** and is worth a brief visit, if only to capture the feeling of what it must have been like to live in Sanur a half century ago. You can't watch the sunset in Sanur, but on a good day you can see Lombok's Rinjani volcano soaring above the clouds. During the day, the exotic triangular sails of fishing boats the Balinese call *jukungs* skim across the horizon. At low tide it's possible to walk across the sand and coral to the reef and watch crabs skittering in the shallows. The late afternoon belongs to kites, many of them with spans up to one-and-a-half meters (five feet). Kite flying is the favorite sport for young boys in Sanur and on the nearby "Turtle Island" of Serangan, and many of the shops along the main street sell animal-shaped kites painted in pastel colors.

WHERE TO STAY

Luxury

The **Hotel Grand Bali Beach** ((361) 288511 FAX (361) 287917, Jalan Hang Tuah, is replete with every conceivable amenity, and as the "grand" suggests it's one of Bali's few international style hotels — built upwards rather than outwards (bungalow style). The approach to the hotel is down a long drive with a nine-hole championship golf course on the right. A gamelan orchestra announces your arrival for luncheon each day.

The **Hotel Tandjung Sari** ((361) 288441 FAX (361) 287930, Jalan Danau Tamblingan N°41, is a luxury hideaway for celebrities and jetsetters. This was one of the pioneers of bungalow accommodation and many consider it the only place to stay in Bali.

Surrounded by 15 hectares (36 acres) of frangipani, bougainvillea and hibiscus fields, rooms at the **Hotel Hyatt Bali** ((361) 288271 FAX (361) 287693, rejoice in tropical decor, with grass mats on the floors and balconies large enough to breakfast on. There is a another Hyatt resort at Nusa Dua, and a shuttle bus

operates between the two hotels. Guests can use the facilities at either hotel.

Moderate

For those traveling on a mid-range budget, the **Santrian Beach Bungalows** ((361) 288009 FAX (361) 287101, Jalan Danau Tamblingan N°10, is a good choice. It has a small swimming pool and a collection of charming thatched bungalows a few steps from one of the best beaches in Bali. Linked by meandering paths leading through a jungle garden, the bungalows don't have television, but

fresh fruit and flowers arrive every day. You don't need a shirt or shoes to be served at the casual Nirwana Reef restaurant. Set right on the sand, the Nirwana obtains its catch of the day from local fishermen who tie up on the beach.

WHERE TO EAT

Although most of Sanur's best restaurants are in the hotels, there are plenty of very good alternatives to the hotel restaurant scene. You'll even find representatives of familiar fast-food chains.

Hotels like the Tanjung Sari cultivate Bali's mystical allure.

The **Legong Restaurant** ((361) 288066 is popular, not least for its Balinese dance performances, nightly at 8 PM. The menu features European, Chinese and Indonesian food.

Two of Sanur's best restaurants can be found on Jalan Danau Tamblingan, which runs parallel to the beach. The Italian restaurant **Mamma Lucia** ((361) 288498, and the fine Chinese establishment **Telaga Naga** ((361) 281234, extension 8080, each makes for a superb evening out. The latter is run by the Hotel Hyatt, a short distance from the hotel in an enchanting Chinese style garden. Both Sichuan and Cantonese dishes are served.

Traditional Balinese cuisine is available at the **Kul Kul Restaurant** ((361) 288038, but only if you order in advance. The emphasis here, as is the case throughout Bali's tourist areas, is on Western and Indonesian food.

Other popular places include the **Italian Terrazzo Martini** ((361) 288371, the **Legong Restaurant** ((361) 288066, with European, Chinese and Indonesian food, and Balinese dancers performing nightly at 8 PM, and the amiable and cozy **Mandelo's** ((361) 288773. **Café Batu Jimbar** has become the most popular place for health food; the owner grows his vegetables up in the mountains and produces some of the most delicious meals in Sanur. The elegant **Chiku-Tei** ((361) 287159 is the place to go for Japanese fare.

NIGHTLIFE

Kuta is where most Sanur residents go when they want to see the bright lights. But on their own turf there is **La Taverna**, right on the beach, a good place for a quiet drink, as well as **Koki**, on Jalan Bypass. The Hyatt's **Grantang Bar** has live jazz Thursday to Tuesday evenings from 8 PM to 1 AM.

For dancing, there is **Pirates** at the Segara Village Hotel (8 PM onwards) and the rooftop **Bali Hai** at the Hotel Grand Bali Beach.

SHOPPING

In Sanur you are more likely to come across quality items than in nearby Kuta, where anything and everything is up for sale. Be

sure to browse at Kuta, but for a special gift try Sanur's smart boutiques and art shops, almost all of which are on Jalan Danau Tamblingan.

Miralin Collection ((361) 286061 is the place for ceramics. Puppets — some original, some reproduction — and Javanese terracotta figurines are can be found at the **Lama Gallery** ((361) 286809. For leather products, check out **Rafflesia** ((361) 288528. For *ikat* and handwoven fabrics **Nogo** ((361) 288832 is the main shop in a chain of similar stores. **Mama Leon Boutique** ((361) 288044 is a beautiful showroom for clothes that are made in the factory just behind it.

NUSA DUA

The unabashedly upscale and meticulously planned resort of Nusa Dua lies on the eastern tip of the Bukit Peninsula. Unlike the rest of mainland Bali, which is made up of volcanic rock and soils, the Bukit Peninsula is entirely of limestone. In this it resembles the nearby offshore island of Nusa Penida, and indeed it is probable that the peninsula was once an island too: Even today it is only connected to Bali proper by a low-lying, narrow isthmus.

Beaches around the peninsula are among Bali's most splendid, and many of them, notably **Suluban Beach**, are magnets for Bali's surfing fraternity. Elsewhere around the peninsula are the five-star complex of Nusa Dua itself and its exclusive golf course, the fishing village of **Tanjung Benoa**, at the end of a five-kilometer (three-mile) sand strip directly to the north of Nusa Dua, the village and bay of **Jimbaran**, on the neck of the isthmus immediately south of the airport, and, in the west, the magnificent temple and surfing venues of **Ulu Watu**.

Nusa Dua has everything the rest of Indonesia lacks — immaculate sidewalks, tree-lined boulevards, street signs and landscaped traffic circles. For some travelers it will seem too antiseptic, but for families and couples who have no interest in roughing it, Nusa Dua is ideal. Like Sanur Beach to the north, Nusa Dua benefits from an offshore reef that makes beaches perfect for swimming. Restaurants have started to spring up nearby, allowing guests to take a break from expensive hotel food, and there is also a small shopping center with a modern supermarket that is served by a free shuttle bus that stops at the major hotels.

WHERE TO STAY

Nusa Dua Beach Hotel ((361) 771210 FAX (361) 772617, PO Box 1028, Denpasar 80363, numbers King Hussein, Lord Litchfield, Senator Robert Dole and President François Mitterand among is former guests. The rooms are elegantly furnished with teak molding, parquet floors and French doors that open onto spacious balconies. A curtain of coconut palms shades the fringe of a spotless beach.

The **Meliá Bali** ((361) 771510 FAX (361) 771360, PO Box 1048, Tuban 80361, blends Balinese style and Spanish ownership, with daily cabarets and flamenco played by Balinese musicians. Rooms are in four-story blocks.

The **Hotel Putri Bali** ((361) 771020 or (361) 771420 FAX (361) 71139, PO Box 1, Nusa Dua 80363, is another big, traditional hotel at Nusa Dua. Puri means princess.

The **Bali Club Mediterranée** ((361) 771521 FAX (361) 771835, the most luxurious of Club Med's Asian properties, provides a package of three extensive buffet meals a day, sports equipment and instruction, supervised activities for children, and lively cabaret shows by night. Non-residents can enjoy a four-hour "sampler" of the hotel's facilities with lunch or dinner included.

Nearby the huge **Bali Hilton International** ((361) 771102 FAX (361) 771616, PO Box 46, Nusa Dua 80361, Bali successfully brings the Hilton touch to its delightfully landscaped Balinese gardens. It offers all the amenities and facilities of the other five-star luxury hotels and includes five restaurants.

One of Nusa Dua's most recent arrivals is the **Hotel Nikko Bali** ((361) 773377 FAX (361) 773388, Jalan Raya, Nusa Dua Selatan 80363. It's a member of the prestigious Japanese chain and is notable for its dramatic sea views.

Lastly, overlooking Nusa Dua and its immaculate golf course from a nearby hilltop is the ultra-luxurious and exclusive **Amanusa** ((361) 772333 FAX (361) 72335.

Classically beautiful, it's the sister of the Amandari at Ubud and the Amankila near Candi Dasa.

WHERE TO EAT

The Nusa Dua dining scene revolves predominantly around the hotel restaurants, but there are also a few high-quality establishments outside of the hotels such as the Japanese **Matsuri** ((361) 772269, the Mexican **Poco Loco** ((361) 773923 and the seafood place **Makuwa Pakuwa** ((361) 772252. The

Galeria, a large shopping center, has some good restaurants, such as the Spanish **Olé Olé** ((361) 771886.

TANJUNG BENOA

Tanjung Benoa is the name of the fishing village, just north of Nusa Dua, facing the port of Denpasar across Benoa Harbor. Sheltering the entrance to the bay is Pulau Serangan, called Turtle Island by tour operators. Hotels are opening along Tanjung Benoa Peninsula, making it a less resort-like

No new hotel in Bali can be built higher than the surrounding palm trees.

alternative to nearby Nusa Dua, but the big attraction is the area's watersports, which include diving, snorkeling, parasailing and windsurfing.

At the northern tip of the peninsula, the **Beluga Marina** ((361) 771997 FAX (361) 771967 is a smorgasbord of Italian food, live jazz and rock, a diving center, and a jetty where two huge silver catamarans wait to transport you to the island of Nusa Penida, a former penal colony of the kingdom of Klungkung. Also noteworthy is **Lingga Sempurna** ((361) 771457 where you can

of straw-roofed Balinese huts. The **Meliá Benoa** ((361) 771714 FAX (361) 771713, also on Jalan Pratama, run by the Spanish Meliá group, is another luxurious newcomer to this beach area.

Close to the Grand Mirage is the **Rasa Sayang Beach Inn** ((361) 771643, which is on the wrong side of the road for the beach and is consequently very inexpensive. The **Matahari Terbit Bungalows** ((361) 771019 FAX 771027, is north and on the beach side of the road; it has comfortable mid-range bungalows.

sample parasailing, jet-skiing, SCUBA diving, snorkeling and more.

WHERE TO STAY

There are a number of hotels on the peninsula, most of them mid-range to luxury in price and standards, though there are also — unlike Nusa Dua to the south — some budget alternatives.

The **Grand Mirage** ((361) 771888 FAX (361) 772148, Jalan Pratama N°74, Tanjung Benoa 80363, is a vast luxury development with a spa and fitness facilities. The spectacular **Novotel** ((361) 772239 FAX (361) 772237, Jalan Pratama, Tanjung Benoa 80361, is built to resemble a village

---

JIMBARAN

For years a spacious, crescent-shaped beach which seasoned Bali travelers shared only with the local Muslim fishermen, Jimbaran has now rocketed into the world of international tourism. A clutch of medium-priced hotels have been built along its firm golden sands, and more recently it has been favored with three upmarket hotels.

WHERE TO STAY

Expensive
Commanding superb views across the bay is the **Four Seasons Resort Bali** ((361) 701010 FAX (361) 701022, Jimbaran 80361, with its

147 luxury villas, each with its own private plunge pool. The hotel's restaurants are renowned, especially its wonderful **PJs** and **Pantai Jimbaran** beachside restaurants overlooking the beach.

The second major hotel to open here was the **Inter-Continental Bali (** (361) 701888 FAX (361) 701777, Jalan Uluwatu N°45, Jimbaran 80361, a huge 425-room, low rise hotel that hides away in the coconut palms along the shores of the beach. It offers guests four restaurants and is open to non-guests.

The latest arrival on Jimbaran or, more accurately, overlooking Jimbaran from Bukit, is the **Ritz-Carlton (** (361) 702222 FAX (361) 701555, Jalan Karang Mas Sejahtera, Jimbaran 80364, which has 570 rooms, villas and suites, some with private plunge pools. From its commanding position, it offers six restaurants tempting the well-heeled to linger and enjoy the hedonistic mix of Balinese beauty and international-class comforts.

In isolated splendor on the southern cliffs of Bukit and overlooking vast indigo vistas of the Indian Ocean, is the **Bali Cliff Hotel (** (361) 771992 FAX (361) 771993 an expensive hotel which has, perhaps, the best prospect on the entire island.

UBUD

About 29 km (18 miles) north of Sanur Beach, Ubud is the cultural heart of Bali. European painters Walter Spies and Rudolf Bonnet arrived here in the early 1930s, built Balinese homes and founded the Pitha Maha, a society dedicated to encouraging young Balinese artists to experiment with perspective and textures. Young painters from Ubud accepted the challenge, as did woodcarvers from Mas. Today, the early works of European masters such as Spies, Bonnet, Arie Smit, Theo Meier and Han Snel hang in local galleries beside that of their now famous students.

Don't imagine for a moment, though, that Ubud is still the village it was in the 1930s. Times have changed and tourism has transformed the village into a New Age escape from the pub-crawl culture of Kuta Beach. Ubud is about *cappucini*, batik *haute couture*, meditation courses, therapeutic massage and relaxing with a good book. But most of all, Ubud is the best place in Bali to see dance

dramas and to buy paintings. It's all somewhat commercial, but few visitors complain.

GENERAL INFORMATION

Look for the Ubud Tourist Office on Jalan Raya. Its main function is to provide information on the locations and times of daily cultural performances around Ubud.

Getting Around
Ubud is small enough to walk around, but for extended day trips consider hiring a

mountain bike. Rental is inexpensive, and bikes move at just the right speed to enjoy the flow of Balinese life. Car rental is also cheap in Ubud.

WHAT TO SEE AND DO

Museums
Ubud has three museums with fascinating displays of Balinese paintings. The most recent is Agung Rai's Museum of art, ARMA, located amidst the paddy fields near the Monkey Forest. Exhibiting works from his

OPPOSITE: Pampered luxury and seclusion are the hallmarks of the Amandari Hotel. ABOVE: Snoozing in a hammock is as good a way as any other to enjoy Jimbaran.

own collection, art dealer and patron of the arts Agung Rai has produced a fabulous museum giving a comprehensive history of painting in Bali. There is a very good restaurant, **Café Arma**, as well as a small hotel, the **Kokokan Hotel** ((361) 975742 FAX (361) 975332, attached to the museum. The **Museum Neka**, set up in 1982, has 13 rooms and is organized according to style, making this the perfect place to get an overview of Balinese art. The museum is about a kilometer (just over a half mile) beyond the bridge by Murni's Warung; carry straight on up the road on the other side of the river and it's on your right. Open from 8 AM to 4 PM.

The older **Puri Lukisan Museum** (founded in 1954) is in the center of the village and contains 10 rooms — seven in the main building and three in a separate gallery on the left as you arrive. Again, all styles of Balinese art are on show, though less clearly categorized than at the Neka. Nevertheless, many paintings crucial to the history of Balinese art and the changes brought about by the arrival of artists from Europe between the wars can be seen here. Opening hours are the same as for the Neka.

An Artist's House

There are a number of artists' houses in Ubud, but the best is **Antonio Blanco's House** and **Museum**. Erotic illuminated poems hang beside fantasy portraits of the painter's Balinese wife. You are unlikely to meet the venerable Filipino artist himself, but you can certainly look around his studio and gain a sense of what Ubud and Bali once were, both for him and for the other expatriate artists who made it their home. A photo of Blanco talking to Michael Jackson hangs in the reception area, testament to his wide range of acquaintances. Open from 9 AM to 5 PM.

The Monkey Forest

A stroll down to the Monkey Forest in the south of town has long been high on the list of things to do in Ubud. Nowadays the Monkey Forest Road is lined with shops and restaurants, but the infamous tribe of unruly monkeys — always quick to snatch

Ubud's serenity makes the highland town an attractive alternative to Kuta Beach.

Bali

the valuables of the unwary — still haunt the forest.

WHERE TO STAY

Ubud has accommodation to match all budgets and tastes. If you are going to be in Ubud for any length of time, do some investigating first. Along with the luxury hotels there are also many delightful family-run *losmen* that cost next to nothing. In the end it's the less expensive places that bring you closer to the real Ubud.

Luxury

Ubud's most luxurious and most expensive hotels are situated just outside the village. The **Amandari** ((361) 975333 FAX (361) 975335, Kedewatan 80571, with 29 suites, is at Sayan, five kilometers (three miles) out of Ubud. Each of the two-story suites has a private outdoor garden for sunning, an upstairs bedroom with a king-size canopy bed and a private garden off the dressing area with a sunken marble bath. The best suites have private swimming pools. Moments after being escorted to the suite by your personal assistant manager, a chilled bottle of Möet & Chandon arrives. Sip it while listening to the distant tinkle of the gamelan orchestra which performs nightly by the pool from 8 PM to 11 PM. The hotel employs a trekking guide who will escort you free of charge on country walks to local caves, temples and waterfalls. There are several secluded grottoes along the river where the hotel can arrange a romantic picnic. Indeed, one is never far away from the soothing sound of running water since irrigation water for the surrounding rice paddies has been ingeniously channeled to flow around the suites. There is an excellent library with books and tapes that can be borrowed and enjoyed in your room.

More pampering comes in the form of the new **Four Seasons Resort Sayan** ((361) 701010 FAX (361) 701022, at Sayan. There are 28 villas, and the accent is on providing a luxurious retreat where body and soul are relaxed and indulged. Its spa facilities bring a respectability to Bali's burgeoning reputation for health and spa treatments. The hotel naturally offers the usual range of amenities

and sports options. One kilometer (just over a half mile) away, the Indo-Australian-owned **Kupu Kupu Barong** ((361) 975476 FAX 0361-975079, Kedewatan 80571, operates along the same lines. Though not quite as luxurious, the nineteen villas here nevertheless enjoy stunning views down to the river far below. It's reached by funicular. You can put on a sarong and go swim in the river, or take a dip in the pool, which is fed by a natural mineral spring. The restaurant here is particularly fine.

If you want some luxury closer to Ubud itself, **Ibah** ((361) 974466 FAX 0361) 975567 is an excellent choice. Again accommodation is in individual suites, and the surroundings are breathtaking, with gardens and panoramic views.

To the northeast of town there is the **Banyan Tree Kamandalu** (0361-975825 FAX 975851, Jalan Tegallalang, Banjar, with 58 villas, floral themes and four-poster beds (It was formerly called the Puri Kamandalu.) A short drive to the north of Ubud, there's the larger **Chedi** (0361-975963 FAX 0361-975968, with 60 beautiful rooms in two-story blocks, along with top-ranking suites with baths situated amidst carp pools.

Moderate

The **Ulun Ubud** ((361) 975024 FAX (361) 975524, in Sanggingan, offers affordable and tastefully appointed cottages complete with double beds, old Dutch lamps and large balconies where complimentary breakfast are served. Cottages overlook the Campuhan River Valley. The hotel also has a restaurant and pool, but rooms are not air conditioned.

In Ubud proper, the **Hotel Tjamphuan** ((361) 975368 FAX (361) 975137 is a bungalow hotel that sits on the steep-sloping bank of the river. Features include a tennis court and swimming pool. One of the bungalows was once the home of the artist Walter Spies though reservations are required far in advance for this bungalow.

Also recommended and in the center of Ubud is **Han Snel's Siti Bungalows** ((361) 975699 FAX (361) 975643, where eight reasonably priced individual cottages are decorated with the artist's work. There is also a small exhibition of his work in a gallery in his garden. It is also worth persuading Han's wife

Siti, to organize a Balinese dinner, if you are traveling in a group.

Inexpensive

Ubud is teeming with budget accommodation. Providing you don't mind showering with cold water (*mandi* style) and doing without luxuries such as air conditioning, you can stay in a homestay, or *losmen*, for as little as US$5 or even less if you shop around.

The **Ubud Inn** ((361) 975071 is at the far end of the Monkey Forest Road, and is only a slight step down from mid-range accommodation, offering both simple fan-cooled as well as better air-conditioned cottages.

For the authentic *losmen* experience, **Tjanderi's** (also spelled Canderi's) is a long-runner. There are many other similar places around this area, but do look for **Anom**, an intimate homestay with just four rooms, which lies on a small lane off the Monkey Forest Road.

WHERE TO EAT

The **Café Lotus** ((361) 975660, Jalan Raya, is an Ubud institution, and with its picturesque lotus pond it's one of the most atmospheric dining spots in town. Prices are high, however, and the ambitious menu doesn't always live up to its promises. Order local or Indonesian fare rather than some exotic Mediterranean treat and you're more likely to be pleased. Open from 8 AM to 11 PM.

Not far away, also on Jalan Raya, is **Ary's Warung** ((361) 975063, another popular long-runner. The setting is not as soothing as at the Lotus, but those in the know give it the nod on the culinary front. Vegetarian dishes and Indonesian specialties are recommended. Live Indonesian music is often featured in the evenings. Farther west on Jalan Raya is **Casa Luna** ((361) 96283, which is reasonably priced and features a thoroughly international menu, good music, and offers plenty of fresh salads and fruits.

Murni's Warung ((361) 975233, down by the old suspension at the western end of Jalan Raya, is a four-story building with good views over the river. It too specializes in Western food — try their unexpected *vichyssoise* and *gazpacho*. In addition it stocks souvenirs

and books on Bali. Murni's is open from 9 AM to 11 PM, closed Wednesdays.

Café Wayan on Monkey Forest Road has been a favorite of foreigners for years. Wayan the cook, who began her career stirring up *jamus* for the locals, and her husband Ketut Krinting, a painter when he's not serving as *maitre d'*, make everything from scratch. The smoked duck dinner must be ordered a day in advance, but it's worth the effort of planning ahead. Its elaborate preparation begins when 12 herbs and spices are mixed with oil and lemon juice until a paste is formed. This

is spread over the duck which is wrapped in palm and banana leaves and put in a large clay bowl to cook for 12 hours in a fire made of rice and coconut husks. The duck and its juices are served with rice, *sambal* and *lawar*, a Balinese dish consisting of finely chopped green beans and grated coconut. Open daily from 8 AM to midnight.

SHOPPING

Art clamors for your attention (and your wallet) at virtually every street corner in Ubud and environs, but the best place for an overview of what's on offer is the craft

Tourists size up the Elephant Cave (Goa Gajah) near Ubud.

market (go early in the morning) on the corner of Jalan Raya and the Monkey Forest Road. Nearby you'll find dozens more shops selling carvings and paintings on consignment from artists in the surrounding villages. In these places, as in the galleries, prices are marked, but are negotiable nevertheless.

A good first stop for anyone seriously interested in buying Balinese art is **Agung Rai's gallery** (the commercial gallery in Peliatan, not the ARMA mentioned above) open daily from 7 AM to 7 PM. Some 50 art-

ists exhibit their work in the six large galleries. But the best aspect of the gallery is the willingness of its personnel to give tours that explain the evolution of Balinese painting. Painted with modest vegetable dyes, traditional paintings are uni-dimensional. Younger artists of the modern school use tempura and acrylics, and deal with bolder themes. Credit cards are accepted.

A smaller gallery closer to the Campuhan River, **Neka** ((361) 26941 is also worth visiting. Open from 8 AM to 5 PM it shows the work of 40 local artists.

Though stores in Kuta and Sanur offer a wide variety of merchandise, some of the island's best buys can be found in smaller towns north of Denpasar. It is difficult to separate exploring from shopping. For that reason, be prepared to stop when you see interesting shops along the roadside. Many of Bali's best artists sell their finest items directly out of their houses. This is especially true of painters around Ubud, so plan a leisurely pace as you pass through these towns.

NIGHTLIFE

Ubud is not known for its nightlife, but the **Beggar's Bush Pub,** over the river from Murni's Warung, provides a British style drinking atmosphere for those who miss such things.

The main thing to do in Ubud, apart from enjoying a leisurely meal, is to watch a dance performance, and these take place seven nights a week at a variety of venues in and out of town. These are advertised up and down the main street and are aggressively touted, so there's no danger you'll miss out. The inexpensive ticket prices usually include transport for out of town locations. Generally, performances last 90 minutes and start sometime between 7 and 8 PM.

HOW TO GET THERE AND AWAY

Tourist minibuses shuttle backwards and forwards between Ubud, Kuta, Sanur and the airport all day. There is a transport agency at the Nomad Restaurant ((361) 975131.

UBUD TO KUTA

The road between Ubud and Kuta is packed with crafts villages. Many are invaded with coach-loads of tourists on a regular basis, but if you have your own transport and you're prepared to do a little exploring, there are still some delightful galleries to be found.

MAS

Mas is a woodcarving center that is home to some of Bali's best craftspeople; almost everyone in the village is involved in the industry. At each shop there is a group of Balinese working out back: men carving while women sand the finished pieces. Don't be surprised if you see Kiwi shoe polish being applied to a statue. The Balinese use shoe polish to stain the wood. Because Bali is a small, densely populated island, the only locally grown materials are mahogany and light colored hibiscus wood. Ebony comes from Sulawesi (Celebes) and Kalimantan. East Timor supplies sandalwood.

Ida Bagus Tilem is the most famed wood-carver of Mas, and his work can be seen (and purchased) at the **Tilem Gallery** ((361) 975099 Both he and his father are acclaimed craftsmen; their work is expensive and excellent.

Other Mas galleries worth looking into include the **Adhi Art Gallery** (9 AM to 5 PM), on the main road, which has several large rooms filled with carvings in both Balinese and European styles, and **Barong** (7 AM to 8 PM), on the same road, an even larger manufacturer and exporter of carvings. Don't be

center of Sukawati. Most Balinese tour operators offer shopping-oriented day trips to nearby Batubulan and Celuk but few stop in Sukawati. The main reason to visit this busy market town is to take a look at the *wayang kulit* — shadow puppets — that are produced here. Sukawati is Bali's center for *wayang kulit*, with numerous professional troupes and puppet makers based in the town. Prices are higher than you would pay for the souvenir versions in Kuta and Ubud, but these are authentic *wayang kulit*, and the workmanship is bound to be exquisite.

put off by the front building, which is the shipping room. Head directly to the back where there is a two-story display area. The large statues are on the first floor. Smaller items such as picture frames, Balinese masks and animals are located upstairs.

While in Mas be sure to stop at the **Puri Rasa Café** (8 AM to 9 PM) for a Balinese lunch. Owned by a woodcarver, the café accepts only cash for meals, but will take credit cards if you want to buy one of the antique Balinese doors on display.

SUKAWATI

South of Mas, just before the village of **Celuk**, which is famous for its jewelry, is the district

BATUBULAN

About 45 minutes north of Kuta on the road to Mas and Lake Batur is Batubulan, the village of antiques, stonecarving and *barong* dancing. Though there is no hotel or homestay of note here, you will want to spend several hours, if only to catch the *barong* dance, an attraction worth at least three rolls of film, staged every morning at 9:30 AM. Be sure to arrive early since the dance is one of the most colorful on the island. It's a major tourist attraction these days, but still worth seeing providing you don't mind the crowds. At tip:

OPPOSITE: Many travelers spend their afternoons on native *prahus*. ABOVE: The Dirty Duck Restaurant exudes Ubud's rustic ambiance.

Seats near the open-air stage are the best in the temple complex, but tend to be occupied last since they're in direct sunlight. By the time the performance begins they'll be in the shade, so grab the front row if it's free.

If you have an interest in stonecarvings, spend some time after the dance looking at the stores along Batubulan's main road. Stonecarving is a living art in Bali since village temples are constantly reordering new statues. Carved from soft sandstone, the statues weather quickly in the tropical climate, and after a decade or so must be replaced.

CANDI DASA

Candi Dasa (pronounced Chandi Dasa) is a compact resort 13 km (eight miles) southwest of Amlapura (Karangasem), on Bali's southeast coast. It is the only stretch of this coast that has experienced any degree of tourist development. The name probably means Ten Tombs and refers to some ancient monuments near the village of **Bug Bug** (pronounced Boog Boog) two kilometers (one and a quarter miles) to the east.

Few tourists, however, purchase stonecarvings since they are heavy and cumbersome and therefore difficult to carry or ship home.

For an overview of some of the best of local carving (though, of course, in this case not for purchase), take a look at the **Pura Puseh** temple, which is a little east of the main road. Most of the statuary here is of recent provenance, though it is modeled on classical forms.

EAST BALI

The main attractions of East Bali are the massive Mt. Agung and the beach resort of Candi Dasa.

Candi Dasa's tragedy, though, is that in the last 10 years it has lost its beach. Following the construction of a sea wall in the 1980s the already narrow strip of beach was swept away by ocean currents. Concrete groins have been constructed to prevent further erosion, and their rectangular patterns now dominate what's left of the shore. There is still good swimming over a sandy bed at Candi Dasa but, along much of the shoreline, there is now effectively no real beach. Even so, Candi Dasa is cheaper and more peaceful than either Sanur or Kuta. While you are in Candi Dasa don't miss the opportunity of visiting nearby **Tenganan**, the Bali Aga village known internationally for its unique double *ikat* weaving.

Where to Stay

The only hotel in Candi Dasa with a beach-front is the **Candi Beach Cottage** ((363) 41234 FAX (363) 41111, a mid-range place half a mile west of the village center. It has a swimming pool and a lush garden, together with an excellent restaurant.

Also west of town is the exclusive **Amankila** ((363) 71267 FAX (363) 71266, where rates start at US$460 and rise to a giddy US$1,300 a night for a double suite. It commands superb sea views across to Nusa Penida and Lombok. Each room is a self-contained villa

and a road winds down to what is essentially a private beach.

In Candi Dasa proper the mid-range **Puri Bagus Beach Hotel** ((363) 41131 FAX (363) 41290 is at the far east end of the beach, nestled amongst the palms and, though there is no longer any beach as such, the swimming is still good. Also recommended is **The Watergarden** ((363) 41540 FAX (363) 41164, which has 12 villas, five of which have air conditioning, in a delightful garden setting.

For something at the budget end try the **Puri Pandan** ((363) 41541, where you can get a basic but sufficient bungalow for as little as US$10 per night. The attached restaurant overlooking the sea is a pleasant and

popular spot for either lunch or dinner. The nearby **Pondok Bambu Seaside Cottages** ((363) 41534 FAX (363) 41818 is arguably a better establishment, but rates are similar.

Where to Eat

As for food, a superior place to eat in Candi Dasa is the **Lotus Seaview** ((363) 41257, an off-shoot of the famous Café Lotus in Ubud. It's not cheap, but the views, the ambiance and the meals (treat yourself to some fresh seafood) are first-rate.

Check out, too, **Kupu Bali** on the main road, not far from the hotel of the same name. Indonesian cuisine is the specialty, and while prices are several notches up from *warung* standards so are the meals.

How to Get There and Away

The easiest (and most sensible) way to get to Candi Dasa if you are not driving your own vehicle is to take a tourist bus from Kuta or Ubud. The tourist buses are frequent, inexpensive and run direct. Doing the journey by public transport is more trouble than it's worth, involving a change in either Denpasar or Batubulan (or perhaps both).

BESAKIH

The **Mother Temple of Besakih** is Bali's largest and most ancient place of worship. In times past, kings and their courts made annual pilgrimages to Besakih, and even today the temple remains an important place of pilgrimage, with crowds flocking to it daily.

The temple is constructed over a network of terraces that ascend the lower slopes of Mt. Agung, Bali's highest and most revered mountain. The various courtyards and enclosures are connected by flights of steps, and it is these, together with the tall, multi-storied *meru* that, with Agung rising steeply immediately behind the central enclosures, make the prospect of Besakih so very impressive.

OPPOSITE: The beach at Candi Dasa is lined with small hotels along all but this unusually solitary stretch. ABOVE: As in this example from Amlapura, erotic dalliance is in no way alien to Hindu art.

The mountain has not always been kind to the temple: An eruption in 1917 almost destroyed Besakih, and it was again badly damaged in Mt. Agung's 1963 eruption. On both occasions the temple was faithfully restored.

The day-to-day business of the temple is taken care of by the *pemangku*, easily identifiable by their white clothes. They receive take care of the offerings left in the temple, sprinkle the visiting pilgrims three times with holy water as they offer up flowers, also three times, and place clusters of wet rice grains

The wide central staircase, flanked on each side by seven rising stone platforms each carrying six carved figures, leads to the first large court. It contains the usual pavilions for offerings, gamelan orchestras and the like. The second court is similar but contains three ceremonial chairs situated on a high stone platform known as a *padmasana*, or world-shrine, intended for the three major manifestations of God — Shiva, Vishnu and Brahma. The other courts follow on up rather fewer steps and contain many of the thatched *meru* that are characteristic of the temple.

on each temple and on the brow in such a way that they will remain there for some time. The Brahmanic *pedanda*, or high priests, only make an appearance for the great ceremonies, though they can regularly be seen at cremations sitting in their high lofts chanting their mantras and wafting incense to the gods.

The main temple complex, or Pura Panataran, at Besakih (there are other, subsidiary ones, especially off to the right) consists of six walled courts, each higher up the mountain than the last. Before you reach the first of these, there is a small walled shrine containing a seven-tiered *meru* on your right — this is the original shrine of the temple.

THE ASCENT OF MT. AGUNG

Besakih is a popular place from which to begin the attempt on Mt. Agung — but "attempt" is the key word. It is not an easy task. Though it is claimed the climb there and back can be done in a day if a very early start is made, it is far better to go prepared to spend a night on the volcano.

A guide is essential as the early part of the mountain route winds through fields, but more importantly because, in the unlikely event of an accident, it is vital to have someone capable of going back quickly and organizing help. It is relatively easy to find a freelance guide in Besakih for your ascent of Mt. Agung, though the most reliable (and expensive) option is to hire one through the Besakih tourist office.

For the climb you will need to take along a flashlight and an adequate supply of food and water; you'll also need stout boots and a hat.

Your guide will suggest being up on the rim of the volcano to see the rising sun, which means making a very early start — preferably around midnight. It's worth it. If you get to the rim of the volcano too late in the day and the clouds will have rolled in over the views.

SINGARAJA

Singaraja has little to delay the average traveler or vacationer. Most people pause only briefly before heading west along the coast to the black-sand beaches of Lovina.

The **Gedong Kirtya Historical Library** contains a collection of Balinese sacred manuscripts inscribed on palm leaves (*lontar*). It's open from 7 AM to 1 PM, Monday to Friday. Singaraja, like many Asian towns, looks better by night than by day, and the **Night**

How to Get There and Away

Getting to Besakih and Mt. Agung by public transport is no fun. From Denpasar you would have to take a *bemo* to Batubulan, change there for Klungkung and from there change for an infrequent minibus to Besakih. The best way is either to drive yourself in a rented vehicle or to charter a *bemo* in Kuta or Ubud.

NORTH BALI

Northern Bali, where you find the former Balinese capital city of Singaraja and some very fine beaches, is a world far away from the heavily touristed southern parts of the island.

Market, which runs seven nights a week, is well worth exploring.

LOVINA

Lovina is not one place, but a group of mostly inexpensive resorts strung like a necklace along Bali's northern shore west of Singaraja. Although these black-sand beaches are not picture-postcard perfect like Kuta in southern Bali, they are fine for relaxing on once you become accustomed to the unusual color

OPPOSITE: The Mother Temple at Besakih, the island's premier place of worship, situated on the lower slopes of Mt. Agung, Bali's highest summit. The first rays of dawn strike the mountain: A hiker far above the treeline ABOVE in the grayness of first light on Mt. Agung.

of the volcanic sands. Unlike Kuta, the beaches here are protected by a reef and there is no surfing. It's an ideal swimming area. Other attractions are snorkeling along the reef and dolphin-watching at dawn just beyond the reef.

Lovina got its start as a tranquil alternative to Kuta, Sanur and Nusa Dua. Today Lovina is expanding, but more slowly than most other tourist destinations on the island. Most of the smaller homestays still have no phone, though the occasional luxury hotel is starting to appear, standing incongruously amongst the rice paddies.

There are so many people clamoring to take you out to see the dolphins that, even if crawling out of bed at the crack of dawn to sit in a boat and watch marine mammals splashing about is not your thing, you'll feel obliged to do so in the end. You will be collected from your hotel at 6 AM and taken down to a brightly-painted *prahu*. These light-weight but sturdy vessels carry their paying crew of three or four visitors 15 minutes out to sea, where with the sun lightening the eastern horizon, dolphins, first in pairs then in dozens, arch their backs above the still surface as the boatmen rev up their engines to follow them. Dawn is the time to see the dolphins in inland waters — later in the day they feed farther out to sea. After half an hour they will move away and the engines will be switched off and you'll be served a simple breakfast of cold fried bananas and sweet tea.

As for diving, **Spice Dive** ((362) 41305 FAX (362)-41171, will arrange everything for you, including trips to Tulamben and instruction courses, either basic or advanced.

Where to Stay

Lovina is mostly about budget accommodation with fan-cooled rooms and a family ambiance. For something more luxurious, try the eastern end of Lovina, the area nearest to Singaraja, where the mid-range **Sol Lovina Hotel** ((362) 41775 FAX (362) 41659, and the **Hotel Aneka Lovina** ((362) 41121 FAX (362) 41827, both offer very high standards of comfort at fairly reasonable rates. The former has a tennis court, and both have swimming pools. Less expensive, but nevertheless aimed at the better-off visitor and still at this

end of the beach, is the **Banyualit Beach Inn** ((362) 41789 FAX (362) 41563.

The **Ansoka Hotel** (362) 41841 FAX (362) 41023 is excellent value, and it has a swimming pool. Of the many budget-category places on offer, the **Palestis Beach Cottages** ((362) 41035, can be recommended for its friendly atmosphere and clean rooms; it also has a swimming pool. Another recommended lodging is the **Padang Lovina Seaside Cottages** ((362) 41302.

Where to Eat

The **Sea Breeze Café** ((362) 41138 is an excellent beach restaurant that offers such unexpected delicacies as cauliflower cheese, lemon meringue pie and mango crumble. Many consider it the best eating place in

Lovina, informal but comfortable, and offering a varied and imaginative cuisine. Also popular are the **Warung Kopi Bali (** (362) 41361, right in the center of the village and frequently full at dinnertime, and the **Bali Apik Bar and Restaurant (** (362) 41050, well-known for its wide range of drinks and hearty pizzas.

How to Get There and Away

Singaraja is the main transport hub for northern Bali. If you are continuing to Lovina, travel agents or your hotel will arrange for a pick-up in Singaraja. Regular buses from Denpasar arrive at Singaraja's southern Sukasada terminal, and less frequent, but more comfortable tourist shuttle buses are also available. Long-distance buses run to major destinations in Java such as Surabaya and Yogyakarta.

WEST BALI

Tanah Lot, one of Bali's most hyped and touristed attractions is best visited as a day trip from Kuta or Ubud. West Bali's other major destinations, Penelokan and Mt. Batur, deserve more time.

TANAH LOT

Small surprise that Bali's most celebrated view has also become one of the island's

Tanah Lot — Coach loads of tourists come to photograph the temple outlined against the sunset, an icon of Bali.

tackiest tourist attractions. The drawing card is a temple—one of many that dot Bali's south coast — that overlooks the ocean in propitiation of sea spirits. With the setting sun behind it, the delicate outlines of the spectacularly situated Tanah Lot make a stunning image. And this is why people come here — to take the photograph. Linger too long and you'll start noticing kiosks touting myriad versions of the same T-shirts and sarongs, a shop selling Polo Ralph Lauren fashions, and the presiding form of the Nirwana Resort with its 18-hole golf course.

Except at high tide, you can walk across over the rocks to the site of the temple, but you will not be allowed up into the temple itself — it's locked except at festival times. The best photographic vantage points are from the cove itself, from along the low cliff, and from the headland on the right. From this last position a natural arch in the rocks to the north can also be taken, with Mt. Batur in the background.

Where to Stay
Now that two hotels have opened their doors, visitors to Tanah Lot can play lots of golf and relax in luxury spas. **Le Meridien Bali (** (361) 243691 overlooks the village from the top of a nearby hill. **Bali Nirvana Resort (** (361) 815900 FAX (361) 815901 has the golf course.

PENELOKAN

Just beyond Ubud the road begins to climb up to the crest of Bali's mountainous spine. Eventually it leads to Penelokan, which means "the place to look." It's a tiny village, but as the name suggests the views are stupendous and there's a dramatically beautiful **temple**.

There are numerous restaurants in Penelokan that cater to the coach-loads of tourists that arrive daily. The set-priced lunch offerings at these places are all much the same, but the views are knockouts. Bear in mind, that you can opt out of the tour group syndrome and stay up in Penelokan. The **Lakeview Homestay (** (366) 51464 has a good selection of rooms at budget to mid-range prices (the better rooms have hot water, which

is essential if you want to shower), and also has an attached restaurant. Ignore the roadside souvenir vendors — they're amongst Bali's rudest and most tenacious.

MT. BATUR

From Penelokan some travelers venture on toward the Mt. Batur region. It is a breathtakingly beautiful place, with a lake and several small towns situated in a vast caldera, 11 km (seven miles) across, that was created by a massive prehistoric volcanic explosion. Mt. Batur itself, whose broken crest rises 1,700 m (5,600 ft) above sea level, is central to the view, its slopes scarred with lava-flows. Magnificent though the mountain is, it is the product of several more recent and smaller eruptions and its summit is actually only 328 m (1,066 ft) higher than the outer-crater rim at Penelokan. It last erupted in 1926, completely destroying the village of Batur.

Batur, eight kilometers (five miles) long and three kilometers (two miles) wide, fills almost a third of the area of the caldera. A day beside the lake and an ascent of Mt. Batur is the standard, pleasant routine. From **Kedisan**, a small boat landing directly below Losmen Gunawan, you can charter an ancient *prahu* for US$2 and cross Lake Batur to the village of **Trunyan**, the home of the primitive Bali Aga who call themselves the original Balinese. The village itself is extremely primitive and can be bypassed in favor of the lakeside cemetery. The 300 people of Trunyan do not believe in cremation. They place their dead in rows beneath an enormous tree and allow nature to take its course. A nominal donation is expected when entering the cemetery. Place the money next to the skull at the gate.

For the ascent of Batur there's no need for a guide unless you plan to set off in the dark to see the sun rise; in this case you will need to start at 3:30 AM and can easily find a guide by asking around at Toya Bungkah. Even if you are not planning to watch the sunrise, an early start is advisable in order to avoid the heat later in the day. From Toya Bungkah, take the lane that leads toward the mountain from the center of the village. Anyone will point it out to you if you say,

"Batur, jalan jalan" (Batur, walking). It curves gently round to the left until, after about a kilometer (just over a half mile), you reach a temple. Pass the temple, continuing on the very clear track, and follow it as it winds across the now cindery scrubland around the base of the mountain. After crossing the second of two (usually dry) river beds, the path turns upwards, heading directly for the peak.

Next comes a steep, dusty section where handholds are provided. At the top is an orange refuse bin that marks the junction by the Bahasa word for "hot springs", Air Panas. Take some time out for a boat trip on the lake — boats with drivers can be hired at Toya Bungkah.

The only place offering mid-range comforts in this neck of the woods is the **Hotel Puri Bening** ((366) 51234 FAX (366) 51248. At present, Air Panas is mostly visited by backpackers keen to hike in the cool upland air, and the place many of them choose to stay is the inexpensive and friendly **Under the Volcano Homestay** ((366) 51166. It has two locations: one beside the lake, one higher up.

of the track with another coming up from the left. From here the path crosses a level stretch and then diverges into several subsidiaries, all making for the ridge on the right. Once you have achieved this, the path becomes straightforward, running clearly ahead to the summit. Views back over the lake are superb.

Where to Stay

Accommodation and guide services are available at the village of **Kedisan**, which is just below Penelokan on the lake's edge. But the most popular place to stay is **Toya Bungkah**, where there is a good selection of basic *losmen*, a black sand beach and hot springs. Sometimes the village is referred to

How to Get There and Away

Tours to Penelokan are popular from Kuta and Ubud, as well as from the major hotels in Sanur and Nusa Dua. Getting there by public transport is, as usual, time consuming. It's possible to get a *bemo* from Denpasar to Kintamani, which is not far north of Penelokan on the crater rim; from here it is possible to charter a another *bemo* inexpensively to Penelokan or to Toya Bungkah or Kedisan.

It takes about four hours to climb Mt. Batur, the highest peak in Bali.

Sumatra

Toba. Outside Padang and Bukittinggi in the southwest of Sumatra, the *adat* system of ancestral worship prevails. On offshore islands such as Nias, animism still holds sway.

Sumatra's dramatic architecture, seen at its best in the northern and western portions of the island, has received national recogni-

ACCOUNTING for 25% of Indonesia's total land area, Sumatra is the sixth largest island in the world. Lying along the Strait of Malacca, it extends for over 1,600 km (1,000 miles) and contains some of the most exotic and unusual cultures in the Indonesian Archipelago. Though it has less than a third of Java's population, Sumatra produces at least 50% of Indonesia's total export earnings. The island produces three quarters of the country's crude oil. The Minas oil field beneath Sumatra's Riau province has been yielding high quality crude for more than a century. Natural gas tapped at the Arun field in Aceh province fires the industries of Japan. Rubber, palm oil and robusta coffee beans flow out of plantations covering the foothills of the island's Bukit Barisan Range. Tin is mined and smelted in the Bangka Islands. For the Dutch, Sumatra was an unending source of wealth with the richest area being the *cultuurgebied*, or plantation area, around the present city of Medan.

Sumatra is home to a remarkably diverse groups of people who have evolved in relative isolation, cut off from the rest of the country by volcanic mountain ranges and raging rivers. The northern tip of Aceh is noted for its fundamentalist brand of Islam, while Christianity prevails around Medan and Lake

tion. The style is reflected in the typical large rectangular building built atop pilings with a saddle-shaped roof that rises to a point at either end. In the Minangkabau area of western Sumatra high-pitched gables are often decorated with buffalo horns. Elsewhere, carvings adorn the pillars and lintels of Sumatran styled auditoriums, airports and convention centers.

LAMPUNG

The southernmost province of Lampung is Sumatra's window on the Sunda Strait and the nearby island of Java. The provincial capital, Bandar Lampung is a major entry point to the island.

The brooding volcano of **Krakatau**, which exploded in 1883 killing 36,000 people and blanketing the entire southern portion of the island with volcanic ash, sits 29 km (18 miles) off Lampung's southern shore. From within the crater created by this explosion arose a new volcanic mountain, now dormant. Boats can be chartered in the village of Canti to Krakatau volcano, a six-hour journey, but the seas can be treacherous; plan your visit for the months of September or October when the weather is at its most calm (see VISIT THE SON OF KRAKATOA in TOP SPOTS, page 16).

Enriched by Krakatau's volcanic ash, Lampung's soil produces abundant crops of

cloves, coffee and pepper. Fertility has made the province a favorite destination for Javanese transmigrants, who are relocated, at government expense, to create agricultural communities. Today, 12% of Lampung's 5,000,000 people are from Java.

GENERAL INFORMATION

The Regional Office of Tourism, Post and Telecommunications ((721) 251900 is at Jalan Kotaraja N°12 in Bandar Lampung. The Lampung Tourist Service ((721) 428565 also in Bandar Lampung, is at Jalan Dr. Suprapto N°39.

WHERE TO STAY

The best hotel in town is the **Sheraton Inn** ((721) 486666 FAX (721) 486690, Jalan W Monginsidi N°70, where you'll find a swimming pool, tennis courts and a fitness center. In the upper mid-range category, the **Marco Polo Hotel** ((721) 262511 FAX (721) 254419, Jalan Dr. Susilo N°4, also has a large swimming pool with the added attraction of a prospect of Lampung Bay.

Overlooking the Sunda Strait the **Sahid Krakatau Seaside** ((721) 484022 FAX 484356, Jalan Yos Sudarso N°294, is a step down from the Marco Polo but nevertheless not a bad choice.

There's a dearth of decent budget accommodation in Bandar Lampung. One reasonable place with air-conditioned rooms for less than US$20 is the **Kurnia Perdana Hotel** ((721) 262030, Jalan Radan Intan N°114.

HOW TO GET THERE AND AWAY

Ferries from Java arrive and depart from one of Lampung's two ports. Bakauhuni is on the southern tip of Sumatra. Panjang is a bit farther up the east coast.

THE RIAU ARCHIPELAGO

At the southern end of the Malacca Strait, the thousand tiny islands of the Riau Archipelago stretch from Sumatra's east coast swamps to the Malay Peninsula. Rich in oil and tin, the islands were used for centuries as stepping stones by fishermen, merchant sailors and pirates. In 1745 the area came under the control of the Dutch East India Company, which immediately set about sweeping pirates from the Matuna Sea. The task remains unfinished to this day.

Most visitors to the Riaus are vacationers from Singapore, which is just two hours from the popular resort islands of Bintan and 45 minutes from Batam. For travelers making their way between Singapore and Sumatra, these islands make a good stop-over.

GENERAL INFORMATION

There are tourist offices in Pekanbaru ((761) 31562, Jalan Merbabu N°16, and in Batam ((761) 322852, Sekupang Ferry Terminal.

WHAT TO SEE AND DO

The Riau may comprise a "thousand islands" but for most travelers just three places count: **Batam**, **Bintan**, and **Pekanbaru**.

HOW TO GET THERE AND AWAY

From Jakarta there are direct flights with Sempati to Bintan, or more frequent flights to Hang Nadim Airport on neighboring Batam. At Punggur jetty in Batam, there are 35-minute speedboat services to Bandar Bentan Telani Ferry Terminal, which serves Bintan's resorts. Speedboats also operate from Batam to Bintan's Tanjung Pinang harbor. From Singapore, speedboats operate from the World Trade Center wharf to Tanjung Pinang, and from Tanah Merah Ferry Terminal to Bandar Bentan Telani Ferry Terminal in Bintan. High-speed catamarans from Tanah Merah operate approximately hourly from 9 AM to 8 PM and the journey takes around 45 minutes.

Garuda has direct service from Singapore, Jakarta, Medan and Batam to Pekanbaru. Merpati to has flights to Pekanbaru from Batam, Medan, Padang and Palembang plus daily service from Banda Aceh, Jakarta and Tanjung Pinang. Sempati has direct flights to Pekanbaru from Jakarta, Kuala Lumpur and Padang.

Batam

Riau Batam is an island of beach resorts just 30 minutes by ferry from Singapore. It's a duty-free port with cleanish water and dramatic nightime views of the Singapore skyline. Apart from its duty-free status, its greatest lure is golf, and many Singaporeans come over at weekends to play the various courses.

If you plan to stay on Batam, avoid the weekends; rates shoot up and it's difficult to get value for money. In Nagoya, Batam's main town, a favorite is the luxury **Holiday Hotel** ((761) 458616, at Blok B, N°1 on Jalan Imam Bonjol. Elsewhere around the island are a number of resort developments aimed at vacationing Singaporeans such as the **Batam View** ((761) 22825, with a private beach, duty-free shopping, floor shows and expensive seafood dining.

Bintan

Bintan is the largest of the 1,300 islands in the Riau Archipelago. Following a joint agree-

ment between the Indonesian and Singaporean governments in 1990, the island is being developed as a luxury international tourist attraction. Fully a third of the island (about half the area of Singapore) has been earmarked for tourist developments. Beaches and marine sports are the chief draw, but the port of **Tanjung Pinang**, with its surrounding stilt villages and bustling market is not without charm. The village of **Senggarang**, across the harbor from the main port of Tanjung Pinang is worth a visit, mostly for its Chinese temple. Tanjung Pinang is a colorful port and safe harbor for everything from Chinese junks to Bugis schooners. It also makes a good base to visit the remnants of the 300-year old Malay kingdom of Riau on neighboring **Penyengat Island**. Golfers can

hit the links at two 18-hole golf courses designed by Jack Nicklaus, Ian Baker-Finch and Greg Norman.

Riau Bintan Resorts operates an information center in Singapore ℂ (65) 543-0039 FAX (65) 545-9232 where you can survey the bewildering array of luxury accommodation and entertainment options available at Bintan. The **Banyan Tree Bintan** ℂ (771) 81347 FAX (771) 81348, Tanjung Said, is a luxury development that covers a huge swathe of seafront. Villas are constructed in Balinese style and come with en suite bathrooms and outdoor Jacuzzis. Eleven of the villas have private swimming pools. The **Hotel Sedona Bintan Lagoon** ℂ (771) 82888 FAX (771) 82788

Sulfurous clouds from Mt. Sibayak don't bother the orangutans who live on the slopes of this volcano.

is a vast complex that houses a 416-room hotel, 10 international-class restaurants, a sea sports center that offers PADI dive courses, a spa and landscaped gardens. Bookings can also be made on ((65) 223-3223 FAX (65) 421-7878 in Singapore. The **Mana Mana Beach Resort** ((65) 346-1984 FAX (65) 344-9472 in Singapore, is a more intimate choice, featuring 50 hillside chalets and a watersports center. The chalets are rustic in appearance but come with all the amenities you would expect at a luxury hotel: air conditioning, minibars, satellite television and comfortable lounging furniture. The newly opened **Club Mediterranée Riau Bintan** (SINGAPORE (65) 738-4222 FAX (65) 738-0770, has 310 luxury rooms, seven restaurants and bars, conference facilities, as well as a disco and the inevitable karaoke entertainment.

In the upper mid-range category the **Riau Holiday Inn** ((761) 22644 FAX (761) 21394, is popular with Singaporean visitors for its restaurant and watersports. For budget travelers, the most popular place in town is **Johnny's Guesthouse**, Jalan Lorong Bintan II N°22.

Pekanbaru

Pekanbaru is a blue collar oil town surrounded on all sides by dense forest. There are no sights as such, and the jungle is not easily accessible.

Unless you have friends or relatives who work for Caltex, you will have no reason to tarry in Pekanbaru. But if misfortune should strike and you are forced to stay the night, head for the upper mid-range **Hotel Dyan Graha** ((761) 26851, Jalan Gatot Subrato N°7, or the inexpensive and popular **Poppies Homestay** ((761) 33863, Jalan Cempedak, not far from Kacamayang Park, where English is spoken and you can you can get travel information.

PALEMBANG

The provincial capital of South Sumatra is a boom town of nearly one and a half million people, many of whom work in the oil, timber and tin industries. The city is surrounded by rubber, coffee and pineapple plantations, but the main attraction for foreign visitors is the **Musi River** which bisects the city. Along

with the Mahakam in East Kalimantan, the Musi is one of the most interesting rivers in Indonesia, although it must be said that it is very polluted. Negotiate an hourly fare at the quay near the Ampera Bridge and cruise the river banks before heading to Palembang's other attraction, the **Museum Sumatera Selatan**. It's around five kilometers (three miles) north of town on Jalan Srivijaya. Open daily except Friday, the museum is the best and only repository of objects from the Srivijaya empire that ruled much of Southeast Asia from the seventh to twelfth centuries. Behind the museum are two traditional *limas* houses.

GENERAL INFORMATION

The best place for local information is the Palembang City Tourist Office ((711) 358450, Jalan Sultan Mahmud Badaruddin II.

WHERE TO STAY

Palembang has a growing number of hotels aimed at business people and travelers. One of the best is the centrally located **King's Hotel** ((711) 310033 FAX (711) 310937, Jalan Kol. Atmo N°623, which offers upper mid-range comfort at slightly inflated rates. The **Hotel Sandjaja** ((711) 310675, Jalan Kapt. Rivai, to the north of the King's, is a more professionally run luxury hotel. The **Hotel Swarna Dipa** ((711) 313322, Jalan Tasik N°2, is a better deal, featuring well-appointed rooms and a swimming pool, but it's not as centrally located.

Mid-range and budget hotels in Palembang are generally disappointing. The **Hotel Sriwidjaja** ((711) 355555, Jalan Iskanda N°31, is not particularly salubrious, but it does have a wide variety of rooms to choose from; opt for the more expensive air-conditioned doubles if you are not economizing. Palembang's inexpensive hotels are best avoided.

HOW TO GET THERE AND AWAY

Merpati and Mandala both have offices at the Hotel Sandjaja; flights are out of Palembang's Talang Betutu Airport Jakarta. Merpati has limited services to other Sumatran destinations.

Other transport options include trains to Bandar Lampung and buses to Jakarta, although you can expect a bumpy journey taking up to 20 hours if you opt for the latter.

BENGKULU

Bisected by the Bukit Barisan Mountain Range, this seldom visited province is comprised of dense rainforests and fertile soil enriched by the Krakatau's volcanic deposits. Peasants resettled under the *transmigrasi* program do much of the agricultural work.

For the moment, at least, the forests still belong to tapirs, tigers, civet cats and the elusive Sumatran clouded leopard.

Three centuries ago, Bengkulu was the base for Britain's entry into the East Indies pepper trade. The experience was not entirely successful. Malaria so thinned British ranks that it was soon said that "two monsoons were the life of a man" sent to Bengkulu. By the time Sir Stamford Raffles arrived on the scene in 1818 most of the work was being done by the Eurasian progeny of the dearly departed.

Today, Bengkulu is a small town of not much more than 70,000 people. It has no exotic nightlife or fine restaurants. Instead it offers an ambiance, a certain tropical charm,

resulting, perhaps, from the fact that its people have made peace with the towering mountain chain at their back, the tempestuous Mentawai Strait at their feet, and the omnipresent ghosts of the past.

GENERAL INFORMATION

The DIPARDA Tourist Service for Bengkulu ((736) 21272 is at Jalan Pembangunan N°14, inconveniently tucked away in the south of town and probably not worth going out of your way for.

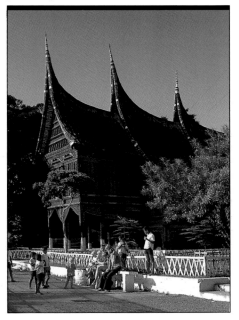

WHAT TO SEE AND DO

Fort Marlborough was the most imposing military structure ever built by the East India Company. It was occupied by the Indonesian army for a long time, who robbed the fort of most of its former grandeur, but it is now a tourist attraction. Its thick front wall has been plastered over with cement giving it the appearance of an adobe-walled prison. But the back of the fort and its windswept parapets remain much as they were when the British and Dutch were fighting over Sumatra. Before leaving the fort, walk

Bukittinggi in Western Sumatra is famous for its horse-drawn carts LEFT and saddle-roofed homes RIGHT.

through the graveyard, preferably at dusk, to read the epitaphs.

A few minutes walk from Fort Marlborough is the former English governor's office, a hilltop ruin whose beauty is enhanced by the fact that the crumbling structure is being devoured by jungle.

Bengkulu's most interesting attraction, from the Indonesian point of view, is Soekarno's house, where he lived for four years during his exile by the Dutch. Next to the tourist office around the corner from Jalan Soekarno–Hatta, the house can be visited in the morning with permission from its present occupants.

WHERE TO STAY

The best area to be based is probably Jalan Pantai Nala, by the beach. Here you'll find the comfortable, mid-range **Horizon Hotel** ((736) 21722 and the inexpensive **Nala Seaside Cottages** ((736) 21855. If you want to be based in town, the popular choice is the inexpensive **Wismar Balai Buntar** ((736) 21254, which has average rooms in a villa setting.

HOW TO GET THERE AND AWAY

Merpati has daily direct flights from Jakarta. Most travelers who make it as far as Bengkulu are on their way to Padang and Bukittinggi. The bus journey to Padang takes 24 hours.

WEST SUMATRA

West Sumatra is the most densely populated area on the island. It has a population of four million, nearly all of whom are Minangkabau, a matrilineal society in which inherited property, land and family surnames are passed on to women. Indeed, the word for family is *saparuik*, which means "from one womb."

Among the Minangkabau of western Sumatra, women are the ones who chose their mates. Men are valued for their virility and have no authority in family or business matters. As a result, thousands of them leave to seek their fortune elsewhere. Sleeping in mosques and eating in restaurants, they become *merantu*, or nomads, who return

home only after striking it rich in the "man's world" of Java. Because many men never return home, Jakarta's Minangkabau population is greater than that of Padang.

The buffalo is a central theme in the architecture and dress of western Sumatra. Minang buildings have peaked swooping roofs that resemble the horns of a water buffalo. Homes of the wealthy can have as many as a dozen of these gables. The pointed headdresses of Minangkabau women, whose dresses are embroidered with gold and silver thread, also appear as stylized buffalo horns.

PADANG

The center of the Minangkabau society is the provincial capital of Padang, Sumatra's third largest city. A sweltering seaport drenched by tropical rain all year round, Padang is one of the cleanest, most orderly cities in Indonesia. It boasts a number of museums and art centers, the most important of which are the **Museum Adityawarman** and the **Padang Art Center**. Located on Jalan Diponegoro, both are open daily except Monday.

Padang is close to the equator, so it never gets cool. Though rain falls throughout the year, it pours from November to March. If the weather weren't disincentive enough to linger, Padang is almost bereft of sights. If you want a beach, **Pantai Bungus**, 22 km (14 miles) south of town is a popular spot that has, sadly, been all but spoiled by the construction of a plywood factory.

General Information

The Provincial Tourist Service (DIPARDA Sumatera Barat) ((751) 34232, Padang at Jalan Jend. Sudirman N°43, is complemented by the West Sumatra Tourism Office ((751) 55711, Jalan Khatib Sulaiman N°22, in Padang Baru. Both offices have maps, handouts and helpful staff.

Where to Stay

Padang's best hotel is the **Hotel Sedona** ((751) 37555 FAX ((751) 37567, Jalan Bundo Kandung N°20, where you can find near five-star levels of comfort along with amenities that include a large swimming pool, fitness center and tennis courts. Inconveniently located in the north of town, the luxury

Pengaran's Beach Hotel ((751) 51333 FAX ((751) 54613, Jalan Ir. Juanda N°79, is a good place to be based if you want peace and quiet.

The **New Pangeran Hotel** ((751) 32133 FAX ((751) 27189, Jalan Dobi N°3–5, is a good mid-range hotel with a central location. The **Dipo International Hotel** ((751) 34261, Jalan Diponegoro N°25, offers still better value for money and has a good, central location.

The most popular backpacker hotel in town is the **Hotel Sriwijaya** ((751) 23577, Jalan Alangawas N°1/15, a small and friendly place whose restful atmosphere belies its central location.

Where to Eat

Padang is the home of Indonesian "fast food." *Nasi padang* is a spicy assortment of meat, fish and vegetables that are served in a dozen or more dishes. Accompanied by a steaming bowl of rice, the food is cooked in chili, coconut milk or curry. You eat only what you want and pay only for what you eat. **Simpang Raya**, Jalan Aziz Chan N°24, across from the post office, is a well managed chain that serves excellent Padang fare at a reasonable price. Also known for *nasi padang* is **Bopet Buyan** on Jalan Aziz Chan.

How to Get There and Away

Padang has international flights to Kuala Lumpur with Sempati and the Malaysian airline, Pelangi Air. Between them there are flights most days of the week. SilkAir and Merpati fly to Singapore regularly. On the domestic front, Merpati, Sempati, Mandala and SMAC fly to destinations in Java and Sumatra. Let a travel agent, such as Desa Air ((751) 23022, Jalan Permuda 23B, deal with the details.

For onward travel to Bukittinggi, buses leave from the central bus station and take just two hours — the blink of an eye in Sumatra. Travel agents in town can book tickets on PELNI boat services to Jakarta and Kalimantan.

BUKITTINGGI

After visiting Padang most travelers head straight for Bukittinggi, the highland center of the culture which has beautiful jungle trails leading out to villages famed for their arts

and crafts. Bukittinggi — the name means "high hill" — is a relaxed place and many visitors who arrive here from the hustle and bustle of steamy lowland Sumatra end up staying longer than they had planned.

General Information

The Bukittinggi Tourist Office ((752) 22403, next to the Clock Tower, is a friendly place that can help with tours and general information. It's closed on Sunday.

What to See and Do

Bukittinggi's main attractions are outside town, but there's also enough in town to keep you busy for a day. In the center of Bukittinggi is the town's foremost landmark, the clocktower, **Jam Gadang**, which has been keeping accurate time since 1827. Close by is the **Central Market**, the best place on Sumatra to find Minangkabau antiques and souvenirs; it expands exponentially on Wednesday and Saturdays, when weavers from Kota Gadang, come to town to sell elaborately embroidered shawls.

Fort de Kock dates back to 1825, when it was built by the Dutch as a defensive structure in the Padri Wars. Although there's not a great deal left to see, the fort ruins offer pleasant views over Bukittinggi and surroundings. From the fort you can take the footbridge to the **Taman Bundo Kanduang Park** where there is a small and uninspired **zoo**.

In the south of town is the **Panorama Park**, which overlooks the Ngarai Canyon, a four-kilometer (two-and-a-half-mile)-long chasm which is at its most impressive in the early light of dawn.

Where to Stay

Bukittinggi has a good range of accommodation. The best hotel in town is the central **Novotel Bukittinggi** ((752) 35000 FAX (752) 31123, at the intersection of jalans H Agus Salim and Istana, which offers luxury standards and facilities in surroundings that complement to a degree the exotic location. Also of a luxury standard and recommended is the **Meliá Confort Pusako Hotel** ((752) 32111 FAX (752) 32667, Jalan Soekarno–Hatta N°7, part of the Meliá group which is earning a fine reputation for hotel management in Indonesia.

In the mid-range bracket, the best deal is what was once Bukittinggi's top hostelry, the **Hotel Denai** ((752) 32920 FAX (752) 23490, Jalan Dr. Rivai N°26. The best rooms are undoubtedly the "superior" doubles. For something cheaper, try the **Benteng Hotel** ((752) 21115 FAX (752) 22596, Jalan Benteng N°1, which has a quiet but central location close to the fort, and has comfortable rooms at very reasonable prices.

There are quite a number of budget hotels around Bukittinggi, catering to backpackers who often linger for a week or more in the area. **Murni's** (no phone), Jalan Jend. Ahmad Yani N°115, is a popular place, as is the nearby **Nirwana** ((752) 21292.

Where to Eat
Padang cuisine is plentiful in Bukittinggi, and a good place to have some is the branch of the **Simpang Raya** chain, at Jalan Lantai N°2. For excellent Indonesian Chinese fare at bargain prices try the **Mona Lisa Restaurant** at Jalan Ahmad Yani N°3. The **Three Tables Coffeeshop**, Jalan Jend. Ahmad Yani N°142, is a popular international café with a good selection of Indonesian dishes and travelers' favorites such as fruit shakes and pancakes.

How to Get There and Away
Because Bukittinggi has no airport travelers are at the mercy of the Sumatran buses. Fortunately, the journey from Padang takes just two hours. In Padang traveling on north to Parapat (Lake Toba) and Medan or south to Palembang and Java, can get onward flights. Buses to Parapat take 12 hours, to Medan 18 hours.

AROUND BUKITTINGGI

Although Bukittinggi itself is a delightful spot to while away some time, the real attractions are outside town. The Minang Highlands is not only a fascinating repository of Minangkabau culture it also holds some splendid natural sights, such as **Lake Maninjau**, about 35 m (22 miles) to the west of Bukittinggi, the **Patuluh Rafflesia Reserve**, about 15 km (nine miles) north of town, the **Harau Valley**, east of Bukittinggi, and to the southeast the awesome volcanic peak of **Mt. Merapi.**

It's also worth visiting some of the traditional Minang villages in the region. Batu Sangkar is where many tourists are taken, but it's disappointingly touristy, even if the setting is magnificent. The village of **Baliambiang**, with its traditional timber houses, 10 km (six miles) to the south, is more rewarding. Pariangan on the slopes of Mt. Merapi is another fascinating Minangkabau village and one of the oldest in the Minang Highlands.

Because Bukittinggi's excursion sights are scattered over a large area, the best way to see them is with one of the many tours advertised in Bukittinggi at the travelers' restaurants and at travel agencies. If you don't want to travel en masse, organizing an individual tour is not particularly expensive. Don't attempt to climb Mt. Merapi without the help of an experienced local guide.

MENTAWAI ISLANDS

Four Mentawai Islands — **Siberut, Sipora, Pagai Utara** and **Pagai Selatan** — are parallel to and about 97 km (60 miles) from the west coast of Sumatra. The Mentawais are submerged mountains peaks that were separated from Sumatra during the Pleistocene Age and have since evolved in splendid isolation, protected by coral reefs, treacherous currents and unpredictable winds.

As late as 1980, the Mentawai islanders, who number 35,000 at most, still wore banana leaves, bark cloth sarongs and gave birth in the rivers. The policy of allowing only anthropologists to visit the islands is now long gone. These days permits are issued on arrival.

All of the schools and social services on the islands are run by missionaries, who have succeeded in converting about half the population to Christianity. Yet in practice, the Mentawai islanders remain animists who believe that everything from a rock to a rainbow contains spirits that must be appeased.

The only town worthy of the name in the Mentawais is **Muarasiberut** on **Siberut Island**. It's essentially a place to stock up on provisions. Accommodation is very limited and extremely basic. There is no reason, however, to go to Muarasiberut if you are not on a guided trek or tour that is going to take you out to some of the Mentawai villages. Be sure that your guide speaks Mentawai before setting out.

How to Get There and Away

Bukittinggi is the popular place to organize tours out to the Mentawai Islands, although it is also possible to arrange them out of Padang. Bear in mind that it can take two or three days to get out to the Mentawai Islands (there are no scheduled air services). A 10-day trek may only mean four to six days of actually being there, and four to six days of get-

Few visitors linger long in Medan. It has little to offer in the way of sights, and the sweltering humidity gives small incentive to seek out what few there are. If you are on a relaxed schedule, it may be worth staying overnight and doing a day tour of the attractions in an air-conditioned taxi or rented car.

GENERAL INFORMATION

The North Sumatran Tourist Office ((61) 538101 on Jalan Ahmad Yani N°107, is the best place for information and maps on

ting there and back. Access is via overnight boat services from Padang's port, Teluk Bayur.

MEDAN

Because its history is shaped by Malays, Javanese, Bataks and a host of Chinese, Arab and Indian traders, Medan is the ethnic melting pot of Sumatra. The largest city (population 2.1 million) on the island, and the fourth largest in Indonesia, Medan is Sumatra's main transportation hub, the place that most visitors see first. This is unfortunate since visitor's first impressions are consequently of the noise and air pollution which almost overwhelm the colonial mansions and old Dutch government buildings.

Medan and northern Sumatra. There's also a small tourist office at the airport, but it is of limited use.

WHAT TO SEE AND DO

Medan's chief attraction is **Maimoon Palace**, Jalan Katamso, which dates back to 1888 and once housed the sultans of Deli. It's a splendid building and the audience hall, which has some period furniture and portraits of the Deli royal family is open to the public. One wing of the building is still inhabited by the sultan's family. Very close by, on Jalan

Medan is famous for Dutch colonial buildings such as its main Post Office.

Sumatra   *187*

Mesji Raya, is the **Grand Mosque**, or Mesjid Raya. It's open to the public and entry is free, but you should give a small donation.

The **North Sumatra Regional Museum**, Jalan H.M. Joni N°51, has a fairly interesting selection of exhibits relating to North Sumatra, including some artifacts from Nias Island. Medan's **Taman Margasawata Zoo** and the much touted **Crocodile Park** are both best avoided.

There is no better way to end a day in Medan than with a pleasant stroll along Jalan Jend. Sudirman in the city's **Polonia** colonial quarter. Stately old plantation homes can also be found along Jalan Imam Bonjol and Jalan Balai Kota. Notable buildings include the **British Council** building and the central **Post Office**.

Products from all over Sumatra find their way to Medan, and most end up being sold in shops along Jalan Jend. Ahmad Yani. The chances of finding antique batik are slim, but reproductions of Batak calendars, statues and betel nut boxes are well made and worth buying after some spirited bargaining.

WHERE TO STAY

Luxury

The **Hotel Novotel Soeichi** ((61) 561234 FAX (61) 572222, Jalan Cirebon N°76A, is the best hotel in town, with foreign management, full health facilities, tennis courts, swimming pool and business facilities.

The **Danau Toba Hotel** ((61) 557000 FAX (61) 530553, Jalan Imam Bonjol N°17, is better located, not far from Merdeka Square, though not quite as professionally run as the Novotel. Nevertheless, with similar recreational facilities, along with some superb restaurants, it's a good luxury choice in the heart of downtown Medan.

The **Tiara Medan Hotel** ((61) 516000 FAX (61) 510176, Jalan Cut Mutiah, is one of Medan's longer-running luxury hotels, and recent renovations have maintained its competitive edge.

Moderate

Recommended in the upper end of the mid-range category is the old Hotel de Boer, now reincarnated as the **Dharma Delhi** ((61) 327011 FAX (61) 327153, Jalan Balai Kota N°2,

a charming place with a renovated colonial ambiance, gardens and a swimming pool. Even if you don't stay there it is worth a visit since its historical value to Medan is similar to that of the Raffles in Singapore or the E&O in Penang (Malaysia).

The **Hotel Garuda** ((61) 718553 FAX (61) 717975, Jalan Sisingamangaraja N°27, is not a particularly charming place, but it has a good location near the mosque, and it offers mid-range comfort at competitive prices.

Inexpensive

Backpackers head to budget *losmen* such as **Irama** ((61) 326416, Jalan Palang Merah N°112S or **Sarah's Guesthouse** ((61) 719460, Jalan Pertama N°10.

WHERE TO EAT

The **Tip Top Restaurant** on Jalan Jend. Ahmad Yani wins top marks for serving not only Western food but also *nasi padang*. The Tip Top has a stylish sidewalk café that is a good place to have afternoon tea. Also popular with expatriates is **Lynn's Bar**, Jalan Jend. Ahmad Yani N°98, which serves reliable generic Western cuisine and is also a good spot for drinks.

Medan is teeming with Chinese restaurants, some of which achieve the astonishing feat of serving porkless Chinese meals. The **Polonia Restaurant**, at the Polonia Hotel, Jalan Sudirman N°14, is a good place to try, as is the **Jumbo Restaurant**, Jalan Balai Kota.

Highly acclaimed by locals for its fried chicken is **Ayam Goreng Kalasan**, Jalan Iskanda Muda N°294. You will also see a familiar fried chicken vendor in several locations around town: **KFC**. The fast-food chain is joined by **Pizza Hut**, which has a branch on Jalan Sudirman.

HOW TO GET THERE AND AWAY

Medan has one of the most active airports in Indonesia and is well served by both domestic and international carriers. Singapore Airlines ((61) 537744 and SilkAir ((61) 514488 fly from Singapore; MAS ((61) 519333 flies from Kuala Lumpur and Penang; Thai International ((61) 514483 flies from Bangkok via Phuket; and Garuda ((61)

538527 flies direct from as far afield as Frankfurt, Germany.

Domestic connections are also excellent, with most major Indonesian destinations being served by the usual array of carriers: Garuda, Merpati ℂ (61) 514102, SMAC ℂ (61) 537760, Bouraq ℂ (61) 552333, Mandala ℂ (61) 516379, and Sempati ℂ (61) 537800.

For onward travel to Malaysia, an alternative to flying is to take one of the high-speed hydrofoil boat services between Penang and Medan's port of Belawan. The hydrofoils do the crossing in four or five hours.

renowned as a fierce and forthright people, were still eating each other until quite recently. Lake Toba wasn't "discovered" until the 1850s, though once it was the European missionaries moved in quickly to guide locals away from the errors of their pagan ways.

Though many of the northern Batak groups remain animist, a century of Christian missionary work has transformed the population around Lake Toba into Protestants. The Batak are skilled woodcarvers who decorate many of their artifacts with graphically carved fertility symbols.

THE BATAK HIGHLANDS: LAKE TOBA AND SAMOSIR ISLAND

Sumatra is home to about two million Batak tribespeople, the majority of whom live in the Batak Highlands around Lake Toba, a volcanic crater lake 732 m (2,400 ft) above sea level.

The origin of the Bataks is uncertain. They may have migrated from the highlands of Burma and Thailand; they may have come from Borneo and the Philippines. Whatever their origins, when Europeans first came across them in the eighteenth century, the world was startled to hear of this remote people with a writing system and complex society who were also cannibals. The Bataks,

Lake Toba, 161 km (100 miles) south of Medan, is a pristine crater lake that surrounds **Samosir**, an island larger than that of the Republic of Singapore. It is one of the most beautiful natural attractions in all of Southeast Asia. On Samosir it is possible to rent traditional Batak houses right on the lake, though many travelers head for the more commodious lodgings found in **Parapat**, on Lake Toba's eastern shore. Whatever sort of accommodation you decide on, Lake Toba is a cool and tranquil alternative to the traffic and humidity of towns along the coast.

Samosir Island has excellent examples of Indonesian architecture.

Samosir is regarded by many as a place to relax and swim, but travelers who opt to leave their bungalows can take one of several cross-island treks through beautiful alpine forest land.

WHERE TO STAY

Accommodation at Lake Toba is concentrated in two areas: Parapat, on the eastern shore of the lake, and the Tomok–Tuk Tuk area directly adjacent Parapat on Samosir. Rates are slightly higher at Parapat, but in

both areas accommodation rates are expensive in comparison to rates in Medan. A ferry connects the two areas.

In Parapat, the better hotels are by the lakeside. Be warned that heavy bookings are the norm on weekends and public holidays, when vacationers from Medan, Singapore and Malaysia descend on Toba. The **Patra Jasa Parapat** ((625) 41706 is a bungalow hotel in the Parapat suburb of Siuhan near Lake Toba. It has a swimming pool, tennis courts and a golf course, and it commands splendid views of the lake.

The **Hotel Natour Parapat** ((625) 41012, Jalan Marihat N°1, is a restored Dutch hotel with a beachside location. It has long been the best of Parapat's hotels.

Close to the Samosir ferry pier, the **Danau Toba International Cottages** ((625) 41583 Jalan Nelson Purba, are a less expensive option, with comfortable rooms by the lakeside.

On Samosir Island the bulk of the accommodation is found at **Tuk Tuk**. It's not the kind of place where you make reservations. Travelers typically just turn up here and look around for a vacancy, choosing from dozens of family-run bungalow guesthouses such as **Bagus**, **Rumba**, **Romlam** and **Tony's**.

For something a little more upmarket, the **Toledo Inn** ((645) 41181, is a long-running and popular mid-range hotel with a good swimming beach. Another good choice is **Carolina's** ((645) 41520, an extremely popular place where bungalows range from functional and cheap to well-appointed and mid-range. The hotel has an excellent restaurant, an isolated swimming cove, and it rents motorbikes to guests. Reservations are essential, especially in the summer.

HOW TO GET THERE AND AWAY

Access to Lake Toba and Samosir Island is via Parapat. With a car or by bus the journey takes four to five hours. Most travelers book a seat in a van operated by one of Medan's numerous travel agencies.

Once on Samosir you can get around by walking, renting a motorbike or waiting for a *bemo* to come your way.

NIAS ISLAND

The Indian Ocean island of Nias, just north of the Mentawais, is studded with reminders of a megalithic stone age culture that once measured wealth and status in terms of pigs and human skulls taken in battle. Priapic obelisks and stone monoliths guard villages decorated with intricate stonecarvings and paved with flagstones.

The Nias Island sport of jumping one-and-a-half-meter (five-foot) stone columns

ABOVE: Lake Toba is the ancestral home of Sumatra's Batak highlanders. RIGHT: Boats provide transportation around Lake Toba communities.

was originally a way of training warriors, who needed to be able to jump over stone walls when they attacked enemy villages. In ancient times, bamboo spikes affixed to the top of the pillars provided additional incentive for the jumpers to strive for that extra height.

Today, stone jumping is a gymnastic practice rather than a preparation for battle. But villages such as Bawomataluo and Hili Simaetano, where stone houses are covered with bas-relief carvings, evoke images of the villages' combative past.

WHERE TO STAY

There are two main centers for lodging: **Gunung Sitoli**, which is where flights arrive; and **Lagundri Beach**, in the southern part of the island.

Accommodation is limited at both locations, but it is particularly limited at Gunung Sitoli. If you fly in to Nias and have the energy to continue on the same day, head for Lagundri, though be aware that the mere 80-km (50-mile) drive south can take longer

Travel Advisory: Chloroquine-resistant malaria is a problem on Nias. If you plan to visit the island, consult your doctor before you setting out.

WHAT TO SEE AND DO

From all over the world, surfers come to Nias' **Lagundri Beach**, 13 km (eight miles) from the port of **Teluk Dalam** in the south of the island. For non-surfers the favored activity here is lounging about in the sun.

Ask at hotel about treks to Nias' megalithic villages. A wide variety of trips are available, ranging from one-day outings into the hills to two- or three-day excursions staying in villages en route. Prices are inexpensive.

than four hours depending on the state of the road.

In Gunung Sitoli, the popular place to stay — some would say the only place to stay — is the **Wisma Soliga** ((639) 21815, which has a good range of rooms from simple fan-cooled to air-conditioned. It's four kilometers (just over two miles) out of town, but transport is easy to organize, and it has a good restaurant.

The choice of lodgin in Lagundri is much wider. The **Sorake Beach Resort** ((639) 21195, offers package-tour type beach huts at lower luxury rates, and discounts are usually available for anyone who asks politely. For inexpensive guesthouse accommodation, **Sea Breeze**, right on the beach, has better than average bungalows and a good restaurant.

HOW TO GET THERE AND AWAY

The quickest way to get to Nias Island is to take the SMAC flight from Medan to Gunung Sitoli. SMAC ((61) 537760 has an office at Jalan Imam Bonjol N°59, where you should certainly go a day prior to your departure to confirm your flight, as SMAC's tiny commuter aircraft can keep an erratic schedule.

There are regular ferry services from Sibolga (in North Sumatra) to Nias Island.

ACEH

Aceh, at the northern tip of Sumatra, is one of the least-visited provinces of all Indonesia. Staunchly Islamic, it has gained a reputation for unfriendliness and even xenophobia. But while this is not an easy province to find your way around in — some Indonesian is essential if you're traveling independently—it's by no means the haven of zealotry that some make it out to be. That said, unescorted women would be wise to

Boats which make the nine-hour trip to Gunung Sitoli leave from the new harbor of Pelabuhan Baru. Ferries making the 12-hour trip to the more popular destination of Teluk Dalam in southern Nias leave from the old harbor of Pelabuhan Lama.

Apart from being the jumping-off point for crossings to Nias Island, **Sibolga** is also well known for its offshore diving. In Sibolga itself, **the Sibolga Marine Resort** ((631)-23588 FAX (631)-23338, North Sumatra, conducts dives out to such attractions as Bata Memara (Tower Rock), where divers can swim amongst clownfish, cardinal fish and blue-spotted stingrays. For SCUBA diving enthusiasts, Sibolga is a great destination to aim for.

avoid this province, and those accompanied by a man should nevertheless wear long dresses and a veil.

Aceh was the first Indonesian region to come into contact with the outside world. Chinese chronicles written in the early sixth century speak of a kingdom on the northern tip of Sumatra called Po-Li. By 1292, when Marco Polo passed through the area, more than six trading posts were active in region of Aceh.

Islam is believed to have reached Aceh sometime between the seventh and eighth centuries, and the first Islamic kingdom,

OPPOSITE: The Grand Mosque in Banda Aceh symbolizes Indonesia's Islamic revival. ABOVE: Acehnese fishing trawlers ply the Malacca Strait.

Perlak, was established in 804. When the Portuguese captured Malacca in 1511, most of the Arab spice traders moved their facilities to Aceh, further enriching the area. By the start of the nineteenth century Aceh found itself in the middle of the struggle between Britain and Holland for regional hegemony. The 1824 Treaty of London gave the Dutch control of all British possessions in Sumatra, but when the Dutch finally moved north of Medan to impose their authority the Acehnese rebelled. The Aceh War, which continued intermittently from 1873 to 1942, was the longest ever fought by Holland, and cost 10,000 Dutch lives.

WHAT TO SEE AND DO

The capital of Aceh province is **Bandar Aceh**, an interesting city to explore on foot, though much of its architectural legacy was destroyed in the struggle against the Dutch in the late nineteenth century. The **Regional Tourist Office** ((651) 23692 is at Jalan Cik Kuta Karang N°3.

Start your sightseeing rounds at the **Grand Mosque** (Mesjid Raya Baiturraman) in the center of town. It was built by the Dutch in 1881 to replace the one they had destroyed in earlier fighting. To the south, on Jalan Teuk, is the **Gunongan**, all that remains of the Royal Pleasure Grounds built during the early seventeenth century by Sultan Iskanda Muda. Opposite is the **Dutch Cemetery**, otherwise known as the Kerkhof, where over 2,000 Dutch and Dutch-employed Indonesian soldiers lie buried, casualties in the Aceh War. The **Aceh Museum**, to the east, located on Jalan Alauddin Mahmudsyah, has an interesting collection of artifacts related to Aceh.

WHERE TO STAY

The **Kuala Tripa Hotel** ((651) 21455, at Jalan Ujong Rimba N°24, is a good upper mid-range place to stay, with a swimming pool and other luxuries. For something less expensive, try the **Hotel Parapat** ((651) 22159, Jalan Jend. Ahmad Yani N°17, a clean and well organized place with both inexpensive fan-cooled rooms and slightly more luxurious air-conditioned rooms.

HOW TO GET THERE AND AWAY

Garuda ((651) 22469 flies daily to Bandar Aceh from Medan, while Pelangi ((651) 21705 connects Bandar Aceh with Penang and Kuala Lumpur in Malaysia.

AROUND BANDAR ACEH

The main attraction in the vicinity of Bandar Aceh is Weh Island, a beautiful retreat with snorkeling and palm-fringed beaches. The most popular beach is **Iboih**, and there is simple beach-hut accommodation there for those who don't mind doing without their comforts. There is more accommodation in the main town of Sabang, but again it is fairly basic. There are ferries to Weh, daily from the port of Krueng Raya, which is around 30 km (19 miles) east of Bandar Aceh.

GUNUNG LEUSER NATIONAL PARK

Gunung Leuser National Park, accessible from either Kutacane or Takingeun, is Indonesia's largest and has research facilities for the study of birds, insects and small mammals. I It is of interest mostly for its **Orangutan Rehabilitation Center**, which is accessible from **Bukit Lawang** on the eastern edge of the park.

Orangutan is a Malay word that translates as "man of the forest," and orangutans do resemble humans in many ways. Unlike chimpanzees or gorillas, orangutans can walk upright, pick up tools and "reason" in a way that suggests the species has human-like thought processes based on logic. Sumatra and Borneo are the only two places where orangutans exist in the wild, and here they are dwindling fast because of unrestricted logging and their susceptibility to human diseases when captured.

The Dutch started the practice of capturing baby orangutans, killing their parents, and raising the young primates as household pets. Though outlawed in 1931, Indonesians continue the practice. When domesticated orangutans are discovered by

police (often they are abandoned once they grow old), they are sent to the rehabilitation center which tries to teach them the skills they need to return to life in the forest.

GENERAL INFORMATION

In order to enter Gunung Leuser you need a permit and a guide. Both can be organized at the Park Headquarters (no phone), which is in the town of Tanah Merah, around five kilometers (three miles) north of Kutacane. There is also a small tourist information office in Kutacane itself. The same applies for the Orangutan Rehabilitation Center, and permits can be obtained with no fuss and a small fee at the Indonesian Directorate of Nature Conservation (PHPA) office in Bukit Lawang.

WHERE TO STAY

There is budget accommodation in Bukit Lawang (where the choice is wider) and in Kutacane.

HOW TO GET THERE AND AWAY

Bukit Lawang is three hours from Medan by bus or car. Kutacane is a longer, six-hour journey from Medan.

Infant orangutans in a pensive moment.

Sulawesi

ous destinations around the archipelago. For the latest schedules check with PELNI ((411) 313393, Jalan Sudirman N°38, or with a local travel agent.

PARE PARE

Sulawesi's second largest city, Pare Pare, has virtually nothing in the way of sights; however, some travelers opt to stop here for the night in order to break their 10-hour bus journey to Tanatoraja into two five-hour segments. Pare Pare is also the place to catch boats to Kalimantan.

The top accommodation in town, the **Hotel Gandaria** ((421) 21093, Jalan Baumassepe N°171, is decidedly mid-range verging on budget. All the same, it's a friendly place,

and the attached alfresco restaurant is a pleasant spot for a meal.

Boats leave for Balikpapan and Samarinda in Kalimantan on a regular basis, though some of the non-PELNI services are best avoided — take a look at the boat you will be traveling on before committing yourself to anything. PELNI ((411) 21017 has an office at Jalan Andicammi N°130.

TANATORAJA

Sulawesi's most exotic locale, Tanatoraja, is a scenic highland where the Toraja people place their deceased in caves and limestone niches overlooking their villages. Many of

The dead watch the living in Tanatoraja.

the dead are interred standing up in tree trunk sarcophagi. Others are placed alongside wooden effigies carved to resemble the deceased. In the villages of **Lemo** and **Londa** past generations sit in their limestone balconies, watching over their progeny and paddy fields.

According to the Toraja, death is the main event in the cycle of life. Though mourning families wear black and symbolically sacrifice a cat to underscore their grief, funerals are actually celebrations replete with feasts and dancing that can last up to a week, depending on the importance of the deceased. Tourists are welcome to attend and photograph funerals, which culminate with the blood sacrifice of pigs and water buffalo.

The Toraja live in large saddle-shaped houses whose high pitched roofs are covered with geometric designs and adorned with buffalo horns, the number and size of which are determined by the family's rank in the community.

RANTEPAO

The main town in Tanatoraja, Rantepao has a number of hotels and restaurants as well as tour operators who can arrange trips to colorful villages such as **Kete** where life-size statues guard coffins. **Londa** offers more of the same with the additional attraction of visits to caves where you can wander among the skeletons.

One way to get to see the area and to meet locals (and perhaps be invited to a funeral) is to join a small group on a trek into the countryside. A reliable trekking agency that does two- to five-day trips is **Satrya** ((423) 21336, in Rantepao.

If you don't join an organized tour you will need to spend some time in Rantepao and the nearby villages in order to get to know locals before an invitation to a funeral comes your way.

Where to Stay

Rantepao, long the preserve of budget travelers, is now home to some quite luxurious hotel developments. The **Marante Highland Resort** ((423) 21616 FAX (423) 21122 is, like most of the better places, out of town, but if

you're staying here it's unlikely you will need to venture into Rantepao. The resort has tasteful Toraja style units and a swimming pool. More of the same, but at slightly lower rates, can be found at the **Toraja Prince** ((423) 21304 FAX 21369.

Built around a quiet courtyard, the **Hotel Indra** ((423) 21583 FAX 21547 has been completely rebuilt in recent years and is now a good mid-range value. The building, which employs traditional Toraja architecture, has a reasonably priced restaurant that looks out over a tropical garden.

One of Rantepao's most popular mid-range hotels is **Toraja Cottages** ((423) 21089 FAX 21369. It sees a lot of tour group traffic but is nevertheless an attractive place, with pleasant bungalows spread around attractive gardens.

There is no shortage of budget *wisma* (guesthouses) and *losmen* (homestays) in Rantepao. Some recommended places are the **Mace Homestay** ((423) 21852, Jalan Tenko Saturu N°4, the **Wisma Maria** ((423) 21165, Jalan Ratulangi N°23, and the **Wisma Martini**

OPPOSITE and ABOVE: The size of the horns decorating a home indicates the family's status in the community, South Sulawesi, Toraja. OVERLEAF: The pageantry of a Torajan funeral ceremony.

((423) 21240, Jalan Ratulangi N°62, all of which have peaceful garden areas and a homey ambiance. Rates are very inexpensive.

Where to Eat

Most of the budget *wisma* and *losmen* have attached restaurants, and it's worth dining in at least one of these if you're in Rantepao for a couple of days.

The **Restaurant Rachmat** on Jalan Abdul Gani in Rantepao has the best European cuisine in Tanatoraja. Almost as good, and quite a bit cheaper, is **Kiosk Mamba**, a modest yet excellently managed restaurant on Jalan Ratulangi, just north of Wisma Monika.

The friendliest restaurant in Rantepao is **Chez Dodeng**, a family-run café on Jalan Mappanyuki diagonally across from the Hotel Victoria. The café provides excellent food and the staff can also furnish information on upcoming ceremonies and other attractions. On the same street is **Indograce**, a slightly more upmarket restaurant that along with Chinese and Indonesian favorites also serves some Torajan specialties such as *papiong*, a delicious fish and meat stew.

How to Get There and Away

Most people visiting Rantepao for the first time drive one way and fly the other. Merpati ((423) 21485 has daily flights from Ujung Padang to Pongtiku Airport, around 20 km (12 miles) south of Rantepao. Bear in mind, however, that delays, cancellations and overbookings are not unusual. A bus, which takes 10 hours from Ujung Padang, is a less comfortable but more dependable mode of conveyance.

The best times to visit are May and September. In July and August European package tourists descend on the area.

CENTRAL AND SOUTHEAST SULAWESI

Sulawesi is the third most visited island in the Indonesian Archipelago, but few tourists venture into the rugged and underpopulated central and southeastern peninsulas. The main industry in the southeast is mining. Large nickel mines outside Soroako and smaller silver mines farther south provide some employment and lots of crudely-fash-

ioned jewelry for sale in **Kendari**. The bulk of the province, however, is given over to subsistence farming, mostly by Balinese sent into the jungle under the government *transmigrasi* program. The farmers are essentially pioneers, relocated from overcrowded to undeveloped areas. Because the land is so poor, the failure rate is high.

Beyond the capital of **Palu**, Central Sulawesi is mostly jungle. In theory, the province has an adequate network of roads, but in reality all movement comes to a halt during the rainy season.

Travel in these two provinces can be a fascinating adventure, but a day spent wrenching your jeep out of Central Sulawesi's thigh-deep mud can be tedious indeed, and a night spent camping beside the Wotu to Poso road may have you going *mano a mano* with some of the largest insects in the Indonesian archipelago.

PALU

Palu, a city of 150,000 and the capital of Central Sulawesi, has some nearby beaches, but apart from this its chief interest for travelers is as pit-stop on the overland road from the south to north.

General Information

The Central Sulawesi Tourism Agency ((451) 21793, Jalan Moili N°103, can be skipped unless you're desperate for help.

What to See and Do

As is the case with all provincial capitals, Palu has a museum. The **Museum of Central Sulawesi**, Jalan Sapiri N°23, has an unambitious collection of artifacts mostly of an ethnographic nature. The megaliths outside are reproductions of stone figures of unknown provenance from Central Sulawesi's remote Lore Lindu National Park.

Palu's beach is not a surf and sand paradise, but 35 km (20 miles) north of town is the unspoiled beach resort of **Donggala**. There's a foreign-run budget resort at nearby Tanjung Karang called **Prinz John Dive Resort**, where you can rent snorkeling and diving equipment. If you have time, this is a pleasant place to stay for a day or so. The resort has an informal restaurant.

Where to Stay and Eat

The **Palu Golden Hotel** ((451) 21126 FAX ((451) 23230, Jalan Raden Saleh N°1, has a private beach and a swimming pool but is otherwise an unremarkable luxury hotel. The **Sentral Hotel** ((451) 22789, Jalan Kartini N°6, is a clean and well run mid-range hotel and, all things considered, a better choice at less than half the price of the Palu Golden. The **Purnama Raya Hotel** ((451) 23646, Jalan Wahidin N°4, is popular with budget travelers.

For excellent Chinese food, seek out the **New Oriental Restaurant** on Jalan Hasanuddin II. You'll probably meet other travelers there. On Jalan Wahidin, the **Ramayana Restaurant** does Indonesian and Chinese dishes.

How to Get There and Away

Palu's Mutiara Airport is around six kilometers (four miles) east of town, and receives a surprisingly large number of daily flights from Ujung Padang and farther afield. Merpati ((451) 21271 has the most flights. Bouraq ((451) 21195 has flights to Kalimantan and, importantly, to Manado in North Sulawesi.

Bear in mind that buses to Manado can take as long as 36 bone-jarring hours. It's possible to stop at Gorontalo en route, but it takes 24 hours to get to Gorontalo. However you look at it, bus travel in this neck of the woods is an ordeal.

NORTH SULAWESI

North Sulawesi is a rugged peninsula 777 km (482 miles) long and 103 km (64 miles) wide that is dominated by six extinct volcanoes and enormous coconut and clove plantations. Thanks to the rich volcanic soil the Minahasan people are among the most prosperous in Indonesia.

Because of North Sulawesi's proximity to established trade routes, it was visited early and often by European sailors. The Minahasans hated the Portuguese and Spanish, however, and were forever grateful to the Dutch for ousting the Iberian Catholics. In return for their liberation the Minahasans by the early nineteenth century had embraced Protestantism, volunteered for the Dutch

colonial army and become so loyal that Minahasa soon became known as the "twelfth province of Holland."

The people of North Sulawesi still refer to their province as Minahasa and often appear to have more in common with the Philippines than Indonesia. In contrast to Ujung Padang, which exudes anarchic cacophony, Manado, the province's main city, seems almost European. Here the imam's call to prayer is replaced by church bells, and the large wooden houses are bordered by rose gardens and white picket fences.

MANADO

The center of Minahasan culture is a sophisticated city of approximately 300,000 people. Indonesians consider the fair skinned women of Manado to be the most beautiful in the entire archipelago. Certainly they are the most Westernized, preferring to wear tight T-shirts and blue jeans instead of the traditional *sarong kebaya*.

Largely rebuilt after World War II, Manado has few buildings of historical importance. The heart of the city is a commercial center called **Pasar 45**. From Pasar 45 you can walk south along Jalan Sam Ratulangi to the hotel and restaurant area, or north to the **Kuala Jenki** fish market.

Manado is a favorite destination for SCUBA enthusiasts. **Bunaken**, **Manado Tua** and **Siladen Sea Gardens** are famous coral reefs that ring three small islands just offshore. Boats, snorkeling equipment and certified

The Minahasan people of Northern Sulawesi are English-speaking Catholics more culturally attuned to Manila than Jakarta.

guides can be hired at the **Nusantara Diving Club** ((431) 63988 FAX (431) 60368 at Malalayang Beach. Experienced divers claim that the clear water, myriad varieties of fish and spectacular drop-offs make these reefs some of the best diving in the world. Other local dive operators in Manado include: Barracuda Diving Resort ((431) 854279 FAX (431) 864848, Molas Dusun II, and Murex Manado Dive Resort ((431) 66280 FAX (431) 52116, Jalan Jend, Sudirman N°28.

General Information

While Manado does have a couple of tourist offices, the small number of foreign tourist passing through means that they are unlikely to be prepared for your arrival. The **North Sulawesi Tourist Office** ((431) 64299, is out of town on Jalan 17 Augustus. There's another **tourist office** ((451) 51723 at Jalan Diponegoro N°111, but it has little in the way of practical information.

Where to Stay

The **Sedona Hotel Manado** ((0431) 871205 FAX (0431) 871206 at Tateli Beach, 25 km (16 miles) from downtown Manado opened in 1998. The 247 rooms and suites all have private balconies overlooking the sea.

The **Kawanua City Hotel** ((431) 67777 FAX (431) 65220, Jalan Sam Ratulangi N°1, has a central location, but despite luxury pretensions it's not particularly good value for money. For central living, you're much better off opting for the moderately priced **Hotel New Queen** ((431) 65979 FAX 65748, Jalan Wakeke N°12–14, a small, quiet and friendly place.

The inexpensive **Rex Hotel** ((431) 51136, Jalan Soegiono N°3, is a no-nonsense basic hostel, but popular all the same.

Where to Eat

Minahasan food is an acquired taste. Sure, you may like it, but will you feel the same way when you discover that the juicy *kawaok* you washed down with Bintang beer was a fried forest rat? Stewed bat, goldfish (*ikan mas*) and dog cutlets with chili (*rintek wuk*) are also local favorites. If after this introduction you still want to try Minahasan fare, go to **Tinoor Jaya** at Jalan Sam Ratulangi. Along the same street are a good number of Chinese

restaurants, such as the popular and recommended **Xanadu**.

With stewed bat and goldfish on the menu, you may find yourself longing for familiar culinary treats. If so look for **KFC** on Jalan Sam Ratulangi, next to the Matahari department store.

How to Get There and Away

Manado has international connections to Singapore with SilkAir ((431) 863844 or (431) 863744 and to Davao in the Philippines with Bouraq ((431) 62757. The latter has the most efficient schedule in and out of Manado; its office is at Jalan Sarapung N°27. In addition to daily flights from Gorontalo, Palu and Ujung Padang, Bouraq also has reasonably priced daily service from Jakarta, Yogyakarta and Balikpapan. Sempati (JAKARTA (21) 51612 also has some useful connections.

As in many Indonesian cities the permutations of getting away by air can be confusing. Pola Pelita Express ((431) 60007, Jalan Sam Ratulangi N°113, can give you the run down on who flies when and for how much.

Also on Jalan Sam Ratulangi is the PELNI office ((431) 62844 which sells tickets for the bewildering number of passenger ships that wend their ways around the archipelago. Again, local travel agents such as Pola Pelita can help with schedules and bookings.

There are three bus stations in Manado and, in theory, one can drive all the way to Ujung Padang, a three-day bump-fest that is only for the mad or foolhardy.

Coral just below the surface of the clear, placid waters of Manado Tua.

negara, a few kilometers inland from Mataram. Built in 1720 to unify Lombok's various Hindu factions, the inner courtyard has three pagodas symbolizing the Hindu trinity of Brahma, Wisnu and Shiva. The **Mayura Water Palace** is notable mostly for its artificial lake filled with pink and white lotus in the middle of which sits a pavilion that once served as the court of justice and meeting place for Lombok's nobles. The gardens here make for a pleasant stroll.

On Jalan Panji Tilar Negara in Ampenan is the **Museum Nusa Tenggara**, which has

pool and restaurant but has significantly less expensive rates. If you like, you can easily take a look at both of these hotels, as they are within easy walking distance of each other.

There are a large number of budget *losmen* in Ampenan. The **Wisma Triguna** ((364) 31705, Jalan Koperasi N°76, is a good choice. It's slightly away from the center, but the large rooms and quiet courtyard and restaurant make up for this.

In Ampenan try the popular **Cirebon Restaurant**, Jalan Yos Sudarso N°113, which

informative displays on Lombok and Sumbawa, particularly on local *kris* and textiles. The museum is open 8 AM to 4 PM every day except Monday.

Where to Stay and Eat

Few travelers stay in town, the vast majority of them opting to head out to Senggigi, Lombok's most developed beach area, 15 km (nine miles) to the north.

The best hotel in the area is the **Hotel Lombok Raya** ((364) 32305 FAX 36478, Jalan Panca Usaha N°11, Mataram, which is a high-class mid-range hotel with business facilities and a swimming pool. Just around the corner is the **Hotel Granada** ((364) 36015, Jalan Bung Karno, which also has a

has a good selection of Chinese and Indonesian favorites. Cakranegara is the place to look for fast food.

Shopping

Antique shops in Ampenan carry three grades of baskets ranging from delicate ones made of horse hair-sized fibers to ones large and sturdy enough to be used as clothes hampers. Jug-shaped, round-bellied baskets sell for US$20 on Lombok, about half what they go for on Bali and a third of what they cost in Jakarta. There are two or three excellent stores (credit cards are not accepted),

OPPOSITE: A boy and his net in Lombok.
ABOVE: Fishermen cast their nets off the Lombok coast.

the best of which is **Sudirman**, Jalan Pabean N°16A.

Lombok textiles use a rainbow of colors to create striped panels which are sewn together to make sarongs. Equally distinctive is the terracotta ware, especially in the village of Penujak where a cooperative of local artisans turns out bowls, jugs and mammoth water jars. In contrast to sinuous Balinese masks and statues, Lombok woodcarvings tend to have strong, primitive lines. Sexual motifs are common, as are dragons which decorate the tops of medi-

cine containers and special boxes that hold spurs for fighting cocks.

How to Get There and Away

Lombok's Selaparang Airport is close to Ampenan and there are plenty of moderately priced taxis available. Sweta, to the east, is the place to go for bus connections to destinations around the island. *Bemo*s to Senggigi Beach leave from Ampenan as well as Sweta.

SENGGIGI

Senggigi, a developed beach resort, is Lombok's Kuta Beach, though it never reaches the excesses of the latter. (If you want something pristine, head for the beaches farther north or to the Gili Islands.) The beaches slope steeply down into the Lombok Strait — the so-called Wallace Line between Asia and Australasia.

Just a little south of Senggigi, look for the only bona-fide "sight" — **Batu Belong Temple**, a Balinese temple oriented in such

a way that it makes a good vantage point to watch the sun set over Mt. Agung.

In Lombok, Baruna Watersports ((364) 93333 FAX (364) 93140, at the Sheraton Senggigi Beach Resort (see below), can organize dives around the island, where beaches and the diving tend to be better than on its nearby and much more heavily touristed neighbor, Bali. The best diving and snorkeling is on Lombok's Gili Islands (see below).

Where to Stay and Eat

The **Sheraton Senggigi Beach Resort** ((364) 93333 FAX (364) 93140, with its extensive palm-fringed lagoon and poolside rooms is Senggigi's best accommodation and indeed one of the best on the island. Among its many selling points are its special facilities for children.

More luxury beachside accommodation can be found at the **Holiday Inn Resort** ((364) 93444 FAX (364) 93092, which is a good alternative to the Sheraton, especially out of season, when substantial discounts are available.

The first luxury hotel to be built on Senggigi was Aerowisata's **Senggigi Beach Hotel** ((364) 93210 FAX (364) 93200, and it is still one of the most attractive hotels on the island with possibly the best position. Good food, great sunsets.

For moderately priced accommodation a good choice is the **Pacific Beach Cottages** ((364) 93006 FAX 93027 at the quieter, less developed northern end of Senggigi. Like a scaled down version of a luxury hotel, the Pacific Beach has a small swimming pool and cottages that come complete with air conditioning, televisions and hot water.

Continue farther north from here towards Mangset and prices begin to drop, and the cottage operations take on a family-run atmosphere. The **Santai Cottages** ((364) 93038 conform to this tendency; this is the perfect spot to get away from it all.

Senggigi's restaurant scene is dominated by the hotels and cottages. Feel free to explore them. You are by no means obliged — though cheaper hotels prefer it — to eat at your hotel. One of the few independent restaurants in Senggigi is the **Café Wayang**, a branch of the celebrated Ubud restaurant on Bali. It's well worth visiting for an evening meal.

How to Get There and Away
Senggigi is easily accessible from Ampenan and Sweta by *bemo*. If you're flying in to Lombok, you can take a taxi direct to Senggigi from the airport for under US$5.

AROUND SENGGIGI

To get to Senggigi's outlying attractions by public transport you will need to backtrack to Sweta. It's a better idea to rent a vehicle. With a car you can visit **Narmada**, where there is a Balinese temple and an artificial lake both dating back to 1805. Close by, to the north, is **Lingsar**, another Balinese temple that faces Mt. Agung. It was built in 1714. **Suranadi**, to the east of Lingsar, is another temple complex worth visiting.

GILI ISLANDS

As anyone who's been to Indonesia can tell you, the Gili Islands, a popular tropical idyll, are inappropriately named, since *gili* means "island." Nevertheless, that is the name, and even locals will know where you want to go when you say effectively you're going to the "Island Islands."

There are three islands here — **Gili Air**, **Gili Meno** and **Gili Trewangan** — and they're easily accessible from Bangsal on the mainland by way of a 30- to 45-minute boat ride. Gili Trewangan, the largest and farthest away of the three, is the most developed and most popular, but it has also suffered in disputes over land leases and parts of the island that were once thriving are now "ghost beaches." Still, if it's snorkeling and diving, and perhaps a little nightlife you want, Gili Trewangan is the best choice.

The Gili Islands, despite persistent rumors of luxury resort developments, is mostly a haven for young — predominantly European — backpackers, but it's not all basic *losmen* accommodation.

Where to Stay and Eat
It's almost impossible to make recommendations for the Gili Islands, there are so many similar inexpensive cottage outfits. If you're

looking for some comfort Gili Meno has a couple of good mid-range hotels. The **Gazebo Resort** ((364) 35795 is a lovely place, laid out in the Balinese style, and a perfect retreat for those who can't do without air conditioning and a Continental breakfast. The **Bougenvil Resort** ((364) 27435 is another mid-range option on Gili Meno, but it lacks the charm of the Gazebo, despite the additional allure of a swimming pool.

Elsewhere around Gili Air and Gili Trewangan you will have no trouble finding dozens of inexpensive family-run operations

with simple cottages and home-cooked meals. Take a look at a few places before making a decision.

How to Get There and Away
Access to the Gilis is via Bangsal. Getting there from the airport or from Ampenan means a *bemo* ride to Pemenang, where you catch a *cidomo* — from Lombok's fleet of horse and cart taxis — to Bangsal. It's easiest, however, to charter a taxi all the way from the airport or from Ampenan. Scheduled boats leave for the islands at around 10 AM, but it should also be possible to charter one inexpensively.

OPPOSITE: Lombok nobility built the Puri Mayura water garden. Balinese temples ABOVE can be found along Lombok's western coast.

SIRA

Sira is a newly developing beach resort at Medana on the north coast of Lombok, near the jumping-off point for the Gili Islands. It has picture-postcard white-sand beaches and will probably emerge as one of Lombok's most exclusive getaways in years to come.

The **Oberoi** chain opened a resort here in late 1997, the **Oberoi Lombok (** (370) 38444 FAX (370) 32496, where 50 beautiful, luxury *lumbung* style villas (a *lumbung* is a traditional rice barn) with individual walled gardens, and two fine restaurants give way to the beach. Bookings can also be made through the **Bali Oberoi (** (361) 730361 FAX (361) 730791.

MT. RINJANI

Indonesia's second highest volcano, the 3,700-m (12,200-ft) **Mt. Rinjani** with its sacred waterfalls, hot springs and crater lake, is Lombok's answer to Bali's Mt. Agung. Like Agung, it's still an active volcano, as an eruption in 1994 reminded everyone.

Hikers can make a strenuous two-day ascent of **Mt. Rinjani**, whose pine-rimmed crater lake, Segara Negara, is believed to be the throne room of the mountain gods. Rinjani's summit towers 1,200 m (4,000 ft) above the lake, which feeds streams that cascade over cliffs into hot springs below.

It is possible, but not particularly sensible, to climb Rinjani without a guide — this is a big mountain, and its ascent is no picnic. Organized treks can be found easily in Senggigi and Mataram, and this is the best way to approach the mountain. Costs average US$150 per person for a three-day, two-night round trip. A reliable tour operator is Nazareth **(** (361) 93033 in Senggigi.

KUTA BEACH

Lombok's own Kuta Beach is quite a different kettle of fish from the infamous Balinese beach of the same name. The Lombok Kuta has long been a byword for get-away-from-it-all sun, sand and surf, and the only crowds

to be seen here were those that came for the annual **Nyale Fishing Festival**, held on the nineteenth day of the tenth month of the indigenous Sasak calendar. That's all set to change, as long moot plans to develop this area on Lombok's southern coast finally come to fruition.

Kuta's brave new future is best represented by the recently completed **Novotel Lombok Coralia (** (370) 53333 FAX (370) 53555, which was designed by a Thai architect, mixing and matching traditional Lombok architecture with Sumbanese and African motifs. Along with the Sheraton at Senggigi and the Oberoi at Sira, this is one of the top hotels on the island.

If you're staying at the Novotel, you will no doubt be whisked from the airport upon arrival. For less privileged travelers, there are direct minibus services from Sweta to Kuta.

SUMBAWA

A towering, rugged island dominated by irregularly shaped peninsulas and eroded volcanic ridges, Sumbawa is another transition island in which verdant valleys blanketed with Asian rice paddies gradually give way to antipodean savannas. Barren, rocky and unapproachable by sea, the south coast is largely uninhabited. Nearly all of Sumbawa's 900,000 people live in the northern river valleys which are linked to Sumbawa Besar, the island's capital, by a surprisingly good highway. Traveling across the island is easy even during the November to April rainy season, but explorers will want to take to the dirt roads off the highway to visit the island's Islamic hamlets.

BACKGROUND

For centuries Sumbawa was little more than a resource for slave labor for marauding Makassarese from South Sulawesi. Ironically, the Sumbawans embraced the Islamic religion of those who came to pillage, and formed a series of small sultanates along the north shore. Domination by Makassar was ended by the Dutch East India Company, which established a benign hegemony beginning in 1669. Despite excellent harbors and a fertile interior, the Dutch never established a colonial presence and today there is little tangible evidence of their influence.

The most dramatic event in Sumbawa's history occurred in 1815 when Mt. Tambora exploded, killing 10,000 people outright and forcing two-thirds of the survivors to permanently flee the island. For the past century people have been encouraged to move to Sumbawa from other, more crowded parts of the archipelago. As a result, the present population is a polyglot group.

GENERAL INFORMATION

Sumbawa's main **Tourist Office** ((371) 21632 is on Jalan Garuda in Sumbawa Besar, next door to the Tambora Hotel (see below). Also in the capital city, Indonesian Directorate of Nature Conservation (PHPA) ((370) 21446, Jalan Garuda N°12, is a source of information about Komodo and the nature reserve on Moyo Island at the mouth of Saleh Bay.

WHAT TO SEE AND DO

The main attraction in Sumbawa Besar is the former sultan's palace, **Dalem Loka**. Built entirely of wood and resting on stilts, the palace was remodeled in 1980 but still retains a seedy tropical elegance.

If you have three days to spare and plenty of stamina, take a motorboat from Sumbawa Besar across Saleh Bay to the village of **Cila-cai**, hire a guide and climb 2,800-m (9,185-ft) **Mt. Tambora**. Most travelers forego this adventure, however, and take a bus to **Bima**, Sumbawa's most thoroughly Islamic city, or they travel direct to **Sape** — the jumping-off point for Komodo and Flores islands — on the eastern end of the island.

WHERE TO STAY

Sumbawa Besar has no luxury accommodation. The best hotel in town is the **Tambora Hotel** ((370) 21555, Jalan Kebayan N°2. Room rates range from inexpensive to moderate depending on the amenities. The Tambora's most valuable asset is its visitor information service. Under the same management is the

Hotel Kencana Beach ((370) 22555, a very comfortable place with a swimming pool, restaurants and a beachside location, though at the price of being more than 10 km (six miles) out of town. Those looking for inexpensive accommodation in Sumbawa Besar might try the **Hotel Suci** ((370) 21589, Jalan Hasanuddin, a small but friendly place with a peaceful courtyard.

The top hotel in Sumbawa, indeed one of the top places in Indonesia, is located on the island of Moyo, a wildlife reserve, off the northern coast. **Amanwana** ((351) 22233 FAX (371) 22288, part of the Aman group of hotels and resorts, has 20 luxurious tented rooms to cosset the well-heeled in a novel and beautiful environment.

In Bima, it's slim pickings indeed. The **Hotel Parewa** ((374) 42652, Jalan Soekarno–Hatta N°40, has air-conditioned rooms and a restaurant but little else going for it.

In Sape, where some travelers get stuck waiting for onward connections to Komodo and Flores, the pickings are skeletal. It's impossible to recommend anything in this town, where a room in a "hotel" amounts to a dirty cubical with a shared bath down the hall. The **Mutiara**, next to the port, is where most people end up.

WHERE TO EAT

In Sumbawa Besar, the restaurant at the **Hotel Tambora** is a popular place to eat. Elsewhere around town in the evening you'll see streetside *warungs*. The **Puspa Warna**, on Jalan Kartini, is a good Chinese restaurant.

In Bima the **Hotel Parewa's** restaurant has an extensive Indonesian menu. Another popular spot is the **Losmen Lila Graha**, Jalan Lombok N°20, which serves tasty, reasonably priced food.

HOW TO GET THERE AND AWAY

Merpati has limited flights to Sumbawa Besar from Denpasar with an intermediate stop at Mataram.

The ferry from Lombok to Alas on Sumbawa's northwestern tip takes 90 minutes (see HOW TO GET THERE AND AWAY, page 216 under LOMBOK).

KOMODO

Between the islands of Sumbawa and Flores lies an arid and inhospitable jumble of rock called Komodo. It is the land time forgot, the desolate home of the Komodo dragon.

This large monitor lizards weighs more than 150 kg (334 lbs) and typically attains a length of three meters (10 ft). Its claws are like talons, its serrated teeth razor sharp. The dragon's saliva is toxic, the better to digest the horn and bone of its favorite

meal: goat. One swipe of the Komodo's tail can fell a man.

Komodo is not the place to economize, so don't waste time wandering about alone. Hire a guide to show you around. The dragons feed all year around, but are peppiest during the May to September hot season. For around US$30 a congenial group of fellow travelers should be able to buy a goat, which the guide will butcher and string up. At that point you can switch on your motor drive and wait for dinner to begin (see HERE THERE BE DRAGONS in TOP SPOTS, page 20).

WHERE TO STAY

The **Indonesian Directorate of Nature Conservation (PHPA) camp** at **Loh Liang** consists of a number of wooden cabins, each with four to five rooms arrayed about a common living area. The rooms sleep two people and are inexpensive. There is a small restaurant at the camp, but its menu is limited.

It is possible to walk from Loh Liang into the minuscule fishing village of **Kampung**

Komodo. There are no restaurants here; those spending more than one night on Komodo should bring supplies of canned food and bottled drinks.

HOW TO GET THERE AND AWAY

Permits to visit Komodo are issued on arrival at Loh Liang and are valid for seven days.

The ferry to Komodo leaves Pelabuhan Sape, Saturday to Thursday at 8 AM and takes approximately six hours. There is also a ferry from Labuhanbajo on Flores to Komodo

which leaves daily. If you're in a hurry, boats can be chartered from either Sape or Labuhanbajo for around US$30.

FLORES

Flores was formerly considered so remote that the Dutch exiled Soekarno here during the 1930s. Nowadays, adventurous travelers are discovering the island's natural beauty and fascinating indigenous cultures. Flores is fast becoming a popular backpacker destination; but, it is still early days for travelers who require mid-range and luxury comforts. In addition, some Indonesian is very useful to have when traveling here.

Nusa Tenggara

Located atop Indonesia's most volatile geological fault, Flores is home to 14 active volcanoes, which cause repeated earthquakes throughout the year. Mountains covered with forests and pristine alpine lakes provide a succession of panoramas, and hundreds of narrow gorges bespeak Flores' violent geological past. Earthquakes and landslides make travel difficult on Flores. The island's roads are constantly being cleaved or crumbled. Movement is further slowed during the November to April rainy season when flash floods join the list of natural disasters. With more than one and a half million people, Flores is Nusa Tenggara's most populous island, but the rugged terrain limits development and has preserved many of the cultural idiosyncrasies of the Malay and Papuan ethnic groups.

BACKGROUND

When Java's Majapahit empire collapsed in the fifteenth century, the Islamic sultans of Powa (Sulawesi) and Ternate (Maluku) immediately began fighting to control the island. Their behavior must have displeased the locals because when the Portuguese arrived in 1512 the population quickly embraced the Catholic faith.

The Portuguese called the island Cabo dos Flores, a peculiar description given the fact that the eastern part where they landed is noticeably devoid of flowers. Vivid coral gardens, however, do blossom in the tropical water offshore.

By 1683 the Dutch East India Company had taken over the island's trade in cinnamon and sandalwood, but Portuguese Dominican missionaries managed to hang on for another 250 years. Today 90% of the population is Catholic.

LABUANBAJO

A small fishing village at the western extremity of Flores, Labuanbajo sees a some traffic for onward boat connections to Komodo. There are beaches nearby with basic *losmen*, and some good mid-range accommodation.

The most popular thing to do in Labuanbajo is to join a tour that takes in a deserted beach or two for some snorkeling and swim-

ming, a visit to Komodo for the monitor lizards, and various other local attractions. Such tours may last as long as a week, before depositing tourists in Lombok.

Where to Stay

For central accommodation, the **Bajo Beach Hotel** ((385) 41009 is the pick of an uninspired bunch. Room rates are inexpensive, and the best rooms are still some distance from creeping into the mid-range category in terms of amenities, but it's clean and friendly with some useful services such as car rental. An-

other good option is the **Gardena Hotel** (no phone), where small cottages, some with attached bath, are available.

RUTENG

The mountain market town of Ruteng, which lies at 1,100 m (3,600 ft), makes an interesting base from which to explore the surrounding hill country and to visit the weaving town of **Ciba** as well as the traditional villages around **Bajawa**. Most travelers, however, use it as a pit stop on the long journey to Ende.

Where to Stay

There's not a lot to choose from in Ruteng. The **Hotel Manggarai** ((384) 21008 in the town center of town has some reasonable rooms with attached bath at inexpensive rates. The **Hotel Dahlia** ((384) 21377 is similar.

OPPOSITE (left and right): It's wise to hire a guide on the island of Komodo. ABOVE: Volcanoes and earthquakes keep Flores undeveloped.

How to Get There and Away

Surprisingly, you can actually fly to Ruteng from places as far away as Denpasar (Bali). Merpati ((384) 21197 also flies from Mataram (Lombok) and Labuanbajo (western Flores), although the latter only a couple of times a week.

ENDE

Ende, the largest town in Flores with a population of around 70,000, is where Soekarno was exiled by the Dutch in 1933, back when this small seaside town with its mountainous backdrop was the "ende of the world" — the Indonesian one at least. It's more readily accessible these days. While there's not a lot to see in town, the colored lakes of nearby Mt. Keli Mutu are Flores' major attraction.

On Jalan Perwira, **Soekarno's residence-in-exile** is now a **museum**, though you will have to be fairly entranced with Indonesian history to fall under the spell of the meager collection of objects — mostly photographs — exhibited here. Those with an interest in *ikat* fabric can charter a vehicle and head out to the nearby village of **Ndona**, where some beautiful work is produced.

Where to Stay

There is some reasonable mid-range accommodation in Ende. The **Hotel Dewi Putri** ((383) 21685, Jalan Dewantara, has a central location and a good range of rooms, from basic and fan-cooled to comfortable and air-conditioned. The **Hotel Wisata** ((383) 21368, Jalan Mt. Keli Mutu, is also recommended and is a very similar set-up to the Dwi Putri. For something slightly less expensive, try the **Hotel Safari** ((383) 21499, Jalan Jend. Ahmad Yani, which has some clean and airy economy rooms along with some air-conditioned mid-range ones.

How to Get There and Away

You can fly to Ende from a number of places, but Merpati ((383) 21355, Jalan Nangka, has a bad reputation for the reliability of its outbound flights. Many would-be passengers end up trying their luck at the airport.

The only way to get to Mt. Keli Mutu is by bus to the village of Moni. Buses take

around two hours and depart regularly through the day from the Wolowona bus terminal, four kilometers (two and a half miles) out of town.

MT. KELI MUTU

The magical, **colored lakes** of Mt. Keli Mutu (*keli* means "mountain") are an unforgettable sight and at the top of any list of Flores' attractions. Set in the craters of extinct volcanoes at an elevation of 1,400 m (4,600 ft), the three lakes are constantly changing color, sometimes appearing green, black and red, at other times purple, blue and black. Many locals believe the souls of the dead reside in the lakes. The green lake receives the honest people, while

the enfeebled sink into the red (which is presently a shade of turquoise). Thieves and murderers sink to the bottom of the black lake.

To see the lakes in all their glory — and they really are a magnificent sight—you need a bright, sunny day. This may require a wait of two or three days, but to come all this way and not see the lakes at their best would be a pity. From Moni, a truck leaves for the summit of Mt. Keli Mutu daily at 4 AM, getting you to the summit in time for the sunrise (see GAZE ON THE COLORED LAKES OF FLORES, page 22 in TOP SPOTS).

Where to Stay
For such a small place, Moni has an inordinately large number of homestays.

Despite this, there can be a shortage of rooms at the height of the tourist season (June to August). Standards are almost uniformly low, but then so are room rates. Take a stroll through the village (which takes all of 10 minutes), check out some of the homestays for comfort and cleanliness, and then take your pick.

How to Get There and Away
Most people arrive by bus from Ende, though there is also a helicopter pad for super-luxury travelers. Moni is around 50 km (31 miles) northeast of Ende and buses take two hours.

The crater lakes of Keli Mutu change colors depending on atmospheric conditions and the time of day.

MAUMERE

The dry season is the best time to rent a snorkel and swim around the coral heads off the coast of **Maumere** on the northeast coast. The best place to rent a boat is **Pantai Waiara** just over 10 km (six miles) east of the city. Snorkeling is excellent right off the coast, but more experienced divers may want to head to the offshore islands, part of a marine reserve, where the coral formations are more dramatic.

Maumere itself was razed by an earthquake in late 1992, and the resulting tsunami took a devastating toll on the local population. However, the town has sprung back to life, and there remains little evidence of the awesome damage caused by the earthquake.

Where to Stay

There are accommodations in Maumere itself, but there are few advantages to basing yourself here. Two kilometers (just over a mile) out of town and next to the beach is the **Permati Sari Inn (** (382) 21171, where clean and comfortable moderately priced bungalows are available. At Pantai Waiara, 10 km (six miles) east of Maumere, the mid-range **Flores Sao Resort (Sao Wisata) (** (383) 21555 FAX (383) 21666 or bookings in Jakarta at **(** (21) 370333 extension 78222 is one of the better places to stay. This place is also the longest-running SCUBA diving operator in the region. A small bungalow hotel on the shores of the marine reserve, Sao Wisata offers world-class SCUBA diving and has, indeed, hosted a number of underwater photographic competitions in the past.

Budget travelers head to Wodong, a farther 16 km (10 miles) east along the coast, where a reliable, French-run homestay called **Flores Froggies** has become a popular place to stay.

How to Get There and Away

Maumere has an airport and is reasonably well connected with other islands in Nusa Tenggara. There are even Merpati flights to Denpasar. Buses to Ende take around five hours.

LARANTUKA

With only 30,000 people, Larantuka, the por town on the eastern extremity of the island is where Flores' Portuguese heritage is mos visible. Catholic feast days are celebrated with a passion and sights around town include a **cathedral** and the **Holy Mary Chapel**.

Where to Stay and Eat

The mid-range **Hotel Fortuna II** has spacious fan-cooled rooms; its located two kilometers (just over a mile) out of town.

When it's dinner time in Larantuka, the chef at the popular and inexpensive **Penginapan Rulies Inn** will make Portuguese African chicken on request.

How to Get There and Away

Merpati has infrequent and somewhat ir regular flights from Kupang. Twice weekly ferries depart to Larantuka from Kupang, and the trip takes approximately 14 hours. Buses to Maumere take around five hours and depart daily.

TIMOR

A large island with a split personality Timor for centuries was cleaved down the middle: half Dutch, half Portuguese. Owing to the extended colonial rule, Protestants in West Timor and Catholics in East Timor account for nearly 50% of the island's two million people; the remainder are animists. Twice weekly flights from Darwin (Australia) to **Kupang**, the island's capital on the western peninsula of the island, have opened the island to travelers, but there has been little development beyond Kupang.

Bisected by Gunung Tata Mai, a towering volcanic mountain chain that soars to 2,600 m (8,600 ft) at its midpoint, Timor alternates between periods of drought and torrential rain (November to March). Originally, the economy was based on beeswax and sandalwood, but all the sandalwood trees have been cut down. Today, Timor's broad savanna supports only acacia and lontar palms.

BACKGROUND

Settled by the aboriginal Atoni, Timor was little more than a gaggle of minor kingdoms until the arrival of the Portuguese in the early sixteenth century. When Melaka fell to the Dutch in 1641, the control of Timor and its valuable sandalwood came into dispute. Finally, in 1904 the two European countries divided the island. Occupied by the Japanese and heavily bombed by the Allies in World War II, the island's western half became part of Indonesia following the Dutch departure. But East Timor remained a Portuguese colony until 1974, when Lisbon abruptly decided to give its tiny possession independence.

Fearing that an independent enclave within the archipelago might inspire other islands to rebel, Indonesia invaded East Timor in December 1975 and brutally disbanded the two indigenous political parties. The Revolutionary Front for the Independence of East Timor, known by the acronym FRETILIN, doggedly fought back, but was eventually defeated. The Indonesian army's campaign of extermination resulted in the death of one sixth of East Timor's entire population.

Open to tourism since 1989, East Timor appears tranquil, but lingering tensions and continued police surveillance make it difficult for travelers to speak candidly with the citizenry.

KUPANG

Kupang got its start as a Dutch center of trade in the mid-seventeenth century and is now, with a population of around 120,000, one of Nusa Tenggara's largest cities. It's a pleasant place, but there's not a great deal to see.

General Information
The West Timor Regional Office of Tourism ((391) 21540 is out of town at Jalan Basuki Rakhmat. It's moderately useful, having some brochures and maps.

What to See and Do
The **East Nusa Tenggara Museum** is located in east Kupang on Jalan Perintis Kemerdekaan. Exhibits are labeled in English as well as Bahasa Indonesia, and the museum has some excellent examples of traditional *ikat* weaving; look at them closely before heading to the market to buy your own.

Kupang's main market, **Pasar Inpres**, is in the southern portion of the city on Jalan Suharto. You should bargain for all items you wish to purchase, allowing the seller to initiate the process by giving his price. If you don't see what you want in the way of *ikat* cloth, visit **Dharma Bakti** at Jalan Sumba N°32. In addition to sandalwood oil, this store has well made *ikat* sarongs and blankets from Timor and surrounding islands. The prices are high, but less than what you would pay in either Java or Bali.

The best nearby beach is **Pantai Lasiana**, around 10 km (six miles) east of Kupang. There is excellent SCUBA diving in the area, which has long attracted Australians in search of good "viz" (visibility) and fine diving. Pitoby Watersports ((391) 31634 or 21443 is the best outfit. Avoid Pantai Lasiana on weekends, when it gets very busy with day trippers.

To the east of Kupang the town of **Soe** has an excellent market that hums with activity on Wednesday when people from surrounding villages come into town to sell their crafts. Not much English is spoken here, so practice a few Indonesian phrases before negotiating a price.

A number of travel agents around Kupang offer excellent tours, not only of Kupang and the vicinity but also to traditional villages. Try Ultra Tours ((391) 22258, Jalan Soekarno N°15A, or Pitoby Tours ((391) 21443, Jalan Sudirman N°118.

Where to Stay
The **Orchid Garden Hotel** ((391) 33707 FAX (391) 33669, Jalan Gunung Fateleu N°2, is the most comfortable lodging and has the best location. It's a luxury bungalow style operation with a pleasant garden and a swimming pool. The **Sasando Hotel** ((391) 33334 FAX 33338, Jalan Perintis Kemerdekaan N°1, is another good hotel, but its location five kilometers (three miles) east of town puts guests outside the thick of things.

Less expensive but equally popular is the **Hotel Flobamor II** ℂ (391) 33476, Jalan Sudirman N°21. The **Laguna Inn** ℂ (391) 21559 is centrally located at Jalan Mt. Keli Mutu N°36, an area with quite a few good mid-range hotels. Room rates for fan-cooled rooms are inexpensive, ranging up to lower mid-range for the air-conditioned rooms. Another good inexpensive to mid-range hotel is the **Timor Beach Hotel** ℂ (391) 31651, Jalan Sumatra, a hotel that gets the nod from travelers for its superb waterfront location and restaurant rather than for its rooms.

Wisma Bahagia, Jalan Diponegoro N°72, in Soe has adequate inexpensive rooms and a good restaurant, if you should decide to overnight in this colorful market town.

Where to Eat

At the end of a long hot day, the best place to cool off is **Teddy's Bar** ℂ (391) 21142, Jalan Ikan Tongkol N°1–3. Beloved by Australians, it's the best spot to meet foreigners and to watch life go by in the seaside breezes. The meat pie and chips are a favorite with the Ozzies.

Another convivial spot that sees a fair amount of foreign traffic is the restaurant at the **Timor Beach Hotel** (see above), which has a good selection of Indonesian and Chinese seafood dishes and a wonderful prospect of the sea. The **Happy Café**, Jalan Ikan Paus N°3, is a good place for an inexpensive meal, either Chinese or Indonesian.

How to Get There and Away

Kupang is Timor's transport hub. Along with twice weekly Merpati flights to Darwin (Australia), there are good connections to other destinations around Nusa Tenggara and to Denpasar (Bali).

Buses leave from Oebobo terminal on Jalan El Tari in the east of town. You can get to Soe in around three hours or to Dili in a long 12 hours. Boats leave from Bolok, which is around 12 km (seven and a half miles) west of Kupang. Bookings can be made at travel agents or at the PELNI office ℂ (391) 22646, Jalan Pahlawan N°3.

DILI

Dili, the erstwhile seat of the Portuguese colonial government and now the capital of Indonesian East Timor, is a sluggish, somewhat neglected city that sits square in the middle of a bay surrounded by barren hills. Its sights, by no means overwhelming, are mostly reminders of the Portuguese administration.

General Information

The small but valiant East Timor Tourist Office ℂ (390) 21350, Jalan Kaikoli, has some useful brochures and maps, and there may be English-speaking staff on hand to field questions.

What to See and Do

In the west of town is the **Motael Church**, a Portuguese style structure that was built in the 1950s. The **Governor's Office**, in the center of town, and the statue of **Henry the Navigator** (one of the few remaining Portuguese monuments) in front of it, are also of recent provenance, dating back to 1960. The **Mercado Municipal**, Dili's market, is worth taking a look at. It's housed in a splendid Portuguese-era structure.

If you've never been to Rio de Janeiro, you can pretend you're there by heading out to **Cape Fatucama**, five kilometers (three miles) east of town, where you will find a 27-m (89-ft) **Statue of Christ**, styled after Rio's Christ the Redeemer. Its hilltop vantage point offers stunning views of Dili and the sea. About a kilometer (just over half a mile) short of the statue is **Areia Branca**, a beach area formerly popular with the Portuguese administrators and now a charming but neglected escape from the city.

Three hours from Dili, **Baukau** is East Timor's second largest town and the site of some interesting Portuguese architecture. It's one of those forgotten corners of the world, notable more for its dereliction than for its energy. There are no tourist facilities here, so charter a *bemo* and visit in a long day trip.

Where to Eat

The restaurant at the **Turismo Beach Hotel** is favored by many travelers not only for its inexpensive Indonesian and Chinese dishes but for its Portuguese specialties and reasonably priced wine. The garden atmosphere is another compelling reason to dine here.

Maussau, Jalan Massau, is another recommended restaurant with Portuguese cuisine and a good wine list. The **New Resende Inn** also has a popular restaurant with a combination of Chinese, Indonesian and Portuguese fare.

Where to Stay

The top hotel in Dili is the **Hotel Makhota Plaza** ((390) 21662 FAX (390) 21063, Jalan Aldes Aideia. Lacking in character, it does at least manage to maintain high mid-range standards in the rooms, which are of course air-conditioned and come complete with mini-bars and televisions.

The **Turismo Beach Hotel** ((390) 22029, Avenida Marechal Carmona, has large rooms with balconies and a view of the sea. It's easily the most popular hotel in town, having a range of rooms to suit most budgets and an excellent restaurant. Another good mid-range hotel, though not as popular as the Turismo, is the **New Resende Inn** ((390) 22094, Avenida Bispo Medeiros N°5.

How to Get There and Away

Merpati flies direct from Denpasar daily. For flights from Kupang, Sempati has a more frequent schedule than Merpati. You can travel by bus from Kupang or Baukau. PELNI boats arrive from time to time from locations around the archipelago.

SAWU

South of the Sulu Sea midway between Roti and Sumba lies the enchanting island of Sawu. Neither strategic nor economically important, Sawu was largely ignored for

A traditional Sawu welcome for seafaring visitors to the island.

centuries. The result today is a culture organized around a succession of animistic festivals, animal sacrifice, clan alliances and the phases of the moon. When Capt. James Cook and the crew of the HMS *Endeavor* accidentally stumbled across the island in 1770, they were so entranced that they stayed for five weeks.

On Sawu the men consider themselves warriors. Instead of entering into ritual combat, however, they exhibit controlled aggression in dances with sensuous maidens in tight fitting sarongs. The highest ranking priest on the island is called the *deo rai* or "lord of the earth." His assistant, the *apu lodo*, is "the descendant of the sun." Together they worship a variety of spirits; but, practically speaking, life for the 60,000 people of Sawu springs from the lontar palm.

From the palm comes a juice that is cooling and sweet when fresh, and mildly intoxicating when allowed to ferment into a wine called *tuak*. Boiled into syrup palm juice becomes the base for a soup. If boiled a bit further it turns into palm sugar that can be molded into blocks and stored for months without refrigeration.

When a baby comes into the world on Sawu he is given a symbolic sip of palm juice before receiving mother's milk. And when that child grows old and eventually dies he will be buried in a coffin hollowed from the omnipresent lontar palm.

HOW TO GET THERE AND AWAY

Merpati flies to Sawu once a week but, as is usually the case with such routes, it is an unreliable service. Ferries from Kupang arrive twice weekly.

SUMBA

Known for its intricate *ikat* fabric, distinctive architecture and sculptured stone tombs, Sumba, like neighboring Sawu, has resisted the advances of the twentieth century. With a population of 400,000, this 11,250-sq-km (4,350-sq-mile) island midway between Sumbawa and Timor is covered with dusty grasslands and eucalyptus savannas. Sporadic rain from November to March sustains subsistence agriculture on the western half

of the island, but on the scrubby plateaus of the east there is little to do save weave *ikat* and raise horses.

Life on Sumba revolves around fortified villages. Here, ancestors are worshipped by extended families living in enormous clan houses which are built on raised platforms and topped with high-pitched thatch roofs. In the past, girls who reached puberty were tattooed and had their teeth filed, but these customs are dying out. Ancestor worship and the custom of preserving sacred textiles remain strong.

The period from July to October is marked by festival dances, bloody *pajura* boxing matches in which men pummel each other with fists wrapped in thorny leaves. In West Sumba simulated battles called *pasolas* in which clans bash shields and scream are conducted in February and March. Accompanied by a chorus of women trilling the *karakul*, a high-pitched cry, once used as a greeting for conquering headhunters, the mock wars are fought by mounted horsemen with wooden swords. **Kodi** and **Lamboya** are popular battle sites, as are **Gaura** and **Wanokaka**.

OPPOSITE: A modern addition to Sumba's traditional dress. ABOVE: Sawu horsemen delighted Capt. James Cook when he sailed through the archipelago.

The most elaborate ceremonies accompany the re-internment of briefly buried mummies in concrete vaults that are sealed with elaborately carved stone slabs. Performed in traditional coastal villages such as **Mani** and **Rende** the funerals are accompanied by vigorous dancing, costumed processions and bloody animal sacrifices.

Village courtesy demands that the local chief welcome foreign visitors into his home. In return, travelers should be prepared to reciprocate his generosity with gifts of *tuak* wine, cartons of cigarettes and canned foods.

Farther afield is the village of **Melolo**, which takes around one and a half hours to reach from Waingapu. Charter a *bemo* if you can, or if you are budgeting take one of the hourly *bemo*s that travel out to Melolo. The village has a market where you can find *ikat*, and if you don't mind roughing it Melolo even has a *losmen* that makes a good base for more adventurous excursions into southeastern Sumba. Very close to Melolo, be sure to visit **Rende**, another *ikat* producing village that offers the additional attraction of some fascinating megalithic stone tombs.

WAINGAPU

Sumba's largest town, Waingapu has a population of 25,000 and feels more like an overgrown village than a city. The town divides into two areas: an old town, nestled around the harbor, and a new area about a kilometer (just over a half mile) inland from the harbor. There's nothing in particular to see around town; Waingapu's chief interests is as a base from which to make excursions.

What to See and Do

For many visitors the prime reason for visiting Sumba is the local *ikat* weaving. Visits can be made to the nearby village of **Prailiu** to buy *ikat* and see it being produced.

Some of the hotels in Waingapu offer tours out to the *ikat* villages and megalithic tombs around eastern Sumba. The Hotel Sandal Wood's tours are a reliable choice, but it pays to shop around.

Where to Stay

The **Hotel Merlin** ((386) 21300 FAX (386) 21333, Jalan Panjaitan, offers mid-range comfort. It's an airy place with a challenging staircase and large comfortable rooms, the better ones air-conditioned. The **Hotel Sandal Wood** ((386) 117, Jalan Panjaitan N°23, has long been a favorite, with its garden and unassuming and friendly ambiance. It provides near mid-range comforts at inexpensive rates and is recommended.

How to Get There and Away

Waingapu is not particularly well connected with the rest of Indonesia by air. Bouraq and Merpati fly from destinations such as Bima (Sumbawa), Denpasar (Bali) and Kupang (Timor). To get to **Waikabubak**, the main town in western Sumba, there are Merpati flights three times a week or you can take a bus, which takes around four to five hours. PELNI ((386) 21285 has boats to destinations as diverse as Ende in Flores and Kupang in Timor. The Hotel Sandle Wood is a good source of information on travel out of and around Sumba.

location and tombs, is virtually *in* town and is the first sight on most visitor's agendas.

You can rent a motorbike or a car with a driver (at most hotels) to see the outlying areas. **Anakalang** to the east of town is one of the more popular regions to explore. **Kampung Pasunga** is the site of a particularly impressive tomb that was carved in 1926. Nearby **Kampung Kabonduk** is also worth visiting.

Where to Stay

Hotel Mona Lisa ((387) 21364 may not have a prime location, but it is a well-maintained

WAIKABUBAK

Waikabubak, with a population of 15,000, is little more than a merging of villages in a setting of verdant (compared to arid eastern Sumba) rice paddies. At an altitude of around 600 m (1,970 ft), it's cooler here, too.

What to See and Do

Unlike Waingapu, Waikabubak has some attractions that can be seen on foot. From most of the hotels it is a pleasant stroll to the nearby *kampungs* (villages), where you can find *ikat* and the megalithic tombs that this part of Sumba is famous for. **Kampung Tembelar** in the north of town has some of the best tombs. **Kampung Tarung**, with its scenic hilltop

mid-range hotel with a charming restaurant. Accommodation here is bungalow style, and some of the bungalows have excellent views.

For inexpensive to mid-range lodgings with a more central location, the most popular choice is the **Hotel Manandang** ((387) 21197, with its garden area and spacious rooms.

How to Get There and Away

Although Waikabubak has an airport, flights are infrequent and often heavily booked. Buses to Waingapu depart daily and take four to five hours.

OPPOSITE: In the distance a village nestles in the palms in Sumba. ABOVE: A traditional Sawu dance performance.

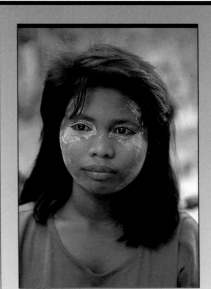

Maluku

Jaya's Bird's Head Peninsula. For the adventurous, a trip on the *Rinjani* is a memorable experience, but when booking passage remember that June to September is the monsoon season during which the Halmahera and Maluku seas are tossed by tropical squalls.

THE BANDA ISLANDS

Banda, "the Jewel of the Indies," was Holland's first outpost in what later became the Dutch East Indies. In 1601 the Bandanese gave the Dutch East Indies Company exclusive rights to purchase nutmeg and mace, the red membrane surrounding the nutmeg seeds. Conflicts over pricing, however, led to several massacres, the last of which established Dutch control over the commodity they sold in Europe for 320 times its purchase price.

By the end of the eighteenth century, smuggled nutmeg seeds planted by the British in Malaya and on the West Indies island of Grenada had broken the Dutch monopoly. The advent of refrigeration reduced demand for spices that had been used as preservatives; public tastes changed; nutmeg prices plummeted, and the Dutch East Indies Company went bankrupt. By 1900, Banda was an impoverished backwater, a remote area where the Dutch exiled dissidents until Indonesia won independence in 1949. Mohammed Hatta, Indonesia's first vice-president, and Sultan Sjahrir, one of the country's first prime ministers, lived on Banda for nearly six years.

The Banda Archipelago consists of nine volcanic peaks surrounded by the azure Banda Sea.

BANDA NEIRA

Banda Neira is the only island large enough to support a town. Restored and developed by Des Alwi, a former Indonesian diplomat turned hotelier, the island is improving its basic amenities, while preserving its rich colonial heritage.

What to See and Do

The seclusion coupled with a rich history and scenic splendor gives the Banda Islands great

charm. Virgin coral reefs ring the island. An underwater garden of rainbow-colored tropical fish suddenly disappears into an ocean 2,000 m (6,650 feet) deep and alive with more marine mammals than any other spot on the globe.

Banda Neira island has many large mansions, some of them more than three centuries old, that once belonged to Dutch *perkeniers*, or estate managers, and Chinese and Arab merchants. An old Dutch church stands at the center of town not far from the ruins of **Fort Nassau**, built in 1609, and **Fort Belgica**, completed two years later. The presence of so many forts in so remote a location attests to Banda's former importance to the Dutch.

Two and a half hours away from Banda Neira by slow boat is the island of **Run** a barely inhabited hummock of sand and coconut palms that produces the most valuable nutmeg in the world. In the geopolitical history of the world, Run merits a fairly large asterisk. In 1667 the Dutch consolidated their grip on the Spice Islands when the British traded Run to the Dutch in return for an undeveloped chunk of real estate in North America called Manhattan.

In Banda Neira it's possible to rent boats, diving equipment and windsurfing boards. Speedboats and launches, large enough to reach Lontar Island — where **Fort Hollandia** is located — can be rented quite inexpensively for the entire day if you shop around and bargain a little. The Lontars are perfect for shallow SCUBA diving since both have colorful reefs. Run Island is better for deeper diving. Be sure to bargain since the price for boats and equipment depends on the volume of tourists and the season of the year.

Where to Stay

The **Maulana Inn** ((910) 21022 FAX 21024, Jalan Pelabuhan N°27, is an overpriced mid-range hotel that has long commanded the top end of the market in Banda Neira, largely one suspects because of its influential owners. Nevertheless, if the rooms are disappointing the views are not. Elaborately decorated longboats large enough to carry 30 men are beached along the shore. Bluefin tuna dart through luminescent swirls of tropical fish. Across a narrow strait, the Gunung Api volcano emits occasional puffs of fire. The smell of nutmeg and mace mixed with cloves permeates the air, conjuring up visions of colonial powers who three centuries ago vied for hegemony in the Spice Islands.

The **Laguna Inn** ((910) 210018 is the Maulana's sister hotel next door, and is operated by the same owner, Des Alwi. Staying at the Laguna can be just as satisfying as the Maulana if your room looks out on Gunung Api, so economize elsewhere and pay extra for the room with a view.

Pinioned between these two mid-range hotels is the unassuming **Likes Homestay** ((910) 21089, which deserves support for providing inexpensive accommodation in a garden setting. As at the Maulana and Laguna inns, superb views of the ocean and Gunung Api are a feature of this homestay. Additional atmospheric and inexpensive homestay accommodation can be found at the **Flamboyan** ((910) 21233, Jalan Syahrir.

Where to Eat

Most visitors to Banda Neira eat at their hotels or homestays. One of the few alternatives is the **Nusantara**, a few blocks down Jalan Pelabuhan, which is a unassuming eatery that can produce grilled fish caught just hours before, served with sliced lime, cold beer and a side dish of *sambal*.

How to Get There and Away

Merpati ((910) 21040 flies 14-seat Cessnas (which is about all that Ambon's small landing strip has room for) from Ambon to Banda Neira six times a week. The flight depends on a mostly-full plane, however, and there is a severe weight restriction on the amount of luggage that can be carried. It's a popular route and should be booked well in advance.

A number of small coastal craft also make the 16-hour overnight trip from Ambon, but none really can be described as comfortable. The PELNI *Rinjani* swings through southern Maluku every two weeks, stopping at Banda en route.

The rainy season lasts from June through August, and the west monsoon which runs from January until February can cause rough seas. The best time to visit the Bandas is from October to December and again from March

through May when the seas are calm, the breeze is gentle and each day ends with a spectacular sunset.

NORTH MALUKU

Just to the west of pinwheel-shaped Halmahera the volcanic islands of Ternate and Tidore rise majestically from the floor of the Maluku Sea. Three centuries ago the two islands and their precious crops of cloves and mace were the focus of international intrigue and warfare.

Ternate and **Tidore** are separated by only a one-kilometer (just over a half-mile) stretch of ocean. As a result, a small fleet of power boats is constantly available to shuttle passengers between the two islands or to nearby **Mare**, **Moti** and **Makian**.

Rugged, very sparsely populated and largely undeveloped, North Maluku's largest island, **Halmahera** is rarely visited. SCUBA diving enthusiasts, however, may wish to explore the island's coastal reefs, which are rich with lobster. A bit farther, but also well worth a detour for SCUBA divers, is the island of **Morotai** which lies just off Halmahera's northern tip. Occupied by the Allies durng World War II after a fierce battle with the Japanese, Morotai became the site of a huge air base used in the retaking of the Philippines. Submerged in the shallows off the coast of Morotai are the coral-encrusted remains of destroyers, P-51 Mustangs and Japanese Zeros.

Golden sunsets and local lore are best enjoyed on the verandah of the Maulana Inn on Banda Neira.

TERNATE

The tiny volcanic island of Ternate, dominated by Mt. Gamalama, may no longer be the focus of world attention, but, after Ambon, it remains the most important commercial center in Maluku. First reached by the Portuguese, it was later claimed by Spain, but the Portuguese succeeded in expelling the Spanish and eventually bought the island from the Spanish Crown.

In 1547 Francis Xavier passed through Ternate, but his Jesuitical precepts were lost on the island's administrators who enraged Ternate's inhabitants by poisoning the local sultan. After throwing the Portuguese off the island, the new sultan Babullah packed his warriors into longboats called *kora-kora* and for the next 13 years attacked every European he could find.

In 1592 Portugal's nominal rule of Maluku became even more tenuous when a Dutchman working for a Portuguese trading company in Goa published the heretofore secret sea routes to the East Indies. By 1621 the Dutch East India Company (VOC) had displaced the Portuguese and established a spice monopoly, declaring that cloves could only be grown on Ambon. To enforce the monopoly, the VOC exterminated the entire workforce of Banda and uprooted all clove trees on Ternate. The Dutch monopoly gradually eroded as more and more clove seedlings were planted in other parts of the world. But the VOC policy remained in force and every few months, until the start of the Napoleonic wars, Dutch officials would come to Ternate to crush clove saplings.

Today, Ternate boasts a robust economy and a laid-back lifestyle. Its Islamic citizenry is gracious and welcoming to foreigners, who should not be alarmed by the frequent earth tremors.

General Information

The **North Maluku Tourist Office** ((921) 22646, Kantor Bupati building, Jalan Pahlawan Revolusi, can provide basic information as well as maps. For organized tours get in touch with **Indo Gama** ((921) 21681, Jalan Pahlawan Revolusi N°17.

What to See and Do

Once the home of the most powerful sultan in the Spice Islands, **Ternate City** (population 50,000) is a pleasant tropical port. Bypassed by World War II, it gives a better picture of Maluku's history than does Ambon.

Looking out over the city of Ternate the 758-year old **Sultan's Palace**, or *kraton*, on Jalan Babullah now serves as a public museum where you can see old Dutch cannons, Portuguese swords and Han ceramics brought to the island as trade goods by Bugis merchants.

A brief taxi ride down the hill from the *kraton* leads to the **Benteng Oranye** or Fort Orange, a massive Dutch trading post built in the early years of the seventeenth century.

Still guarded by Dutch cannons and emblazoned with the VOC crest, the outpost now serves as a garrison for the Indonesian Army which, in contrast to its behavior elsewhere in Indonesia, is happy to greet camera-toting tourists.

A 30-minute walk north from Fort Orange will take you back a century in time to **Benteng Toloko**, a Portuguese fort built by Alfonso de Albuquerque in 1512. In contrast to many other colonial ruins, Benteng Toloko has been lovingly preserved, ironically, by Dutch renovators who mistakenly assumed it was one of their own structures.

Benteng Toloko commands a panoramic view of the city that includes **Benteng Kayu Merah**, an old coastal Portuguese fort the Dutch clearly recognized as Portuguese.

Allowed to slowly disintegrate, the roundish, wave-splashed ruin is still worth a look. A more dramatic trek leads to **Gunung Api Gamalama** the active volcano to which Ternate City clings. It is possible to climb into the steaming crater with the help of a guide from the mountain village of Marikrobo, but most people are content to simply enjoy the view.

Where to Stay

The best hotel in town is the **Neraca Golden Hotel** ((921) 21668, Jalan Pahlawan Revolusi N°30, a relatively new place with a good location and air-conditioned rooms with hot water and other amenities. Nearby, at N°58,

Old forts built by the Portuguese and Dutch dot the Spice Islands.

the **Hotel Nirwana** ((921) 21787 has slightly lower standards but considerably lower rates. Take a look at both before checking in.

The **Chrysant** ((921) 21580, Jalan Ahmad Yani N°131, has both air-conditioned and fan-cooled rooms at lower mid-range rates.

Where to Eat
Most restaurants in Ternate are found along Jalan Pahlawan Revolusi and offer basic Chinese and Indian food at inexpensive prices. The specialty is coconut crab, a beach-dwelling creature that exists entirely on coconuts. One restaurant that rises above the norm in Ternate is the **Siola** ((921) 21377, a short stroll from the center of town on Jalan Stadion. As with other area restaurants, coconut crab is the specialty here, but unlike that of the competition it comes in unusually generous portions.

How to Get There and Away
Merpati ((921) 21651, Jalan Bousori N°81, has a daily flight linking Ambon and Ternate. There is also daily service to Manado in northern Sulawesi. Be sure to arrive at the airport early since both flights are often overbooked. Bouraq ((921) 21288, Jalan Ahmad Yani N°131, also flies to Ternate from Ujung Padang, Sulawesi via Manado three times a week.

PELNI ((921) 21434, has an office in the Komplex Pelabuhan on Jalan Ahmad Yani, where you can book space on several boats that make long loops around the archipelago. There are myriad other services fanning out to other Maluku destinations.

TIDORE

Tidore is a beautiful island that visitors usually arrive at on Tuesday and Saturday, when the towns of **Rum** and **Soa Siu** have their market days. The jungle-covered ruins of an old Spanish fort lie atop a hill at the entrance to Soa Siu. Local children will lead you to the ruins of the old sultan's palace.

Where to Stay
Few foreign travelers stay on Tidore, but if the mood grabs you, try the inexpensive **Losmen Jangi**, in the town of Soa Siu. It's probably the best on the island.

How to Get There and Away
Small outboard boats to Tidore shuttle passengers from Pelabuhan Bastiong on Ternate to Run on Tidore's northwest coast. The boats run from 7 AM to 6 PM and cost less than 50 cents.

SOUTHEAST MALUKU

Out on the far edge of the Banda Sea, in the most distant corner of the archipelago, lie the almost completely forgotten island groups of **Aru**, **Kai** and **Tanimbar**. Populated by 260,000 natives of Papuan stock, these seldom-visited islands are of no strategic or economic importance. Historically, the only recorded struggle has been the battle for men's souls waged between Christian and

Muslim missionaries. All three island groups have palm-shaded beaches, people making traditional handicrafts and coral reefs swarming with miniscule tropical fish, but the time necessary to travel to and between islands must be counted in weeks, and food and accommodation are often difficult to come by.

KAI ISLANDS

Undiscovered by Westerners until the late nineteenth century, the Kai Islands were once covered with forests. The Melanesian natives were renowned boat builders who subsisted happily on a diet of yams, sago and fish. Today, the hills have been largely deforested by Javanese timber companies,

and although problems of modern society has prompted many Christians to revert to animism, the Kai islanders' artistic talents carry on undiminished.

Carved stone and wooden statues and finely woven baskets can be purchased in small villages on the two large islands of **Kai Besar** and **Kai Kecil**. On **Palau Tayandu**, just west of Kai Kecil, villagers produce pottery in the shape of animals and forest spirits. Though villagers will gladly accept rupiah, barter is an accepted practice on all three islands, with inexpensive digital wrist watches and calculators being much in strong demand.

A narrow strait separates Banda Neira from the Gunung Api volcano.

How to Get There and Away

Merpati and Bouraq have flights from Ambon to Langgur most days of the week. There are also two flights a week linking Langgur with Saumlaki on Tanimbar. Boat connections are mostly of the every two or three weeks variety.

TANIMBAR ISLANDS

In 1645 the Dutch tried to establish a colony on **Yamdena**, the largest island in the Tanimbar group, but departed with some

alacrity after learning that the Tanimbarese were headhunting cannibals. Catholic missionaries later subdued the Melanesian ferocity, but they did not completely dispel the islanders' animism. These days, the missionaries have been joined by botanists who come to observe the islands' unique assortment of orchids.

Of the 66 Tanimbar Islands, only seven are inhabited and the total population of these islands amounts to fewer than 70,000. Despite miles of deserted beaches and rainbow-colored coral reefs, there is no organized tourism. Those who venture this far south, however, will find some of Indonesia's finest *ikat* weavers and talented silversmiths who make ceremonial headdresses from old coins.

Because the rest of the world is so far away, everything is in short supply here. T-shirts, ballpoint pens, leather belts and brandy are valued items that can be traded for textiles, shell jewelry and carvings. One can only imagine what you might receive in return for a Swiss Army knife.

There are several places to stay in **Saumlaki**, notably the **Harapan Indah**, a tidy place with some air-conditioned rooms. Those going beyond this town should carry canned food and bottled drinks to share in return for shelter.

How to Get There and Away

Merpati has three flights a week from Ambon to Saumlaki. PELNI's *Tatamailau* also stops every month on the way to and from the Aru Islands.

ARU ISLANDS

Nearly 700 km (400 miles) southeast of Ambon, the Aru Islands are Maluku's most distant land masses. Located on the edge of a marine plateau, the 21 islands in this group are sparsely populated, covered with mangrove swamps and surrounded by deep trenches that lead into the shallow Arafura Sea. Wallabies and kangaroo share the land with the Alfuro natives, but the main attraction here are birds of paradise which display their brilliant plumage each summer when it comes time to mate.

Unlike the neighboring Tanimbarese, the dark skinned Alfuro are peace-loving farmers who cultivate melons on their swampy, low lying islands and make tortoise shell jewelry in their spare time. **Dobo** on the island of **Wokam** is the only town of any size. There it is possible to buy painted cassowary eggs and artifacts made from mother-of-pearl.

How to Get There and Away

There is an airstrip outside Dobo, but the Merpati flights, which in theory wing twice weekly from Ambon to Dobo via Langgur are irregular. PELNI provides the only scheduled transportation to Aru, but the journey from Ambon takes three weeks.

LEFT: A souvenir of Ambon. RIGHT: Tropical greenery swathes the gentle waters around Ternate Island.

Kalimantan

BORNEO. The name evokes images of impenetrable jungles, sluggish rivers, screaming gibbons, leeches and communal longhouses occupied by tattooed Dyak headhunters. It's all true — except for the headhunting which in recent years has fallen out of fashion.

Kalimantan, which means "Rivers of Precious Stones," occupies the southern two-thirds of Borneo, the world's third largest island. It is a brooding, exotic place that has captivated generations of writers. In *Heart of Darkness*, Joseph Conrad's character Marlow confesses his childhood fascination with maps that depicted Borneo as a sprawling expanse of jungle patterned by enormous, undulating rivers. "It fascinated me as a snake would a bird — a silly little bird."

Maps of Borneo contain many of Asia's most storied locales. Across the border in East Malaysia the state of Sarawak once belonged to the British "White Rajah" James Brooke. Sandakan the pirate prowled the sea off the coast of modern day Brunei. In addition to inspiring *Heart of Darkness*, Kalimantan's rivers were often the focus of Somerset Maugham's *Borneo Stories*.

Kalimantan has a population of only seven million, but because of the oil and timber industries its four provinces are well-served by the airlines. Daily nonstop flights keep things going between Banjarmasin in South Kalimantan and the East Kalimantan oil town of Balikpapan with flights to Jakarta and Surabaya. Moving between Kalimantan's major towns is also easy since Garuda, Merpati, Bouraq and Dirgantara Air Service (DAS) have overlapping services.

Kalimantan is relatively flat with no active volcanoes, but transportation inland from the coast can be difficult. There are no major highways because of the swamps, peat bogs and thick jungle. This means that all commerce must move on rivers such as South Kalimantan's Barito, East Kalimantan's Mahakam and the Kapuas River in West Kalimantan. During the rainy season, when the rapids are transformed into foaming torrents, boats reminiscent of *The African Queen* must slowly zigzag up the broad rivers, carefully avoiding the tree trunks sent floating down river by the timber companies. Once the rivers reach the coastal flatland, however, they turn the color of ocher and meander

aimlessly until their final transformation into mangrove swamps.

Some of Kalimantan's towns can be bypassed without fear of missing much. Balikpapan, for example, has little save a disproportionate number of expatriates divided in two categories: "oilies" in the petroleum business and "chippies" who work for logging companies. West Kalimantan's capital of Pontianak, which sits atop the equator is a humid city of Chinese shopkeepers. The beauty of Kalimantan is found on and around its rivers which drain the planet's last great

primary forest. With some 25,000 species of flowering plants (all of Europe has fewer than 6,000; Africa fewer than 13,000) Kalimantan's the richest rainforest in the world.

BORNEO'S DYAKS

Dyak, it should be noted, is a term that is now falling out of use in Indonesia because of its pejorative associations. Orang Pedalaman (Inland People) is a polite way to refer generically to the 200 tribal groups native to Borneo and who altogether number about one and a half million.

OPPOSITE: Dyak settlements line Borneo's many rivers. ABOVE: Dyak women welcome visitors with freshly-cut pineapple.

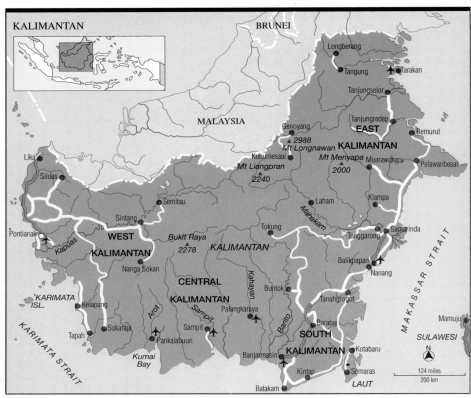

Dyaks such as the Iban, Kayan and Punan, are neolithic animists who live along the banks of the island's many rivers. Originally, they lived along the coast, but when Arab traders arrived in the fifteenth century the Dyaks moved inland to escape Islam and its prohibition against their favorite food: pork.

Dyaks are skilled boatmen and hunters who transform their bodies into works of art with tattoos. They are also known for their *ikat* cloth and ornaments. The Tanjung Dyaks make a kind of cloth called *daun doyo*, which is woven from plant fibers and used for certain rituals in traditional longhouses.

The Dyak's highly-structured society revolves around the longhouse. Wooden structures built on pilings that reach 130 m (150 yards) in length, longhouses can shelter as many as 100 families. Though each family has a their own apartment, most of their days and evenings are spent in the unpartitioned corridor that runs the length of the house.

Frontier hospitality prevails in nearly all of Kalimantan's longhouses. Visitors receive a welcome tour, an explanation of how the human heads hanging from the rafters were taken, dinner and a place to sleep on the split-bamboo floor. In return you are expected to provide cartons of cigarettes and several five-gallon cans of rice wine. The extent and intensity of the festivities that follow will be largely determined by how much wine you bring. It's also deemed thoughtful to bring several bags of hard candy for the kids, but only wine and cigarettes are mandatory.

HEADHUNTING

When Sir James Brooke, the nineteenth century British adventurer who became the "White Rajah" of Sarawak, first met the Dyaks he wrote that "they are the most savage of tribes — and delight in headhunting and pillage."

According to Dyak lore, nothing prevents plague, increases fertility or insures a bountiful harvest like a brace of freshly-severed heads. Heads brimming with the spirit of the departed are the perfect wedding gift and are basic to any respectable dowry. For Dyaks, taking heads was essential to the well-being of a community. Indeed, following a death in the family, heads taken from an enemy tribe served as a spiritual transfusion.

Because a head's power faded as it aged, fresh skulls always were needed. Those taken from rival warriors received VIP treatment. After being drained of its brains and dried over a fire, a head often would be stuffed with rice or betel nuts. On occasion a cigar would be inserted between the desiccated lips.

Tolerated by the Dutch, who viewed it as a primitive form of population control, headhunting fell out of fashion after Indonesia gained independence. The last confirmed case of headhunting occurred in the early 1960s when Iban warriors loyal to the British lopped off the heads of Soekarno soldiers who had ventured too far inside northern Borneo. Today, it is a serious felony. But new legislation doesn't completely dispel old beliefs, and in most upriver longhouses heads smoked over generations of cook fires continue to occupy a place of honor.

EAST KALIMANTAN

BACKGROUND

Indonesia's petroleum industry got its start in East Kalimantan at the end of the nineteenth century when British Petroleum discovered oil outside Balikpapan and on the offshore island of Tarakan. Oil, natural gas and timber have made the province of East Kalimantan vital to the economy of Indonesia. Indeed, more than 25% of Indonesia's export earnings comes from East-Kal's natural resources.

Logging is concentrated in the forests west of Balikpapan and Samarinda. It was here that 35,000 sq km (13,500 sq miles) of woodlands burned from 1982 through 1983, when fires started by peasants using the slash-and-burn method of cultivation got out of control. The fire devastated an area the size of Holland and cost Indonesia US$6 billion worth of timber. The fires continue. In 1997

The jungles of Kalimantan are home to some of Indonesia's most reclusive and colorful minorities.

the same slash-and-burn clearing methods led to massive fires that cast a pall of health-damaging smoke over places as far away as Singapore and Kuala Lumpur.

BALIKPAPAN

Balikpapan offers nothing in the way of sights, but as an oil and logging town with a large number of American, European and Australian expatriates it is Kalimantan's most organized city and has the highest accommodation standards. The foreign presence

and wealth, however, underscores Indonesia's lack of development. It is incongruous to see two-cylinder *becak*s parked in front of gleaming office towers. Foreign workers for Pertamina, Total and Union Oil live in a leafy enclave atop the hill where they enjoy the benefits of a country club and other suburban amenities.

Where to Stay
The best hotel in Balikpapan, indeed in all of Kalimantan, is the **Dusit Inn Balikpapan** ((542) 20155 FAX 20150, which is situated on the airport road, a five minutes' drive east of town. It has everything from international-class cuisine and live entertainment to tennis courts.

The **Hotel Benakutai** ((542) 31896 FAX (542) 31823, Jalan Ahmad Yani, was for many years Balikpapan's best. Nowadays it offers comfort and high service standards in the center of town, but falls considerably short of the Dusit. Close by, at Jalan Sudirman N°2, is the **Bahtera Hotel** ((542) 22563 FAX (542) 31889, an older hostelry that has been completely renovated to three-star standards. It gets a lot of custom from oil workers and loggers, who are not as rowdy as you might imagine.

A recommended mid-range hotel is the **Mirimar Hotel** ((542) 33906, Jalan Pranoto N°16, which has a good selection of rooms and a decent restaurant off the lobby. An expatriate favorite with a lively restaurant and bar is the more upmarket **Blue Sky Hotel** ((542) 22268 FAX (542) 24094, Jalan Suprapto N°1. It's a modern place with a swimming pool, in-house movies. Its only drawback is its location, just north of the Pertamina Oil Refinery in the north of town.

Where to Eat
Because of East Kalimantan's swampy terrain, most of the food served in restaurants is imported. For this reason, dining out in East Kal is more expensive than in many other regions of Indonesia.

Steak and grilled seafood are popular with Balikpapan's expatriate community. **Bondy's**, just north of the Hotel Benakutai is one of the most popular places to dine on these two treats. The garden setting is pleasant, particularly on balmy evenings.

For good dining, try the Hotel Benakutai which has an excellent seafood restaurant, or the Dusit where you'll find Thai, Chinese and Indonesia restaurants. Excellent seafood served in a lively atmosphere can be found at the **Rainbow Coffeeshop and Restaurant** at the Blue Sky Hotel.

For top quality Chinese cuisine, **Dynasty**, Jalan Ahmad Yani N°10/7, has a large selection of mostly Cantonese dishes and some Indonesian dishes too.

How to Get There and Away
Balikpapan is the main transportation hub for Kalimantan. Garuda, Merpati, Sempati and Bouraq all have daily flights from Jakarta and Surabaya. Shop around for tickets, as

prices can differ considerably on long-haul domestic flights. Sempati ((542) 31612 has its local office at the Hotel Benakutai. The Bouraq ((542) 23117 and Garuda ((542) 22300 offices are both on Jalan Ahmad Yani, close to the Hotel Benakutai. Merpati ((542) 24477 has its office at Jalan Sudirman N°22.

From Balikpapan, low cost buses run on a regular basis to Samarinda and Banjarmasin. The trip to Samarinda takes two hours. The 12-hour journey to Banjarmasin is an interminable, gut-wrenching experience that will leave you wishing you had flown.

Most of the Mahakam is navigable year-around, but travelers bound for remote destinations such as **Long Pahangai** should plan to journey from September through December when increased rain makes it easier to negotiate upriver rapids.

SAMARINDA

A colorful town on the Mahakam River, Samarinda is the center of East Kalimantan's timber industry. Its bustling riverine harbor is packed with freighters and water taxis

PELNI ((542) 21402, Jalan Yos Sudarso N°76, sells tickets for several passenger steamers that sail to Jakarta, Surabaya and Ujung Padang (Sulawesi); these voyages have intervening stops at Toli Toli, Tarakan and Pantoloan.

THE LOWER MAHAKAM RIVER

An enormous river that is more than three kilometers (two miles) wide in many locations, the Mahakam functions as the aorta of the East Kalimantan region. Ocean-going freighters steam up the Mahakam River as far as Samarinda, which serves as the final destination for thousands of logs floating downstream.

and lined with businesses and homes from which children dive into the river. Indeed, the city's biggest attraction is its harbor, and travelers are well advised to rent a boat with a wooden roof on which they can sit and observe the passing scene. A variety of canals and tributaries branch off from the river. Some extend through commercial neighborhoods, others meander through residential areas. The journey will offer an insight into the nature of Kalimantan's aquatic culture that no book or land-based tour can provide.

OPPOSITE: Kalimantan timber sent down the Mahakam River often clogs the port of Samarinda. ABOVE: For many of the inhabitants of Kalimantan, life is lived on the rivers.

General Information

The regional Tourist Information Center ((541) 21669 in Samarinda is not particularly useful, and most travelers do their information gathering from travel agents.

Where to Stay

The **Hotel Mesra International** ((541) 32772 FAX (541) 35453, Jalan Pahlawan N°1, at the northwest edge of Samarinda, is a resort-style hotel with tennis courts, a large pool and several restaurants. It's quiet and a good value for the money. Similar in standards and

Where to Eat

The specialty of Samarinda is *udang galah*, huge freshwater prawns that nearly every *warung* can grill to specification. Travelers who don't speak Indonesian, however, may find it easier to spend a little more money and have their seafood repast at the **Haur Gading Restaurant**, Jalan Pulau Sulawesi N°4, a wonderfully ambient spot for an evening meal. For a change of pace foreigners often head for **Pondok Indah**, a steak restaurant on Jalan Panglima Batur. Prices there are a bit higher than elsewhere, but the

rates is the **Hotel Bumi Senyur** ((541) 41443 FAX (541) 38014, Jalan Diponegoro. It has a central location and upper mid-range rates for its comfortable, well appointed rooms.

The **Swarga Indah** ((541) 22066 FAX 23662, Jalan Sudirman N°43, has air-conditioned rooms, a souvenir shop and a restaurant. It also has a central location, making it a good mid-range choice.

Unlike neighboring Balikpapan, Samarinda has some inexpensive accommodation options that are popular with backpackers taking budget tours up the Mahakam River. Pick of the pack is probably the **Aida Hotel** ((541) 42572, Jalan Temenggung, a small and friendly budget place where they bring you breakfast in the morning.

beer is cold and the person sitting next to you at the bar probably speaks English.

The Hotel Bumi Senyur has that most unexpected of things: a Japanese restaurant. The **Daisaku** does an eclectic range of Japanese favorites at mid-range prices.

How to Get There and Away

Merpati, Garuda and Sempati ((541) 43385 share an office and phone number at Jalan Sudirman N°20. Between them they'll get you to most major coastal destinations in Kalimantan and to destinations elsewhere around the archipelago too.

For destinations upriver, DAS ((541) 35250 is the major carrier, though getting on flights often requires long waits.

There is a PELNI office where you can book passage, but boats are infrequent.

TENGGARONG

Forty kilometers (25 miles) up the Mahakam River from Samarinda is Tenggarong, capital of the Kutai regency and formerly the seat of the Kutai sultanate. The sultan's palace at the riverside is now a **museum** where the royal paraphernalia is kept, as well as an excellent collection of antique Chinese ceramics. Every September 24 the **palace** is taken

ketingtings are powered by a swivel-mounted engine attached to a long propeller shaft which allows the boat to pick its way through extremely shallow water.

For travelers with time to spare, a trip upriver can be the experience of a lifetime. Surrounded by rippling streams, waterfalls and produce gardens, the villages of **Barong Tongkok** not only provide an opportunity to hike through shimmering rice fields and groves of bamboo, but also view a particularly undiluted form of tribal animism. Around Barong Tongkok jungle trails lead

over by dancers and musicians who celebrate the town's anniversary.

Tenggarong is the is the last town of any consequence before the interior, though it's little more than a village. It is better to organize a tour in Samarinda or Balikpapan than in Tenggarong.

THE UPPER MAHAKAM RIVER

A fascinating variety of boats travel up the Mahakam from Tenggarong. Unlike the taxi boats in Samarinda, which have long wooden hulls, a canvas roof and a small diesel motor, long-distance upriver vessels are sleeker longboats with more powerful engines that allow the boat to skim up the rapids. Smaller

past carved statues and spirit offerings of rice and flowers to villages where the beating of drums and the clanging of gongs punctuate rituals carried down through the centuries.

Half way up the Mahakam is **Long Iram**, an equatorial village that offers the last call for cold beer and restaurant food. Long Iram is one of the Mahakam's larger transportation hubs with boats leaving frequently for towns both up and down the river.

Upriver of Long Iram, Dyaks with tattoos and earlobes elongated by dangling brass rings become more visible. Elaborately carved longhouses can be visited at **Long**

OPPOSITE: A whirl on Kalimantan's version of the open road. ABOVE: A pastoral upriver scene on the Mahakam.

Bagun, but before settling in for the evening visitors are expected to announce their presence to the local police.

SOUTH KALIMANTAN

Bisected by the Barito River, Kalimantan's smallest province is a relatively trackless expanse of jungle which is rapidly being denuded by timber companies. Turned into plywood and rattan products, the rainforest is disappearing at an alarming rate at the hands of Indonesian "chippies" whose long logging tractor-trailers roar along the Trans-Kalimantan Highway, which begins just outside Banjarmasin.

BANJARMASIN

South Kalimantan's greatest attraction is the 460-year-old provincial capital of Banjarmasin — a veritable Venice of the East — whose canals ebb and flow with the tides. Located 16 km (10 miles) from the sea at the confluence of the Martapura and Barito rivers, Banjarmasin is a riverine city in which houses, cafés and produce markets ride the tidal swell. "Banjar" is a good place to buy Dyak handicrafts and semi-precious stones, though the latter may be purchased more cheaply in the "diamond city" of Martapura, 40 km (25 miles) east of Banjar.

Background

Banjarese kingdoms on the northern edge of the Java Sea fell to Java's Majapahit kingdom at the end of the fourteenth century. Many Dyak tribes later retreated into the interior to escape the advance of Islam, but the area was forcibly converted and was controlled by the Sultan of Banjarmasin when the Dutch finally arrived. In 1857 Dutch colonialists who had come in search of diamonds tried to depose the Sultan. Their goal finally was achieved but only after a costly 50 year insurgent war thinned both sides.

General Information

The best place for information about Banjarmasin and South Kalimantan is the Provincial Tourist Office ((511) 68707, next to the Grand Mosque at Jalan Panjaitan N°3. This office can also help you get in touch with

qualified local guides for tours of Banjarmasin's canals and for tours farther afield.

What to See and Do

Banjar's canals are worth at least a half day. Leave early in the morning so that you'll arrive at one of the city's **floating markets** or *pasar terapung*, between 9 AM and 10 AM, when they are most active (see FLOAT OFF TO MARKET, page 23 in TOP SPOTS).

After a leisurely lunch and a nap, rent another boat for the eight-kilometer (five-mile) trip down river to **Pulau Kaget**, an island inhabited exclusively by long-nosed proboscis monkeys. In addition to their long noses, the animals have red faces and pot bellies — characteristics that prompted Indonesians to dub them *kera belanda*, or Dutch monkeys.

Another proboscis monkey island, **Pulau Kembang** is much closer to Banjarmasin, but it is more difficult to visit because the mischievious long-tailed macaques that inhabit the area tend to pester tourists.

Where to Stay

The best hotel in Banjarmasin is the **Barito Palace** ((511) 67300 FAX (511) 52240, Jalan Haryono. It's by no means exceptional, but it has luxury amenities such as a swimming pool, restaurants, a bar and basic fitness facilities. The **Kalimantan Hotel** ((511) 66818 FAX (511) 67345, a luxury hotel in central Banjarmasin which once had the edge on the Barito Palace was damaged by rioting in 1996.

In the mid-range category, the **Nabilla Palace Hotel** ((511) 52707, Jalan Ahmad Yani, is a resort hotel on the road out to the airport. If you don't mind being out of town, you can enjoy excellent facilities at very reasonable rates, though it's difficult to imagine how anyone summons the energy to swing a tennis racket in Banjarmasin's sweltering equatorial heat. (The Nabilla was formerly known as the Fabiola.)

The **Hotel Mentari** ((511) 68944, with a central address at Jalan Lambung Mangkarat N°32, has seen better days, but the lobby restaurant is good, and there's a lively disco on an upper floor. The mid-range rates are overvalued by local standards.

Budget travelers should head straight to the **Borneo Homestay** ((511) 57545 FAX (511)

57515, near the river, just off Jalan Pos, Borneo's most friendly and efficiently run homestay operation. Along with simple fan-cooled rooms, there are a couple of slightly more expensive air-conditioned rooms.

Where to Eat

For the homesick, the **Rama Steak Corner**, in the Arjuna Plaza, is a popular place to wolf down a T-bone, particularly amongst those who have just traipsed back into town at the end of a Borneo trek.

Banjarmasin's most popular Chinese Restaurant is the homey and inexpensive **Lezat Baru**, Jalan Pangaran Samudera N°22. One of Banjarmasin's top seafood restaurants is **Kaganangan** close by on the same street at N°30. A variety of dishes, both grilled and fried, are accompanied by steaming bowls of rich vegetable soup.

How to Get There and Away

As in so many other places in Indonesia, there are a bewildering number of airlines taking to the skies from Banjarmasin; it's best to let a travel agent figure out who flies where when and for how much. Garuda and Merpati ((511) 54203 on Jalan Hasanuddin N°31, do the long-haul flights to and from Java and Denpasar, as does Bouraq ((511) 52445, which also offers some internal flights; DAS flies into the center of Kalimantan ((511) 52902.

PELNI passenger ships sail twice weekly from Surabaya to Banjarmasin. In Banjarmasin return tickets can be booked at Borneo Homestay (see above) or at travel agencies. Speedboats travel upriver to Palangkaraya daily and take about six hours.

CENTRAL KALIMANTAN

The largest and most sparsely populated of Kalimantan's four provinces, Central Kalimantan, or Kalimantan Tengah, is blanketed by a thick rainforest that rises abruptly from the coastal mangrove swamps to the serrated ridge lines of the Schwaner and Muller mountain chains drained by four enormous rivers: Arot, Barito, Kahayan and Sampit.

Central Kalimantan's 900,000 inhabitants are predominately Islamic (65%) with the bulk of the remainder clinging to native Dyak animism.

GENERAL INFORMATION

The Regional Tourist Office ((541) 21416, Jalan Parman N°21, is a useful place with English-speaking staff. If you've come this far, you may as well pop in for a visit.

WHAT TO SEE AND DO

During the early 1960s, Soekarno began to challenge the region's old colonial powers with a policy called *konfrontasi*. He forced

the Dutch out of Netherlands New Guinea (now Irian Jaya) and tried to wrest control of Sarawak and North Borneo, British protectorates destined to join the new nation of Malaysia. To win support from Kalimantan, Soekarno announced a series of Moscow-financed development projects. His main target was **Palangkaraya**, a dusty, impoverished village bereft of historical importance or geographical advantage. Despite the town's undistinguished past, Russian engineers went to work building a road that would link the town with the village of

---

Equatorial torpor and intrusive police prevent Pontianak from becoming the Venice of Indonesia. OVERLEAF: The floating markets of Kalimantan are one of Indonesia's least touristed attractions.

Tangkiling 35 km (22 miles) distant. The result today is advertised as Kalimantan's "Highway to Nowhere," an all-weather turnpike that stretches between towns where people ride bicycles and on bullock carts.

Central Kalimantan's main attraction is the **Tanjung Puting National Park**, a 3,000-sq-km (1,180-sq mile) preserve inhabited by orangutans, pythons, crocodiles and several species of monkeys. The entrance to the park is located an hour's drive east of Pangkalan Bun at **Kumai**. Located on the

Kumai River, the small town is home to dozens of longboat captains who provide the sole means of transport into the park. Inside the park there are piers where one can get off and hike through the foliage, but except for a few locations such as Camp Leakey, where the Orangutan Research and Conservation Project is located, the heat, humidity and the buzz of circling insects keep most visitors in their boat.

It is possible to direct your boatman down the river to Tanjung Keluang beach on Kumai Bay, but a more rewarding experience lies up the Sekonyer tributary at **Camp Leakey** where Dr. Birute Galdikas

Off to market in Banjarmasin.

teaches captive orangutans to reenter the wild. Because of their gentle disposition, baby orangutans are often captured by Indonesian peasants (in violation of the law) who try to turn them into pets. When they realize that the jungle creature is incompatible with urban life, they try to release the orangutan back into the jungle, but by that time it is too late. The best time to visit Camp Leakey is in the late afternoon when orangutans, proboscis monkeys and other primates come down from the trees to feed. Longboats take about four hours to reach Camp Leakey from Kumai.

A permit from the Indonesian Directorate of Nature Conservation (PHPA) is required to enter Tanjung Puting. This involves producing photocopies of your passport's information Indonesian visa pages for the police in Pangkalan Bun, then proceeding to the PHPA office in Kumai, where you pay a small fee. The procedure can be time-consuming and a serious bother if you are on a day trip into the park.

WHERE TO STAY AND EAT

Pangkalan Bun has a couple of surprisingly good hotels. The **Hotel Blue Kecubung** ((532) 21211 FAX (532) 21513 has comfortable air-conditioned rooms, some of which look onto the garden. It also has a good restaurant. You can phone the Blue Kecubung for information about staying at the **Rimba Lodge**, an inexpensive resort style hotel that is within the boundaries of Tanjung Putung Park.

Back in Pangkalan Bun, the **Hotel Andika**, Jalan Hasanuddin N°51, has none of the pretensions of the Blue Kecubung, but it's a well-run place with some good mid-range air-conditioned rooms. The downstairs, open-front restaurant is a pleasantly breezy place to eat in the evenings.

Don't expect much luxury in remote **Palangkaraya**. Accommodation here is mostly of the cheap but spartan *losmen* variety. An exception is the **Hotel Dandang Tingang** ((514) 21805, Jalan Yos Sudarso N°13, a hotel on the outskirts of town where you will not only find English speaking staff but also air-conditioned rooms, a restaurant and a bar.

HOW TO GET THERE AND AWAY

Though the easiest way to reach the provincial capital of Palangkaraya is by river boat from Banjarmasin, travelers in a hurry may wish to take Merpati, Sempati, DAS or Bouraq. Bouraq has two flights a day into Palangkaraya from Banjarmasin and Sampit, plus daily service to Pangkalan Bun. In addition to daily service from Jakarta, Garuda has nonstop flights from Balikpapan. All of the major airline offices and travel agents in Palangkaraya are located along Jalan Ahmad Yani.

WEST KALIMANTAN

PONTIANAK

West Kalimantan is a rugged, sparsely populated area that sees very few tourists. Prior to the arrival of the Dutch it was composed of the states of Sukadana and Sambas. British adventuring along the coast in the eighteenth century prompted the Dutch to install a puppet sultan in Pontianak. Though West Kalimantan produced some diamonds and precious gems, it was never targeted for large-scale development by the Dutch.

During World War II, West Kalimantan was the scene of numerous atrocities committed by the invading Japanese army. Though figures are imprecise, mass graves uncovered after the war indicate that as many as 15,000 people may have been exterminated.

General Information

The Provincial Tourism Agency ((561) 36172 in Pontianak is at Jalan Ahmad Sood N°25, but no one has a good word for the place. You will probably find the staff at your hotel more useful.

Where to Stay

The **Kapuas Palace** ((561) 36122 FAX (561) 34374, Jalan Imam Bonjol, is Pontianak's best hotel. The hotel's most distinctive feature is a 100-m-long swimming pool which dominates the interior courtyard.

In the same price category the **Hotel Mahkota Kapuas** ((561) 36022 FAX (511)

36200, Jalan Sidas N°8, is closer to the center of town. Foreign businessmen tend to stay here because of the discotheque, health club and rooftop restaurant.

Across the river from City Hall right in the middle of Pontianak is the **Kartika Hotel** ((561) 34401, a nicely appointed hotel, catering predominantly to business travelers, that looks like it has seen better days. If you choose to stay here, take one of the rooms with a view of the river.

Where to Eat

West Kalimantan is a coffee growing province, so Pontianak has plenty of coffeebars. For more substantial dining try the night *warungs* near the Kapuas Indah ferry terminal or the Chinese cafés along jalans Diponegoro and Tanjungpura.

The **Gajah Mada**, Jalan Gajah Mada N°202, is a popular mid-range Chinese restaurant that some claim is the best in town. For less expensive Chinese food in a more Indonesian setting, the **Hawaii** on Jalan Pasah Nusa Indah (opposite the Nusa Indah Plaza) is a good spot.

How to Get There and Away

Pontianak's Pelabuhan Udara Supadio Airport is well served by Garuda, Merpati, Bouraq, and DAS. Located in the same office at Jalan Rahadi Usman N°8A, Garuda and Merpati ((561) 21026 between them cover most major destinations in Indonesia and even Singapore. Bouraq ((561) 32371 has an office at Jalan Tanjungpura N°53. MAS flies to Kuching in Sarawak twice a week. DAS ((561) 34383, Jalan Gajah Mada N°6, has flights into the interior.

There are five PELNI passenger ships that depart on an infrequent (mostly twice per week) but regular schedule for Jakarta. PELNI ((561) 34133 sells tickets at the company headquarters on Jalan Pelu Buhan N°2.

Irian Jaya

COMPRISING the western half of the island of New Guinea, Irian Jaya is Indonesia's largest and least explored province. Roughly equivalent in size to California, it accounts for more than 22% of Indonesia's total land area, yet has a population of only two million, about one percent of Indonesia's total. Irian's rugged terrain is as beautiful as it is inhospitable. The southern Casuarina Coast consists of pristine white beaches and malarial mangrove swamps. The Jayawijaya Mountains, Irian's serrated spine, form an impassable, jungled wall that, despite being just four degrees below the equator, is permanently covered with snow at higher elevations. More than 200 landing strips cut into the jungle have tamed the region slightly, but transportation remains expensive and often depends on pilots working for Mission Aviation Fellowship (MAF), an organization known locally as the "Missionary Air Force."

BACKGROUND

When Portuguese explorers first arrived at the world's second largest island, they called it Islas dos Papuas, Island of the Fuzzy-hairs. Dutch colonists changed the name to Netherlands New Guinea since its black-skinned Melanesian people reminded them of natives in the African country of Guinea. The Dutch had little use for the island because of its poor soil, so they turned its remoteness into a dubious asset by using it as an internment camp for Indonesian nationalists.

Partitioned toward the end of the nineteenth century, the eastern half of the island, Papua New Guinea, came under Australian control at the start of World War I and continued as a trust territory until 1975, when it gained independence. The lesser-developed western half remained in Dutch hands after 1949 when the rest of Indonesia gained independence. But Indonesian president Soekarno maintained military and diplomatic pressure on the Netherlands, which finally agreed to withdraw in 1962 to the consternation of most Papuans.

Soekarno promised the Kennedy administration that citizens of Netherlands New Guinea would be allowed to vote in a 1969 "Act of Free Choice" on whether they wanted to join Indonesia. But when the date for the

referendum arrived, Jakarta canceled the election and instead selected 1,025 delegates, who promptly voted to join Indonesia. Indonesia's newest province became Irian Jaya, or "victorious hot land rising from the sea."

Tensions between Javanese bureaucrats and Irianese natives continues to this day. The Irianese, most of whom continue to live in stone age conditions outside the coastal towns, object to the commercial exploitation of their land by Javanese, whose population is increasing disproportionately because of the government's *transmigrasi* program.

Jakarta's transmigration program has the laudable goal of moving landless peasants from the densely crowded islands of Java and Bali to relatively uninhabited places such as Irian, where they are given land and the tools to begin a new, and hopefully more productive, life. Unfortunately, the shock of arriving in the middle of a jungle where natives wear nothing but a *koteka* (penis sheath) and cut down trees with stone axes does not bode well for cultural integration. Many transmigrants work only long enough to earn their fare back to Java, leaving scarred plots of land quickly leached by tropical rains.

OPPOSITE: A Dani man in Irian Jaya sports a feathered crown. ABOVE: A shell talisman.

Despite its thin top soil, Irian Jaya is one of Indonesia's richest provinces — blessed with an abundance of gold and timber, as well as the world's richest copper deposits.

PERMITS

Bear in mind that while Biak *is*, Jayapura *is not* a visa-free airport, though the only international flights into the latter are from Vanimo in Papua New Guinea.

All travel outside the major population centers of Biak, Jayapura, Sentani and Sorong,

require a *surat jalan*, literally a "travel letter." This includes travel to the Baliem Valley, for which a *surat jalan* can be picked up in Jayapura by applying to the police with two passport photographs and a list of the places you wish to visit. There is a small fee. If you are joining a tour, the agent will process your *surat jalan* for you.

JAYAPURA AND THE NORTH

Irian's capital, **Jayapura**, is separated from Jakarta by more than 3,000 km (1,800 miles) of ocean and dozens of islands. From Jayapura, travelers can fly into the beautiful **Baliem Valley**, visit Vogelkop (Bird's Head Peninsula) and the nearby **Raja Empat Islands Nature Reserve** or hop over to Biak, a coral island rich in memories for veterans of World War II's Pacific Theater. Jayapura is also the jumping off point for those heading to the **Yotefa Nature Reserve**, east of the city along Humboldt Bay.

Though occasionally the main course at a feast, pigs are more often used as currency.

JAYAPURA

Originally named Hollandia, Jayapura was founded by the Dutch shortly after they annexed the territory in 1828. It is a small, stultifying city largely populated by Javanese bureaucrats who would rather be elsewhere. There is little opportunity for shopping, and entertainment consists of pool halls, several movie theaters and karaoke bars. For tourists, Jayapura is essentially a transit point heading into the Baliem Valley.

One place of interest is the **Anthropological Museum** at Cenderawasih University in nearby **Abepura**. It has some excellent Asmat carvings. Open Monday to Saturday from 8 AM to 2:30 PM. Beached landing craft and rusting tanks attract amateur historians to the suburb of **Hamadi** where General Douglas MacArthur landed in 1944. MacArthur's first stop on the road back to the Philippines, Hamadi also has a colorful fish market.

If you have an early flight the following day or simply want to escape the torpor of Jayapura, you may wish to spend the night in **Sentani**, the lakeside town 35 km (22 miles) outside Jayapura near the airport, where flights leave for Wamena, the Baliem Valley capital of the Dani tribe.

General Information

The Jayapura Tourist Office ((967) 33381, Jalan Soa Sio Dok II, Jayapura, is probably the best one-stop source of information on Irian Jaya.

Where to Stay

Jayapura's finest is the **Matoa Hotel** ((967) 31633, Jalan Ahmad Yani N°14, which has a central location close to the Merpati office and manages to maintain surprisingly high standards. Room rates at the **Hotel Dafonsoro** ((967) 31695, Jalan Percetakan N°22–24, are about half the price as at the Matoa; but, if you are looking for a no-frills, air-conditioned, mid-range hotel it's a good choice. All rooms have attached bath with hot water, and breakfast is included in the price of the room.

The **Hotel Sederhana** ((967) 31561 is located right in the middle of Jayapura at Jalan Halmahera N°2, and has a good range

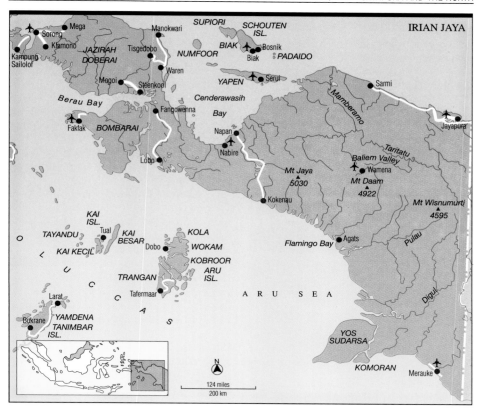

of rooms from inexpensive fan-cooled to air-conditioned. It is convenient to everything of interest in the city, including the night market. Another lodging with inexpensive rooms is the **Hotel Kartini** ((967) 22371, Jalan Perintis N°2, a popular place, despite being somewhat inconveniently located in the southwest of town.

Where to Eat
The restaurant at the **Hotel Dafonsoro** is recommended for its inexpensive but excellent Indonesian dishes. The **Jaya Grill** on Jalan Kota next to the outdoor *warungs* will cost you somewhat more but it's worth it for the seafood and the sea views.

How to Get There and Away
Garuda ((967) 26217, flies to Jakarta three times a week, and Merpati ((967) 33111, also has flights to Jakarta as well as to Denpasar, Biak and Ujung Padang. Merpati also has several flights a day to Wamena, the main town in the Baliem Valley region. You should

reserve well ahead, as flights are typically heavily booked, particularly at the height of the season in August.

PELNI ((967) 33270 has boats that stop in Biak, but they are infrequent.

THE BALIEM VALLEY

About 110,000 Dani live in the Baliem Valley, which was discovered in 1938 by explorer Richard Archbold. "From the air the gardens and ditches and native built walls appeared like the farming country of Central Europe," he later wrote in the *National Geographic*. After landing his seaplane on a lake, Archbold discovered that the natives were remarkably friendly. They mostly ate sweet potatoes and gauged wealth by the number of pigs owned by a family. Today, the Baliem Valley continues to maintain its unique culture. Dani women still wear only short grass skirts around their pelvis. Men's fashion consists of a penis sheath called a *koteka* made from a gourd. A decade ago, Indonesian bureacrats tried to introduce clothes, a reasonable suggestion since the 73-km (45-mile) long Baliem Valley is over 1,500 meters (5,000 ft) high. But on cold nights the Dani prefer to smear themselves with pig grease and huddle about a fire in their communal huts.

Wamena is the main town and a growing tourist area. Accommodation is improving here and so are the access roads to more remote locations around the valley. To fully appreciate the Baliem Valley, however, you will need to either join an organized trek or find a guide and organize a trek of your own.

When you arrive in Wamena you will inevitably be approached by would-be guides. Their rates are generally reasonable, and their services have the great advantage of being personalized: You can inexpensively organize your own trek with a porter, cook and guide to the remote valley villages, an experience of a lifetime. The drawback of choosing a guide in this way is that you have little guarantee that he or she knows what they are doing. If you don't mind spending more money, you can put such concerns aside and go with a travel agency such as Chandra Nusantara Tours & Travel ((969) 31293 FAX 31299, Jalan Trikora, Wamena, one of the longest running and most reliable agents in the area.

Where to Stay

One thing you don't get in the Baliem Valley is value for money. It would be ridiculous to expect it this far from the rest of the world.

The **Honai Resort** ((969) 31515 is a local version of a luxury hotel. The Honai would be an average mid-range hotel in most other parts of Indonesia. Rates, however, start at over US$100. Try instead the **Baliem Palace Hotel** ((969) 31043, Jalan Trikora, where rates are much lower and the spacious rooms come with hot water. There's even a pleasant garden area.

The **Baliem Cottages** ((969) 31370, Jalan Thamrin, goes for the traditional Dani look with cottages that are designed to look like thatched Dani huts. There are attached bathrooms with hot water.

For something less expensive, the **Hotel Anggrek** ((969) 31242, Jalan Ambon, can be recommended as inexpensive, clean and friendly. Elsewhere around Walema are a dozen or so *losmen* with inexpensive rates.

Where to Eat

Most of the beef and fruit in Wamena is flown in, which means you should eat the locally grown vegetables when possible. This is not the culinary capital of Indonesia, and to make matters worse (for some at least), Wamena is dry: You won't find anything alcoholic served here. Most people eat at their hotel or *losmen*. One of the better places to eat is the **Rumah Makan Mas Budi**.

Shopping

There is much more to buy in Wamena than Jayapura. Penis sheaths (*koteka*), bark string bags and handwoven bracelets called *sekan* can be purchased in the market or from shops along Jalan Trikora. Individual Dani with items to sell also cluster outside the hotels. Most of the hand-chiseled stone axes will fit in a suitcase and look surprisingly good when mounted on a wall back home. Asmat carvings are also offered for sale, but the selection is better on Biak.

BIAK

The most idyllic destination in Irian is Biak, a coral island 202 km (125 miles) east of Manokwari in **Cenderawasih Bay**.

The **North Biak Nature Reserve** is full of exotic parrots and cockatoos. After watching the birds, head for **Korem Beach** next to the mouths of two freshwater streams that run through coconut plantations. Nearby **Supiori Island** has an even larger nature reserve that is reachable by boat.

P.T. Biak Paradise Tours & Travel ((961) 21835 at the Hotel Arumbai (see below) is a good agency for tours of World War II sites and for diving excursions. Among other places they can take you out to **Bosnik Beach** where United States marines landed, as well as the **Japanese Cave** where 5,000 soldiers loyal to Emperor Hirohito chose to die rather than surrender. Tours out to the remote but gorgeous **Padaido Island**, which was the main Allied base during the war and is now an unspoiled snorkeling and diving getaway, are more expensive but worth the money.

Where to Stay

The Dutch-built **Hotel Irian** ((961) 21139, Jalan Prof. Moh. Yamin, is across the street from the airport, less than one kilometer (just ovr half a mile) from the center of town. The standard rooms, all with an ocean view, are arrayed motel-fashion around a simple garden, while the VIP rooms, only slightly more expensive, are right on the beach. The mid-range room rates include breakfast.

For mid-range comforts in the town center, the best is the **Hotel Arumbai** ((961) 21835, Jalan Sekat Mekassar N°3, a more modern affair than the Hotel Irian, with well appointed mid-range rooms and a swimming pool amongst its amenities.

The **Basana Inn** ((961) 22281, Jalan Imam Bonjol N°46, offers all the essential mid-range comforts (attached bath and hot water) in a pleasant garden atmosphere, making it a good choice for economizing travelers.

Biak has a number of *losmen* but none of them are particularly salubrious. The **Hotel Solo** ((961) 21397, Jalan Monginsidi N°4, is one of the better inexpensive places, but on Biak you're better off going slightly upmarket and staying, for example, at the Basana.

Where to Eat

Nobody has anything good to say about Biak's restaurants. Along Jalan Ahmad Yani are the usual range of Chinese and Indonesian restaurants, among them **Cleopatra** and **Cinta Rosa**, both of which can be recommended as being a notch above the local average. If you are looking for an alternative to these places, try the night *warungs* off Jalan Imam Bonjol where fare runs to satay, pickled cucumbers and *gado gado*.

THE BIRD'S HEAD PENINSULA

Sorong and **Manokwari** on the Bird's Head Peninsula are oil towns completely devoid

of charm, but Sorong may be worth a stopover since it's the gateway to the Raja Empat Islands Nature Reserve, a bird watcher's paradise covering parts of **Waigeo Batana** and **Gag** islands. Like the island of Komodo, the Raja Empat Reserve is administered by the Indonesian Directorate of Nature Conservation (PHPA), with offices in Sorong at Jalan Permuda N°40.

THE SOUTH COAST

The Casuarina Coast of southern Irian Jaya is a dense and malarial region. Poisonous adders dangle from areca palms; man-eating crocodiles rule the mangrove swamps. The Asmat and other cannibal tribes who inhabit the jungle call their home "the land of lapping death." **Agats** on the southwest coast near Flamingo Bay is the departure point for a journey upriver to Asmat villages,

OPPOSITE: Animist artisans use stone axes to carve ceremonial shields. ABOVE: Television programming and stone age technology is a combination that leaves many Irianese bewildered.

but a trip this far afield must be carefully planned far in advance with the assistance of missionaries.

The Asmat are prolific woodcarvers who adorn their villages with two- to three-meter (six- to 10-ft) tall totem poles adorned with copulating animistic spirits. Commercial objects such as shields, spears and blow guns are also produced. Dealers in the primitive arts may find a journey into the Asmat jungle rewarding, but less adventurous souls can purchase Asmat carvings in Jayapura or the Biak Airport.

Until recently, foreign presence in this area consisted of missionaries and officials of the Freeport Copper Company who ran the world's largest open pit copper mine near **Tembagapura**, a prosperous little town perched 3,700 m (12,136 ft) up snow-capped Mt. Jaya. Freeport's announced withdrawal (owing to pressure from environmentalists) complicates transportation to this area, which has never been easy to reach.

For Westerners, South Irian's greatest mystery concerns the fate of Michael Rockefeller, the 23-year old son of the late American millionaire Nelson Rockefeller, who disappeared suddenly in November 1961.

Drawn to Irian because of his "desire to do something adventurous," Rockefeller worked as a sound man on a documentary film sponsored by Harvard's Peabody Museum. After briefly visiting home, he returned to the Casuarina Coast to live with the Asmat, whose art he began to collect for Manhattan's Museum of Primitive Art. Together with Dutch ethnologist Rene Wassing, Rockefeller set out on an expedition to look for elaborately-decorated human skulls, but the small boat they were using was quickly swamped by the rough currents of the Arafura Sea. Rockefeller's two Asmat guides swam for help, but never returned. Wassing told Rockefeller to wait for rescue, but despite the sharks and crocodiles Rockefeller decided to swim for help and was never seen again.

Did Michael Rockefeller drown? Did he arrive safely ashore only to encounter hostile tribesmen? *Argosy* magazine dispatched a correspondent who concluded Rockefeller was killed by an Asmat tribe seeking revenge for earlier indignities suffered from the Dutch. Rockefeller's fate may remain a mystery forever, but recurring stories of his glasses, clothes and skull appearing in the Asmat village of Ocenep persuade some that the heir to one of America's largest fortunes was the victim of cannibals.

HOW TO GET THERE AND AWAY

Garuda's international flights from Los Angeles and Honolulu once stopped at Biak en route to Jakarta, but this service has been discontinued. (Plans to resume this service had not yet materialized at the time of publication.) Inside Indonesia, Garuda has daily services out of Jakarta and Denpasar to Jayapura, Biak and Sorong. Unfortunately, traveling from Java to Irian is a tiring, all day affair. Garuda flights from Jakarta leave early in the morning and stop at Ujung Padang, Ambon, Sorong and Biak before heading to Jayapura. The Merpati flight from Jakarta can take even longer since it makes an additional stop in Surabaya and overnights in Biak before heading to Jayapura the following day.

Within Irian, transportation is provided by Merpati which has service linking Sorong, Jayapura, Wamena, Merauke and Nabire.

There are a large number of boats plying the waters of Irian Jaya. Most of them are best avoided. Stick to PELNI boats and to flying wherever possible. Traveling by PELNI boat is possible all the way from Java, but it's a long (two-week) trip with some rough patches along the way.

Out of the more than 200 airfields in Irian, fewer than a dozen are serviced by commercial airlines. The remaining strips are used by MAF, or its Catholic counterpart, Associated Mission Aviation, both of which have offices across the road from Sentani Airport. Understandably, as the flow of tourists traveling through Irian Jaya increases each year, both MAF and Associated Mission Aviation have become less enthusiastic about carrying passengers. Only contact them in an emergency.

A Dani youth poses with a prize rooster.

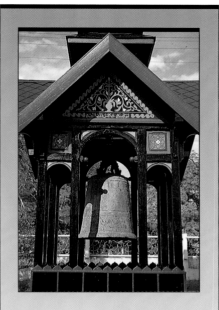

Travelers' Tips

HOW TO GET THERE

BY AIR

A quick look at any map will confirm that Indonesia is not a country in which one "stops over" en route to another destination. That being the case, it is important to plan your trip to Indonesia carefully and shop around for the best travel buys.

Although for many budget travelers, the islands of Indonesia are stepping stones on the Asian overland trail to Australia, the quickest, most economical way to get to Indonesia is by air. From Europe, KLM, Swissair, Lufthansa and Air France all have direct flights. From the United States, Indonesia's national flag-carrier, Garuda Airlines, offers the most efficient, economical service. Flights leave Los Angeles for Jakarta, with stops in Honolulu and Bali's capital of Denpasar four times per week. The only United States airline to fly direct is Continental, which has thrice weekly service to Denpasar via Honolulu and Guam.

If a direct flight to Bali or Jakarta is not your priority, you may want to fly through Singapore, the Southeast Asian hub city with the most connecting flights to Indonesia. Northwest and United both fly direct to Singapore from the United States' West Coast. Singapore Airlines has daily service from San Francisco and Los Angeles, but the flights make several stops and require changing planes in Singapore.

Once you're in Singapore, getting to Indonesia is easy. Singapore Airlines has 10 daily non-stop flights to Jakarta and daily service to Medan in North Sumatra. It also flies to Bali five days a week. Because the number of Singapore Airlines flights between Jakarta, Bali and Singapore is matched by Garuda, the level of service linking the two countries essentially is that of a competitively-priced shuttle.

Executive and full-fare passengers flying with Asian carriers from the United States should look into the availability of free stopovers when flying to Indonesia. Cathay Pacific offers stop-overs in Hong Kong and Malaysian Airlines (MAS) does the same for Kuala Lumpur. Flights from the United States' West Coast to Malaysia via Tokyo arrive in Kuala Lumpur in the evening. MAS will provide a hotel for the evening and take passengers to Jakarta or Medan on connecting flights the following day.

From New York, KLM has direct connections via Amsterdam to Medan in Sumatra and on to Bali. Travelers in Bangkok, another good staging point between Europe and Asia, can take Thai International's daily nonstop to Jakarta or Bali. Qantas has two weekly flights to Jakarta and three flights weekly to Bali from Sydney.

Garuda reservations can be made at the following offices:

Chicago ((312) 443-0060 FAX (312) 443-0036, 20 North Michigan Avenue, Suite 104, Chicago, IL 60602.

Honolulu ((808) 947-9500 FAX (808) 946-9943, 1440 Kapiolani Boulevard, Suite 1503, Honolulu, HI 96814.

Los Angeles ((213) 387-0149 FAX (213) 389-7329, 3457 Wilshire Boulevard, Los Angeles, CA 90010.

New York ((212) 876-2254 FAX (212) 949-3299, 317 Madison Avenue, Suite 621, New York, NY 10017.

San Francisco ((415) 788-2626 FAX (415) 788-3450, 360 Post Street, Suite 804, San Francisco, CA 94108.

Sydney ((02) 334-9900 FAX (02) 223-2216, 55 Hunter Street, NSW.

London (0171 486-3011 FAX 0171 224-3971, 35 Duke Street, W1M5DF London, England.

Paris (01 44 95 15 50 FAX 01 40 75 00 52, 75, avenue des Champs Élysées, 3rd Floor, 75008 Paris, France.

Berlin ((030) 265-1162 FAX (030) 265-1165, Europe Center, 3rd Floor, Tauentzienstrasse 9, 10789 Berlin, Germany.

BY SEA

The great irony of this enormous equatorial archipelago is that it is very difficult to reach by ship. The only two fully established ports of entry are the Medan seaport of Belawan in North Sumatra and Sekupang on Batam Island in the Riau Archipelago. Both are served by hydrofoils and ferries that connect them with Penang in Malaysia and Singapore.

Children play while the grownups pray. Indonesia is the largest Islamic country in the world.

The ferry linking Penang and Belawan runs twice a week and takes 15 hours. In Medan tickets can be purchased from P.T. Eka Sukma Wisata Tour & Travel Service at Jalan Brig. Jend. Katamso N°62 near the Maimoon Palace. In Penang, tickets are sold by Sanren Delta Marine on Jalan Tun Syed Shah Barakbah.

Hydrofoils leave Singapore's World Trade Center at frequent intervals from around 8 AM to 7 PM to Sekupang on Batam. After clearing customs there, it's possible to board another ferry for a two-hour trip to Tanjung Pinang.

USEFUL ADDRESSES

CONSULAR INFORMATION

In addition to visas, Indonesia's embassies and consulates have valuable information on annual events which you may wish to time your visit to coincide with.

United States
INDONESIAN EMBASSY
((202) 775-5200, 2020 Massachusetts Avenue NW, Washington, DC 20036.

INDONESIAN CONSULATES
Chicago ((312) 345-9300 FAX (312) 345-9311, 72 East Randolf Street, Chicago, IL 60601.
Honolulu ((808) 524-4300, Pri Tower, 733 Bishop Street, Honolulu, HI 96813.
Houston ((713) 785-1691 FAX (713) 780-9644, 10900 Richmond Avenue, Houston, TX 77042.
Los Angeles ((213) 383-5126 FAX (213) 487-3971, 3457 Wilshire Boulevard, Los Angeles, CA 90010.
New York ((212) 879-0600 FAX (212) 570-6206, 5 East 68th Street, New York, NY 10021.
San Francisco ((415) 474-9571 FAX (415) 441-4320, 1111 Columbus Avenue, San Francisco, CA 94133.

Canada
INDONESIAN EMBASSY
((613) 236-7403 FAX (613) 563-2858, 287 Maclaren Street, Ottawa, ON K29 OL9.

INDONESIAN CONSULATES
Toronto ((416) 591-648 FAX (416) 591-6613, 425 University Avenue, 9/F, Toronto, ON M56 1T6.

Vancouver ((604) 682-8855 FAX (604) 662-8396, 1455 West Georgia Street, 2/F, Vancouver, BC V6G 2T3.

Netherlands
INDONESIAN EMBASSY
((70) 310-8100, Tobias Asserlaan N°8, 5517, KCS Gravenhage.

Germany
INDONESIAN EMBASSY
((0228) 328990, Bernkasteler Strasse 2, 53175 Bonn.

INDONESIAN CONSULATES
Berlin ((030) 472-2002, Esplanade 7-9, 13187 Berlin.
Bremen ((0421) 332-2224, Domhof 26, D-2800 Bremen.
Düsseldorf ((0211) 626151, Moersenbroicher Weg 200/VII 40470 Düsseldorf.
Hamburg ((040) 512071, Bebelallee 15, 22299 Hamburg.
Hannover ((0511) (361) 2150, Georg Platz 1 Hannover.
Munich ((089) 294609, Widenmayerstrasse-24, 80538 München.
Stuttgart ((0711) 226-0341, Klettpassage 39, 70173 Stuttgart.

Great Britain
INDONESIAN EMBASSY
((0171) 499-7661 FAX (0171) 491-4993, 38 Grosvenor Square, London W1X 9AD.

Australia
INDONESIAN EMBASSY
((062) 273-3222 FAX 2733748, 8 Darwin Avenue, Yarralumia, Canberra, ACT.

INDONESIAN CONSULATES
Adelaide ((08) 430-8742, Beulah Park Place 44 Gawler, Adelaide, SA.
Darwin ((089) 410048, 20 Harry Chan Avenue, Darwin, NT.
Melbourne ((03) 9525-2755, 72 Queen Road, Melbourne, NSW.
Perth ((09) 221-5858, 134 Adelaide Terrace, Perth, WA.

Europe's demand for cloves and nutmeg, which were found only on the islands of Ternate TOP and Banda BOTTOM, prompted explorers such as Christopher Columbus to set out in search of the East Indies.

Sydney ((02) 9349-6854, 236-238 Maroubra Road, Maroubra, Sydney, NSW.

Indonesian Tourist Promotion Offices
For additional information and maps get in touch with your nearest Indonesia Tourist Promotion Office (ITPO):
Australia ((02) 9233-3630 FAX (02) 9357-3478, Level 10, 5 Elizabeth Street, Sydney, NSW.
Germany ((069) 233-6778 FAX (069) 230840. Wiesenhuettenplatz 17, 60329 Frankfurt am Main.
Singapore (534-2837 FAX 533-4287, 10 Collyer Quay, 15-07 Ocean Building, Singapore 0104.
Great Britain ((171) 493-0030 FAX (171) 493-1747, 3-4 Hanover Street, London W1 9HH.
United States ((213) 387-2078 FAX (213) 380-4876, 3457 Wilshire Boulevard, Los Angeles, CA 90010.

ARRIVING

TRAVEL DOCUMENTS

All travelers to Indonesia must possess passports valid for at least six months after arrival and proof of onward passage.

Neither visas nor immigration fees are required for nationals of the following countries: Australia, Austria, Belgium, Brunei, Canada, Denmark, Finland, France, Germany, Greece, Iceland, Ireland, Italy, Japan, Liechtenstein, Luxembourg, Malaysia, Malta, the Netherlands, New Zealand, Norway, the Philippines, Singapore, South Korea, Spain, Sweden, Switzerland, Thailand, the United Kingdom, the United States. Citizens of countries not listed above can obtain one-month, non-extendable visas from any Indonesian embassy or consulate.

Entry to and exit from Indonesia must be made either through air or seaports in Ambon, Balikpapan, Bandung, Batam, Belawan, Benoa, Biak, Denpasar, Dumai, Jakarta, Manado, Mataram, Medan, Padang, Pekanbaru, Pontianak, Semarang, Surabaya and Tanjung Pinang. Visas are required for arrival or departure through any other ports in the country.

Extensions on two month visas are granted only under exceptional circum-

stances. It is easier to leave the country and re-enter.

CUSTOMS

A maximum of two liters (three and a quarter pints) of alcohol, 200 cigarettes or 50 cigars can be brought in duty-free. Importing of television sets is prohibited. All video cassettes are subject to seizure and editing by the Film Censor Board.

WHEN TO GO

Indonesia has an equatorial tropical climate tempered by tradewinds. Temperatures hover around 28°C (82°F) in the coastal areas, but drop rapidly at higher elevations. The average humidity is 81%. The wet season is from October to April, and the dry season is from May to September. It can rain any time, however, with the heaviest rains coming in December and January. Kalimantan receives 330 cm (130 in) of rain a year, while eastern Nusa Tenggara gets less than 100 cm (40 in). Bogor is the wettest spot on the island of Java.

WHAT TO WEAR AND BRING

Casual and light clothing is best suited to the climate, but for travel in the mountain areas of West Java and Irian Jaya one should have a sweater or jacket. A coat and tie is always appropriate for diplomatic functions, but long-sleeved batik shirts are acceptable almost everywhere else.

Most essentials can be bought in the major cities of Indonesia, but if you have brand preferences for any particular product it is a good idea to come stocked with your own supplies.

GETTING AROUND

BY AIR

Indonesia has a large number of domestic airlines. How safe some of them are is open to debate and testimony, but most visitors to Indonesia fly at one point or another simply

Flag bedecked pier at Jakarta Bay.

because flights save so much time and because ground travel in Indonesia can be so arduous.

Garuda flies to all of Indonesia's large cities and many of its smaller ones. There are booking offices throughout Indonesia. If you are entering the country with Garuda, you are entitled to a "Visit Indonesia Decade Pass." At approximately US$100 per sector, the pass is only really cost-effective if you are planning to fly long routes from Jakarta, for example, to destinations in Nusa Tenggara or farther afield. The pass must be bought overseas or within 14 days of arriving in Indonesia and is valid for Merpati flights too.

There are a number of Garuda Indonesia offices in Jakarta. The two most convenient are in the Hotel Indonesia ((21) 320-0568, Jalan M.H. Thamrin, and in the Hotel Inter-Continental ((21) 231-1991, Jalan Lapangan Bateng.

Merpati Nusantara Airlines ((21) 654-0690, Jalan Angkasa N°B-15, Kav 2, Jakarta, is the second national carrier and flies to a huge number of destinations, the more obscure ones, it should be added, on an irregular basis. It also has a few cross-border flights to Darwin, Australia, Brunei Darussalam and the East Malaysian state of Sarawak. Merpati is particularly active in the smaller islands of eastern Indonesia and the interiors of Kalimantan, Sulawesi and Irian Jaya. Though Merpati and Garuda have made connections more convenient by coordinating their route structures, you still have to buy a Merpati ticket from Merpati Airlines.

Three privately-owned airlines, Bouraq, Mandala and Sempati, try their best to compete with the state-subsidized carriers. Of the three, Bouraq (named after the horse on which the Prophet Mohammed rode to Heaven) has the larger route structure and is particularly useful in getting to coastal cities of Kalimantan and Sulawesi. In Jakarta Bouraq ((21) 629-5364 is located at Jalan Angkasa N°1–3, and Sempati ((21) 809-4407 is at Jalan Medon Merdeka Timur N°7.

An airport tax of Rp25,000 is levied on all departing passengers on international flights and Rp11,000 for domestic flights. This may rise in the future. Check with your hotel concierge before leaving for the

airport, or call the airline to get the current amount.

BY TRAIN

Train service is only available on Java and Sumatra. The most heavily traveled route is between Jakarta and Surabaya. The most comfortable trains by far are the air-conditioned *Bima* sleeper train and the *Mutiara*, which also runs at night. The *Bima* passes through Yogyakarta and Solo, while the *Mutiara* takes the northern route through Semarang. Another train, the *Senja Utama*, offers express service to Yogyakarta and Solo, but it has no air conditioning. Bandung is well serviced by the *Parahyangan Express*, which makes four three-hour round trips a

day between Jakarta and the mountain city the Dutch built to escape the heat.

BY TAXI

Metered taxis operate in the major cities of Java and in some parts of Bali, but elsewhere you will need to haggle over your fare before you set off. Metered taxis are inexpensive.

Jakarta has a number of taxi companies. Blue Bird, President and Steady Safe are the best. Blue Bird cabs are clean and the drivers are courteous, but often their English is minimal, so it's always advisable to have a written address for your destination.

Taxis also serve as an efficient and economical way to move about West Java. A number of companies shuttle between Jakarta and Bandung, and one even offers service to Bandar Lampung on the southern tip of Sumatra.

BY SHIP

PELNI, the state-owned shipping company, traverses the archipelago with a fleet of nearly 20 ships (and still growing) that carry up to 1,800 passengers in five classes of service. Not luxurious but comfortable, the ships are air-conditioned and have cabins with attached bath and television sets in the first-class.

Bugis schooners from the Celebes and beyond make the port of Sunda Kelapa a favorite of photographers.

BY BUS

Buses are cheap, fast and crowded. Inner city buses are labeled *bis kota* on the side. Long-haul buses that travel overnight between large towns are called *bis malam*. Because Indonesian roads are poorly lit and crowded with trucks, a trans-Java excursion can have its share of close calls. Indonesians who can afford to fly, do so, and you should too.

If your budget dictates land travel, there are a variety of ways to move between cities. In addition to a *bis malam* you can take a Colt minivan between towns. Cheaper still are *bemos*, small pickup trucks with a bench along each side.

BY CAR

Avis, Hertz and National have self-drive and chauffeured rentals in Jakarta, Yogyakarta and at other major tourist areas, but before you rent your own car think twice. Road rules, as most Westerners will know them, are not much in evidence and if you're involved in an accident and a local is injured the legal ramifications can be Kafkaesque. Worse still, in rural Indonesia, traffic accidents often result in extremely ugly and dangerous "scenes." The best solution is to rent a car or minibus with a driver who is used to local conditions and who will know what to do if anything happens.

As a rule, driving is not worth the hassle. The exception is Bali where traffic is less intense and jeeps can be rented at normal prices from shops along Legian Road in Kuta Beach. If you decide to drive, remember that Indonesians drive on the left side of the road and call gasoline *bensin*. If you get lost on Java, ask for the *kepala kampung* (village chief) or the *bupati* (district chief). Avoid police unless you speak Indonesian, and never surrender your driver's license unless forced to do so at a central police station.

BY HITCHHIKING

Only the poorest of Indonesians begs a lift, and even then payment is expected. Sticking your thumb out at roadside may create some confusion. Hitching is not recommended.

TOURIST INFORMATION

Each of the 27 provinces of Indonesia has its own tourist office which goes by the abbreviation DIPARDA (Provincial Tourist Service) or BAPPARDA (Provincial Tourism Agency). Some of these offices are useful, some aren't. The greater the tourist traffic in an area, the better the quality of service and volume of hand-outs in the local tourist office.

In Jakarta the Directorate General of Tourism ((21) 383-8217 is located at Jalan Merdeka Barat N°16–19.

EMBASSIES AND CONSULATES

AMERICAN EMBASSY ((21) 360360, Jalan Merdeka Selatan N°5, Jakarta.
AUSTRALIAN EMBASSY ((21) 522-7111, Jalan Rasuna Said, Kav 15–16, Jakarta.
BRITISH EMBASSY ((21) 330904, Jalan M.H. Thamrin N°75, Jakarta.
CANADIAN EMBASSY ((21) 510709, 5/F, Wisma Metropolitan I, Jalan Jend. Sudirman, Kav N°29, Jakarta.
FRENCH EMBASSY ((21) 314-2807, Jalan M.H. Thamrin N°20, Jakarta.
GERMAN EMBASSY ((21) 394-9547, Jalan Raden Saleh N°54–56, Jakarta.
JAPANESE EMBASSY ((21) 324308, Jalan M.H. Thamrin N°24 Jakarta.
NETHERLANDS EMBASSY ((21) 511515, Jalan Rasuna Said Kav N°83, Jakarta.

HEALTH

Western doctors advise getting a battery of vaccinations before setting out for Indonesia. That said, the worst that usually happens to most visitors is an upset stomach — a rite of passage for anyone new to the tropics.

The most serious health risks in Indonesia are malaria and dengue fever. Both of these mosquito-spread diseases make their appearences in isolated spots throughout the archipelago, but unless you get a long way off the beaten track the risks of catching either are minimal. See your doctor about the appropriate malaria prophylactic to take before you go and make sure you cover up each evening, when the female (malaria-carrying) mosquitoes come out.

Komodo Island is a bad place to have a toothache, so have a dental check up before leaving home. Also, bring any prescription medication you may require. Fungal infections can be a problem because of the heat, so you may want to travel with talcum powder or an anti-fungal spray.

If a medical problem arises, there are a variety of Western-educated doctors practicing in Jakarta. The most centrally located office is the Medical Center ((21) 52-5435, Jalan Rasuna Said, Kav C21. If you prefer a clinic where all the doctors speak English

credit cards are widely accepted in Jakarta hotels and restaurants, some travelers charge every expense believing the interval between the time of their purchase and the time the credit company bills their bank will result in a more favorable rate of exchange. Though deficient in other areas, Indonesian businesses are remarkably efficient at processing card charges because of the rupiah's declining value. After returning home don't be surprised if all your expenses appear on the first credit summary you receive in the mail.

or Dutch, call the Medical Scheme ((21) 515597 in the Setiabundi Building on Jalan H. Rasuna Said.

MONEY

Indonesia's national currency, the rupiah, was highly unstable at the time of researching this book, varying between 2,500 rupiah and 16,000 rupiah per United States dollar. When this book went to press a United States dollar was worth 11,250 rupiah. Check with your bank, or an international newspaper like the *International Herald Tribune* before departing for Indonesia.

In tourist haunts prices tend to be expressed in United States dollars. Because

Outside Jakarta, Yogyakarta and Bali you must pay cash for goods and services. Carry rupiah in small denominations; large bills are often difficult to change. Personal checks are useless and travelers' checks, if accepted at all, can take hours to negotiate. Only the most tourist-wise businessmen accept credit cards, so their usefulness is extremely limited. Though you may opt for greater security, the best way to finance a trip through Indonesia is to carry US$100 bills, which can be exchanged for rupiah when needed at a rate slightly above what is offered for travelers' checks. Don't exchange money until you need it since those unspent rupiah in your

Lake Toba passenger ferries provide the only transportation to Samosir Island.

pocket lose a bit if their value every day. Neither, however, should you wait until you get to an out of the way place such as West Kalimantan, Irian Jaya or Nusa Tenggara since the rate moneychangers offer there is not competitive with that available in places such as Java and Bali.

Banks are generally open from 8 AM to 2 or 3 PM. Branch banks in hotels stay open longer and moneychangers may be open until midnight.

TIPPING

Hotels add a service charge of 10% to the bill. Restaurants each have their own policies, so you must look at your bill and add five to 10% if service has not been included. Tipping is not mandatory anywhere. Taxi drivers and hotel porters do not expect a tip, though one will be happily received. Baggage handlers at airports do expect to be tipped US$.50 for every bag they carry, plus a bit more if the suitcases are large and heavy.

ACCOMMODATION

Despite promotions such as "Visit Indonesia Decade," tourist levels have stagnated in recent years, while at the same time there has been a furious scramble to provide new luxury hotel accommodation. The result is low occupancy rates and plenty of bargains for visitors.

Better hotels list their room rates in US dollars. Small *losmen* or guesthouses that require payment in cash list their rates in rupiah, as do some of the older and longer-running mid-range hotels. All major hotels in the larger cities accept credit cards.

ETIQUETTE

Handshaking is customary for men and women alike when being introduced or greeting another person. Be sure to shake hands with everyone when greeting a small group of people. To give or receive anything with the left hand is unacceptable, as is touching an adult on the head. It is considered impolite to call people by crooking the finger or to point to an individual or to

objects on the ground with your foot. Neither should you stand with your hands on your hips, since the posture evokes unpleasant memories of plantation overseers. Though the majority of Indonesians are Muslims, it is permissible to eat pork and drink alcohol in their presence, except around Bandar Aceh in North Sumatra where fundamentalism prevails. Beyond the beach communities on Bali women should never wear shorts. If you visit an Indonesian home or office and food and drink is placed before you, do not eat or drink until

invited to. Often, steaming coffee or tea will be allowed to cool as the conversation continues and will be verbally offered late in the meeting, after which it should be drunk rather quickly as the meeting is considered at an end.

Naughty Indonesian children are pinched instead of spanked. A child is also sometimes pinched as a sign of affection. If you are traveling with children, be sure to warn them of this custom.

TELEPHONE

Indonesian telephone numbers vary in the number of digits depending on the location. Offices with several telephone lines in some cities often list a six digit number and a seven digit number. The system is not as confusing as it initially appears; Indonesia simply adds new numbers as they are needed and small towns such as Jayapura have five digit numbers while Jakarta has six and seven digit numbers. Add "0" before city code when calling within Indonesia.

Outside of the major hotels, you won't find many public telephones. Those you happen to find take a Rp100 coin for a local call. In smaller towns the best place to make

New Zealand   64
Pakistan   92
Singapore   65
Spain   34
Thailand   66
United Kingdom   44
United States   1
Russia   7

INDONESIAN CITY CODES

Ambon   911
Balikpapan   542

a call is the Telephone and Telegraph Office. The offices are remarkably efficient at putting through normal (*biasa*) calls. For even faster service, pay a modest premium for immediate (*segara*) service.

COUNTRY CODES

Australia   61
Denmark   45
Egypt   20
France   33
Germany   49
Hong Kong   852
India   91
Japan   81
Mexico   52

Banda Aceh   651
Bandung   22
Banjarbaru   5119
Banjarmasin   511
Banyuwangi   333
Bekasi   99
Belawan   619
Bengkulu   736
Biak   961
Binjai   619
Blitar   342
Bogor   251
Bojonegoro   353
Bondowoso   332

Sumatra's Grand Mosque OPPOSITE is the pride of Banda Aceh. ABOVE: Colorful celebrations occur throughout the Indonesian year.

Bukittinggi   752
Cianjur   263
Cibinong   99
Cilacap   282
Cimahi   229
Cipanas   255
Cirebon   231
Denpasar   361
Gadog/Cisarua   251
Garut   262
Gresik   319
Jakarta   21
Jambi   741
Jayapura   967
Jember   311
Jombang   321
Kabanjahe   628
Karawang   267
Kebumen   287
Kediri   354
Kendal   294
Kendari   401
Kisaran   624
Klaten   272
Kotabaru   622
Kuala Simpang   641
Kudus   291
Kupang   391
Lahat   731
Langsa   641
Lhok Seumawe   645
Lhok Sukon   645
Lunajang   334
Madiun   351
Magelang   293
Malang   341
Manado   431
Manokwari   962
Mataram   364
Medan   61
Merauke   971
Metro   725
Mojokerto   321
Nusa Dua   361
Padang   751
Palangkaraya   514
Palembang   711
Palu   451
Pamekasan   324
Parapat   622
Pare Pare   421
Pati   295
Pekalongan   285

Pekanbaru   761
Pematang Siantar   622
Ponorogo   351
Pontianak   561
Parapat   622
Prigen   343
Probolinggo   335
Purwakarta   264
Purwokerto   281
Rantepao   423
Sabang   652
Salatiga   298
Samarinda   541
Sekupang   778
Semarang   24
Serang   254
Sibolga   631
Sidoarjo   219
Sigli   338
Situbondo   332
Solo   271
Sorong   951
Sukabumi   266
Sumbawa Besar   27
Sumedang   261
Surabaya   31
Tangerang   99
Tanjung Karang   271
Tarakan   551
Tasikmalaya   265
Tebing Tinggi   621
Tegal   283
Ternate   921
Tulung Agung   355
Ujung Padang   411
Yogyakarta   274

NEWSPAPERS AND MAGAZINES

One thing Indonesia is short of is news from the outside world. There are several English-language newspapers published in Indonesia — all are dreadful. Imported newspapers are available, but they are heavily taxed. A *Bangkok Post* or *South China Morning Post* from Hong Kong can cost US$4. *Time* magazine is widely available. If you crave news of the world, bring along a small short wave radio.

Even English-language books printed in Indonesia are expensive. If you transit at Changi Airport in Singapore, make the most of your transit time and buy books there.

BASICS

TIME

Indonesia has three time zones. Jakarta, in the West Indonesia time zone, is Greenwich Mean Time plus seven hours. Thus, when it's midnight in London, it is 7 AM in Jakarta, 8 AM in Lombok and 9 AM in Irian Jaya. Because Indonesia is so straddles the equator, the days are the same length all year around.

ELECTRICITY

Electrical outlets in Indonesia supply 220–240 volts at 50 cycles current and require two-prong plugs. Transformers normally are available in hotels for travelers carrying laptop computers or hair dryers. Power surges are not common, but brown-outs are, so be sure to save information often when using a computer.

WATER

Drink only bottled or boiled water. Most hotels, and many small *losmen*, provide bottled water at no charge. Mineral water or purified water in plastic containers can also be purchased in small grocery stores. Every restaurant offers *air minum* or boiled water.

HYGIENE

In Bahasa Indonesia the term for "to wash" is *mandi*. *Mandi* is also the name for the large square water tank in most Indonesian bathrooms. Instead of taking a shower, Indonesians use a plastic bucket or dipper to splash themselves with water from the *mandi*. After lathering up, they rinse off by sloshing more water. It is a thoroughly refreshing way to take a bath, especially at the end of a long, hot day. The *mandi* is refilled periodically and used by everyone. Nothing should be washed or rinsed in the *mandi* itself.

Beyond the tourist centers of Java and Bali toilets tend to be nothing more than a hole in the floor with footrests on either side. The toilet is flushed with water dipped from the *mandi*. Indonesian toilets in restaurants and gasoline stations normally don't pro-

vide toilet paper, so you may wish to carry your own.

CRIME

In comparison to the United States and Australia, Indonesia is a very safe country. There is very little violent crime of the sort encountered in cities such as New York and Chicago. Robbery and pickpocketing can be a problem, however, for people who are careless or imprudent. When traveling in remote areas where traveler's checks are not readily accepted, it is advisable to wear a money belt.

In Jakarta and Bali, employees at the better hotels are carefully selected. In general, it is quite safe to leave cameras or travel documents in a locked hotel room. Money and jewelry, however, probably should be put in a safety deposit box or closet safe.

LANGUAGE: BAHASA INDONESIA FOR TRAVELERS

More than 250 distinct languages and dialects are spoken throughout the Indonesian Archipelago, but the unifying tongue is Bahasa Indonesia. A refinement of classical Malay spoken on the Malay Peninsula, it is a relatively new language that has been officially recognized only since Indonesian independence.

Indonesians in large cities tend to speak several languages. In Yogyakarta, for example, Javanese is spoken in the home, while Bahasa Indonesia is the language of the workplace. English is taught in public schools and widely spoken by those in commercial trade service industries. Dutch is also an elective course that some students are beginning to study again. Indonesian professionals age 60 and older usually were educated in the Dutch language. But the general preference for a second language today is English.

GRAMMAR AND PRONUNCIATION

Bahasa Indonesia is a relatively easy language to learn because sentence structure is simple, it is written in Roman script and, unlike other Asian languages, it is phonetic, not tonal. There are no articles: *peta*, for example, means "a map." To make a noun plural, just double it, so that *peta-peta* (or *peta2* as it might be written in a newspaper) becomes "maps." Neither are there verb tenses. Past and future are denoted by the use of adverbs such as *sudah* (already) and *belum* (not yet).

In speaking the language remember that adjectives always follow the noun, and the order of sentences is subject–verb–object, as in *Saya* (I) *angkat* (carry) *peta* (the map). The possessive is accomplished by putting the personal pronoun after the noun. *Peta saya* means "my map."

In 1972 the country simplified spelling, making it conform to Malay. Some Indonesians prefer the old spelling, especially when it comes to their names, so that's why you'll see newspapers spelling their president's name Soeharto instead of Suharto. Pronunciation is roughly as follows:

a   a short sound, as in "father"
c   "ch" sound as in "church"
k   hard at the start of a word, as in "kite," and silent when it comes at the end
kh slightly aspirated
j   as in the word "James" (Under the old spelling dj substituted for j. That's why on old maps Jakarta is sometimes spelled Djarkata.)
r   rolled
u   full as in "ukulele," never as it sounds in "but"
y   as in "you"

15	*limabelas*
20	*duapuluh*
21	*duapuluh satu*
30	*tigapuluh*
40	*empatpuluh*
100	*seratus*
200	*duaratus*
243	*duaratus empatpuluh tiga*
500	*limaratus*
1,000	*seribu*
2,000	*duaribu*
10,000	*sepuluh ribu*
100,000	*seratus ribu*

Numbers

0   *noi*
1   *satu*
2   *dua*
3   *tiga*
4   *empat*
5   *lima*
6   *enam*
7   *tujuh*
8   *delapan*
9   *sembilan*
10   *sepuluh*
11   *sebelas*
12   *duabelas*
13   *tigabelas*
14   *empatbelas*

first   *pertama*
second   *kedua*
third   *ketiga*
fourth   *keempat*
fifth   *kelima*
sixth   *keenam*
seventh   *ketujuh*
eighth   *kedalapan*
ninth   *kesembilan*
tenth   *kesepuluh*
½ (half)   *setengah*
¼ (one quarter)   *seperempat*
⅔ (two thirds)   *duapertiga*

Calendar

Sunday   *Hari Minggu*
Monday   *Hari Senen*

Tuesday   *Hari Selasa*
Wednesday   *Hari Rabu*
Thursday   *Hari Kamis*
Friday   *Hari Jum'at*
Saturday   *Hari Sabtu*
day   *hari*
today   *hari ini*
tomorrow   *besok*
yesterday   *kemarin*
week   *minggu*
month   *bulan*
year   *tahun*
season   *musim*
hot season   *musim panas*
dry season   *musim kemarau*
wet season   *musim hujan*
January   *Januari*
February   *Februari*
March   *Maret*
April   *April*
May   *Mei*
June   *Juni*
July   *Juli*
August   *Agustus*
September   *September*
October   *Oktober*
November   *Nopember*
December   *Desember*

Time
morning (dawn to 11 AM)   *pagi*
good morning   *salamat pagi*
noon (midday, 11 AM to 2 PM)   *siang*
good day   *salamat siang*
evening (3 PM to 8 PM)   *sore*
good evening   *salamat sore*
good night   *salamat malam*
always   *selalu*
before   *dahulu*
soon   *nanti*
now   *sekarang*
right now   *baru saja*
quick   *cepat*
very flexible ("rubber time")   *jam karet*
about (approximately)   *kira-kira*
then   *kemudian*
What time is it?   *Jam berapa sekarang?*
Eight o'clock   *jam delapan*
Half-past eight   *setengah sembilan*

Key Words and Phrases
yes   *ya*
no   *tidak*

I'm sorry   *Ma'af.*
I beg your pardon   *Saya mohon ma'af.*
Thank you.   *Terima kasih.*
What is your name?   *Siapa nama saudara?*
My name is…   *nama saya…*
I come from…   *Saya datang dari…*
Mr.   *Tuan, Pak, Bung*
Mrs.   *Nyonya, Ibu*
Miss   *Nona*
and   *dan*
but   *tetapi*
this/that   *ini/itu*
here/there   *disini/disana*

more/less   *lebih/kurang*
much/very much   *banyak/banyak sekali*
very nice   *bagus*
big/small   *besar/kecil*
young/old   *muda/tua*
clean/dirty   *bersih/kotor*
hot/cold   *panas/dingin*
good/no good   *baik/tidak baik*
open/closed   *buka/tutup*
You're right./You're wrong.   *Anda benar./
Anda salah.*
entrance/exit   *masuk/keluar*
push/pull   *tolak/tarik*
no smoking   *dilarang merokok*
I don't speak Indonesian.   *Saya tidak bicara
Bahasa Indonesia.*
I speak only a little Indonesian.   *Saya bisa
bicara sedikit saja Bahasa Indonesia.*
please   *silahkan*
Please speak slowly.   *Tolong bicara pelan-
pelan.*

OPPOSITE: When you eat *padang* style you pay only
for what you eat. ABOVE: Some antique *ikat* textiles
are worth hundreds of dollars.

Do you speak English? *Apa saudara dapat bicara Bahasa Inggeris?*
I understand. *Saya mengerti.*
I don't understand *Saya kurang mengerti*
goodbye (to person going) *salamat jalan*
goodbye (to person staying) *salamat tinggal*

In the Post Office
post office *kantor pos*
stamp *prangko*
letter *surat*
package/parcel *paket/bungkusan*
aerogram *warkatpos udara*

airmail *pos udara*
postcard *kartu pos*
tape *isolatip*
overweight *terlalu berat*
I'm looking for the post office. *Saya sedang mencari kantor pos.*
I want to send this letter via regular mail. *Saya mau mengirim surat ini biasa.*
This is a special delivery letter. *Ini adalah surat kilat.*

In Restaurants
restaurant *restoran, rumah makan*
Where is a good restaurant? *Restoran mana yang baik?*
I'm hungry. *Saya lapar.*
dining room *kamar makan*

breakfast *makan pagi*
lunch *makan siang*
dinner *makan malam*
food/drink *makanan/minuman*
water/boiled water *air/air putih*
Is this water drinkable? *Apa air ini bisa diminum?*
I would like to drink boiled water. *Saya minta air matang untuk minum air.*
drinking water *air minum.*
ice/iced water *es/air es*
tea/coffee *teh/kopi*
beer *bir*
milk *susu*
bread/butter *roti/mentega*
rice/noodles *nasi/mie*
soup *soto*
chicken *ayam*
beef *daging gapi*
pork *babi*
lamb *domba*
goat *kambing*
fish *ikan*
shrimp *udang*
vegetables *sayur*
fruit *buah*
banana *pisang*
coconut *kelapa*
mango *mangga*
pineapple *nanas*
egg *telur*
fried egg/omelet *telur mata sapi/telur dadar*
boiled/fried *rebus/goreng*
sugar *gula*
salt/pepper *garam/merica*
sweet/sour/spicy *manis/asam/pedas*
hot/cold *panas/dingin*
soya sauce *kecap*
cup/glass *cangkir/gelas*
plate *piring*
knife/fork/spoon *pisau/garpu/sendok*
Where is the toilet? *Dimana kamar kecil?*
May I see the menu? *Boleh saya lihat daftar makanan?*
Waiter, please bring the bill. *Bung, saya minta bonnya.*

In the Hotel
hotel *hotel*
small hotel, guesthouse *losmen*

ABOVE: Tamun Ayun, at Mengwi in South Bali — Note the *meru* OPPOSITE with several levels, visible in the background.

Where is the hotel? *Dimana ada hotel?*
Do you have a room with a private bath? *Apa anda kamar yang pakai kamar mandi tersendiri?*
How much for one night? *Berapa harganya satu malam?*
Does the price include breakfast? *Apakah sewanya termasuk sarapan pagi?*
room/bedroom *kamar/kamar tidur*
bathroom *kamar mandi*
toilet *kamar kecil*
toilet paper *kertas toilet*
towel *handuk*
soap *sabun*

to wash *cuci*
clothes *pakaian*
Please wash these clothes. *Tolong cuci pakaian-pakaian.*
to iron *gosok*
I want to check out. *Saya mau keluar sekarang.*
Please get me a taxi. *Tolong panggilkan saya taksi.*

On the Road
left/right *kiri/kanan*
bus *bis*
bicycle *sepeda*
train/train station *kereta-api/stasiun kereta-api*
airplane/airport *kapal terbang/lapangan terbang*

I want a ticket to… *Saya mau beli karcis ke…*
What's the fare? *Berapa ongkosnya?*
How long does it take to get from here to… *Berapa lama perjalanan dari sini ke…*
ship *kapal laut*
first class/economy class *kelas satu/kelas ekonomi*
I want to reserve two seats to… *Saya mau pesan dua kursi untuk ke…*
gasoline station *pompa bensin*
city *kota*
central *pusat*
I'm lost. *Saya tersesat.*
What's the name of this street? *Apa nama jalan ini?*
market *pasar*
office building *wisma*
hospital *rumah sakit*
pharmacy *apotik*
taxi *taksi*
How much is this taxi per hour? *Berapa sewa taksi ini per jam?*
Drive faster. I'm in a hurry *Cepat sedikit. Saya buru-buru.*

Shopping
antique *antik*
How much? *Berapa?*
cheap/expensive *murah/mahal*
like this/like that *begini/begitu*
I'm just looking. *Saya hanya melihat-nrelihat.*
What is this? *Apakah ini?*
I want to buy… *Saya mau beli…*
It's too expensive. *Itu terlalu mahal.*
I'll come back later. *Saya akan kembali lagi.*

In Emergencies
I've lost my passport. *Paspor saya hilang.*
Please help me *Tolonglah saya sebentar.*
Is there anyone here who speaks English? *Ada yang bisa berbahasa inggeris disini?*
Please go away! *Pergilah!*
Please call a doctor. *Tolong panggilkan dokter.*

Ramayana dancers personalize the Hindu epic with their own interpretations.

Recommended Reading

History and Politics

BOXER, C.R. *Jan Compagnie in War and Peace (1602–1799)*. Heinemann, Hong Kong 1979.

CROUCH, HAROLD. *The Army and Politics in Indonesia*. Cornell University Press 1978.

GRISWOLDE, DEIDRE. *Indonesia*. World View Publishers, Chicago 1979.

JONES, HOWARD PALFREY. *Indonesia: The Possible Dream*. HBJ, New York 1971.

MAY, BRIAN. *The Indonesian Tragedy*. Graham Brash Ltd, Singapore 1978.

MONEY, J.W.B. *Java or How to Manage a Colony*. Oxford University Press, Singapore 1985.

MOSSMAN, JAMES. *Rebels in Paradise*. Jonathon Cape, London 1961.

NOTOSUSANTO, BRIG. GEN. NUGROHO. *The National Struggle and the Armed Forces in Indonesia*. Center for Armed Forces History, Jakarta 1983. Also *The Japanese Occupation and Indonesian Independence*.

PIGEAUD, T.G. and H.J. DE GRAAF. *Islamic States in Java 1500–1700*. Martinus Nijhoff, The Hague 1976.

SCIDMORE, E.R. *Java: The Garden of the East*. Oxford University Press 1984.

STEINBERG, DAVID JOEL. *In Search of Southeast Asia: A Modern History*. University of Hawaii Press 1986.

WALLACE, ALFRED RUSSEL. *The Malay Archipelago*. Graham Brash Ltd, Singapore 1962.

Culture and Religion

AVE, JAN B. *Borneo: The People of the Weeping Forest*. Netherlands National Museum of Ethnology, Leiden 1986.

GEERTZ, CLIFFORD. *The Religion of Java*. University of Chicago Press 1976.

LEE KHOON CHOY. *Indonesia Between Myth and Reality*. Nile & Mackenzie, London 1976.

NEILL, WILFRED T. *Twentieth-Century Indonesia*. Columbia University Press 1973.

RICHARDSON, DON *Peace Child*. GL Publications, Ventura, CA 1975. Also *Lords of the Earth 1979*.

VAN NESS, EDWARD and SHITA PRAWIROHARDJO, *Javanese Wayang Kulit*. Oxford University Press 1985.

Fiction and Essays

ALLEN, CHARLES. *Tales from the South China Seas*. Futura Publications, London 1984.

BANGS, RICHARD and KALLEN, CHRISTIAN *Islands of Fire, Islands of Spice*. Sierra Club Books, San Francisco 1988 (out of print).

CONRAD, JOSEPH. *Almayer's Folly, An Outcast of the Islands*. Viking Press 1976, 1990. Also *Victory*. Penguin Classics (reprint) 1996.

FORBES, ANNA. *Unbeaten Tracks in Islands of the Far East, Experiences of a Naturalist's Wife in the 1880s*. Oxford University Press, Singapore 1987.

KOCH, C.J. *The Year of Living Dangerously*.

LEWIS, NORMAN. *An Empire of the East*, Jonathan Cape 1994.

LUBIS, MOCHTAR. *Twilight in Djartaka*. Oxford University Press, Singapore 1987. Also *The Indonesian Dilemma, A Road With No End* and *The Outlaw and Other Stories*.

LULOFS, MADELON. *Coolie*. Oxford University Press, Kuala Lumpur 1982. Also *Rubber*.

MAUGHAM, WILLIAM SOMERSET. *Maugham's Borneo Stories*. Heinemann, Hong Kong 1976.

MULTATULI (EDUARD DOUWES DEKKER). *Max*. Penguin Classics (reprint) 1995.

STEVES, RICK and GOTTBERG, JOHN. *Asia through the Back Door*. John Muir Publications, Santa Fe 1990.

NIEUWENHUYS, ROB. *Mirror of the Indes, A History of Dutch Colonial Literature*. University of Massachusetts Press, Amherst 1982.

SUTTON, ANNABEL. *The Islands in Between*. Impact Books, London 1989.

SZEKERLY, LADISLAO. *Tropic Fever*. Oxford University Press 1979.

VAN SCHENDEL, ARTHUR. *John Company*. University of Massachusetts Press 1983.

ZACH, PAUL. *Indonesia, Paradise on the Equator*. St. Martin's Press, New York 1988.

Travel Guides

DALTON, BILL. *Indonesia Handbook*. Moon Publications, Chico, California 1989.

HUTTON, PETER. *Insight Guuides Java*. Apa Productions, Singapore 1998.

MULLER, KAL. *Spice Islands; The Moluccas*. Periplus Editions 1990.

MULLER, KAL. *Underwater Indonesia*. Periplus Editions 1995 (out of print).

OEY, ERIC. *Insight Guides Indonesia*. Apa Productions, Singapore 1990.

OUNSTED, ROSSIE. *Birding Indonesia*, Periplus Editions 1997.

WINTERTON, BRADLEY. *Traveler's Bali Companion*. Globe Pequot (updated) 1998.

Photo credits

All pictures by **Nik Wheeler** with the exception of those listed below:

Adrian Bradshaw: pages 89, 93, 108, 124, 131, 183 *left*, 189, 191, 197, 199, 204, 219, 256, 283, 292.

David DeVoss: pages 253, 270.

Jill Gocher: pages 10, 11, 12, 13, 14, 15 *top and bottom*, 17, 20 *top and bottom*, 21, 25, 26, 28, 31, 33, 35, 37, 38, 39, 41, 43, 51, 52 *top*, 55, 57, 60 *top and bottom*, 61 *top and bottom*, 67, 71, 73, 76 *bottom*, 84, 96, 97, 111, 122, 136, 137, 139, 167, 177, 190, 195, 207, 209, 211, 216, 229, 231, 257, 258, 261, 263, 266, 267, 268, 269, 274, 275, 276, 287.

Robert Harding Picture Library: pages 74, 75, 76 *top*, 81, 85, 92, 100 *left and right*, 105, 127, 129, 181, 183 *right*, 196, 198, 205, 217, 223, 225, 250, 252, 265, 272, 273, 296.

Leonard Lueras: pages 147, 171.

Image-Link: pages 23, 29, 30, 40, 41, 52 *bottom*, 53, 54, 67 *bottom*, 160, 161, 230, 232, 233, 25, 259.

Chris Stowers: page 123.

Bradley Winterton: page 155.

Joseph R. Yogerst: pages 118, 119, 159, 213, 218, 222 *left and right* 293.

Quick Reference A–Z Guide
to Places and Topics of Interest with Listed Accommodation, Restaurants and Useful Telephone Numbers